GODDESSES AMONG US

Book 2

KIMBERLY ANDERSON

HAVANA BOOK GROUP LLC

43537 RIDGE PARK DRIVE

TEMECULA, CA. 92590

COPYRIGHT 2021 All rights reserved.

ISBN: 979-8-9851905-8-8

EPUB ISBN: 979-8-9851905-3-3

Dedication

This book is dedicated to all the women out there; you are a Goddess; always have been always will be. Everything about you is what makes you, uniquely you! Everything in your life up to this point has been preparing you for that next chapter in your life, and preparing you to stand in your brilliance.

You are powerful, and it is time to step into your power, speak your truth and Unleash Your Inner Goddess!

Table of Contents

About The Author

Kimberly Anderson

Kimberly Anderson is a writer, life coach, speaker, Tv Show host, and intuitive healer who helps women tap into their power.

A recipient of the Presidential Lifetime Achievement Award, the Presidential Service Award, Volunteer Award from the United States Congress, All Women Rock Award, Red Blazer Award, She Inspires Me Award, Heroes of Change Award, and many others. She is heart lead, and truly has a passion to help others.

As an intuitive transformational coach & business creative, Kimberly speaks to the soul within, smoothing out energy blocks and emotional ruts.

Her coaching begins with inner sovereignty work. Teaching women to understand and trust their intuition is an essential tool for their success, her philosophy, change your mindset, change your life will set you free.

Through deep listening, humor, and gentle guidance, she identifies their deepest goals, recognizes the challenges they face in taking steps to fulfill them—and begins creating solutions they would never have dreamed of on their own.

Her signature method helps people change old habits into new beliefs while tapping into their inner wisdom and finding happiness along the way.

She believes every woman has a unique identity and an innate gift to share with the world. And that is why she has created this massive global platform called Unleash Your Inner Goddess.

KimberlyAcoaching.com
https://www.facebook.com/AphroditeEnterprisesInc/
https://www.instagram.com/kimberlyacoaching/

Kimberly Anderson

Introduction

Once again, it is my great honor to introduce to you, 21 dynamic women in this second book of the series, Goddesses Among Us. These women have stepped into their power, and are speaking their truth, by sharing their stories.

As the title implies, these Goddesses walk among us. They are your friends, sisters, aunts, mothers, daughters, grandmothers, and neighbors. Just like you, they are the Goddesses Among Us. Overcoming heart wrenching traumas, obstacles, limiting beliefs, and adversities. They have graciously stepped into the spotlight to share their powerful stories.

Every one of these women is a blessing to humanity. May we follow in their light, learn from their experiences, and bring their wisdom into our lives.

These transformational conversations bring to light that we all go through "stuff". We are all on journeys of experience, change, choice, and transformation. I hope you take the profound wisdom and enlightenment found in this book to help you on your journey of life and in your own transformation.

With the global reach of this series, the Universe graced us with the magic and brilliance of Fizzy Beard, AKA Olivier Fardel, who collaborated on this project to bring women from around the world to create songs to go with each chapter story. With his incredible ear and the sounds of these women's voices, I hope you are profoundly touched. The QR codes will take you to each song

I am eternally grateful for all of the women in this book. It has been a profound honor to help share their stories. May the words in this book bless you with wisdom and divine energy, gracing you with clarity and empowering you to your next level; and the songs touch your soul.

To your higher consciousness and expansion

Kimberly Anderson

CHAPTER 1

Journey into My Body

Adina Isebelle Ravenswood

Dr. Adina Isebelle Ravenswood is a pharmacist, specializing in all issues pertaining to women's health. Realizing that pharmacy offers only a narrow range of wellness options, she found a way to expand that healing that many women today are seeking. She teaches belly dance classes to help women inhabit their bodies more fully and love themselves, just as they are.

Adina also focuses on teaching women about their inner cycles and the cycles of the natural world that affect them every day. In our patriarchal society, humans are expected to live by the 24-hour sun cycle (masculine) and essentially ignore the 29 ish day moon cycle (feminine). She believes we need a balance for all humans and wants women to understand that they have 4 distinct phases and superpowers every month. She believes that many of the health issues women face today can resolve themselves by following personal inner rhythms.

Please find her on Facebook at Adina Isebelle Ravenswood, or visit her business page at Bliss Belly Dance. Join her free Facebook group, Bliss Belly Dance: Practices to Feel Safe + Powerful.

Contact info

blissbellydance.com

askdradina@gmail.com

She learned it's ok to be herself, and she loves who she is now. ~KA

Kimberly: I am excited today to talk with Adina Isebelle Ravenswood. You are a pharmacist turned embodiment expert. I love this!

Adina: So good to be here, Kimberly. Thank you.

Kimberly: Talk about what you do. You're a pharmacist and an embodiment expert?

Adina: Well, the pharmacist piece is I really love helping people. I always heard the pharmacist is the most accessible healthcare professional, and it's true. I mean, you try, and try to get your doctor on the phone and they're not available; but you can always come in and see us and ask questions. What I found was that over the years, people would come in for the same issues, time after time, and the medicine would get them maybe a little relief, but there's just so much else. The whole personal piece of it is missing, I found a way to... well first, I healed myself through dance and then I found, goodness, this is a good base piece to helping women heal. That is what I do.

Kimberly: I love that. When you say dance, share what it is you do in the dance realm.

Adina: Belly dance has been a passion of mine since 2001. That is 20 solid years of belly dance and teaching since 2013, kind of on and off. And recently I've also become certified to teach a conscious dance modality called TranscenDance TM. I weave conscious dance with belly dance in all my teachings. And it's magical.

Kimberly: It is magical. And it's fascinating because I love to dance! I was a ballerina when I was little, but to incorporate dance, it's sexy, it's sensual, it's empowering. And I love belly dancing, anyway. Really being able to combine all those modalities into belly dancing, that's powerful. It's magical!

Adina: Yes. And I feel like most women know how to do these movements. It's just a feminine art form. What I try to do is just help women remember what it's like, help them remember how the body moves and the shapes that we make. And there's nothing quite like dancing with a group of women, even online.

Kimberly: Lets dive into it. Talk about what you would say is one of your biggest obstacles or experiences that you've had to overcome or get through.

Adina: You know, in thinking about this, it brings up something that I think is common to all women – that inability to express ourselves fully, and then mine has another layer. My inability to express fully started because I was born in Communist Romania, and it was 1978 so it was not good. My parents had to do things they didn't want to do. When I was three years old, they left me behind and they escaped and I stayed with my grandparents in the village. Their escape journey took almost nine months. And nine months later, somehow they were able to get me out, and I reunited with them in West Germany. We stayed there for about a year and then we moved to beautiful Columbia, Missouri, which is where I grew up.

And really the iron curtain didn't fall until 89 and we came to America in 84. That five-year span, I was five and a half when we came here. The whole time I felt like there was this invisible thing, holding me, choking my words, keeping me in bondage of some sort. It was this unspoken message that I had to be quiet. I couldn't stand out. I couldn't draw attention to us as a family. It's not hard to do as a kid, right? But as a teenager it was incredibly limiting. And I still felt that dampening of my spirit, even though my parents were very encouraging, like, hey, do what you gotta do. I always have felt like it's not safe. I can't be different. And for me, this belly dance thing is way out of my comfort zone, but I have to do it. It's this thing that's been calling me for decades. And I'm just going with it now. I think with age really comes freedom and liberation, if you allow yourself to be liberated.

Kimberly: Absolutely. Wow. Your story is amazing. I wanted to touch on a couple of things as you were talking. One thing that it made me think of is there's a sense of abandonment early on I would imagine. You were so little when they left and you're like, why are you leaving me? You don't understand as a child the bigger picture and what's going on. Do you find that affects you still today? And then the other thing I would ask is you learned you had to be invisible really, the word that kept coming out at me. Like you're saying, it's easier when you're a kid, we're still even taught children shouldn't be heard, seen and not heard, and then to be a teenager, and still living in that would affect you, that would affect you on many levels, and even growing up to be a pharmacist, you're still trying to not stand out and not shine in your brilliance.

Adina: Yeah. So true. That abandonment piece, I've thought about that over the years. When things happen to you, when some sort of trauma happens, there are so many directions that you can take it, you know? I think what I really did with that is thought, okay, I'm just going to be independent. Right? I'm going to learn how to do everything kind of on my own. And yet I'm still extremely attached to my parents to this day. Maybe it's a Romanian thing, Eastern Europeans and their big families and closeness and stuff. But I think a lot of it has to do with that early detachment, that is definitely true. Just being invisible, you know, I never really thought of it in that, that word. But totally that's what it is. It's be the gray person, be the person who completely doesn't stand out. It was verbally said that I needed to get some job that is conventional and secure. And that plays into pharmacy as well.

Kimberly: Definitely, one thing that I talk about often is, even as we have overcome or gotten through those moments in our lives, it's like an onion. And I jokingly say Shrek and Donkey put it well, where it's this onion and you're still peeling those layers back and you could be walking through the grocery store and have a meltdown. And you're like, what? Because those things still come up for us even as we maneuver through life, and we've thought we've gotten over it. How do you help people even through, as a pharmacist and as an embodiment expert, when you're talking about those things with your clients, because it's certainly something that's always going to come up? It's not, you get through it and you make it to the other side and then you never have to deal with it again. It's a deeper layer that comes up for you where you're having to heal even more.

Adina: Right. And you have to heal in the moment as you go. Yeah, I do this for myself and do this with clients as well. I think it's about finding the right tools, just learning things to do. One, of course, is conventional medicine. Really, I think that's not the best option and it shouldn't be the first line option. But for many it is, and that's okay. You know, it's there, it's available. Antidepressant medications, stomach acid relievers, insomnia meds... All these issues that are all related to trauma in the past. Then on the embodiment side of it there, over the years, I've had the privilege of learning what different emotions feel like as they're moving through your body and how to do those movements and help the emotions move.

During my dance classes we do several pieces of that, where we can allow whatever comes up to come up and then we release it and we refill, and we soothe, and we do all these wonderful, wonderful things. Every dance class, we have that opportunity. Plus, then those tools are available If you're at the grocery store and you have a meltdown, you could pretend that you're reading a label and if you feel like a wave of grief come over you, do some simple kind of rolling movements. It doesn't have to be big, you don't have to look like a weirdo in the soup aisle or something.

You can just do something simple like that. Or you can just kind of table it and wait until you get to the car and do something, or even, you know, there are lots of societies around the world that don't do things right in the moment. They take it to the tribe and they take it to this, this time where everyone experiences that emotion and its kind of a cathartic group experience.

I think having some tools and figuring out what works for you is super handy because every single person experience that.

Kimberly: Absolutely. One of the things that I love about this series is that we talk about many tools and techniques and tips to help you get through that. And I think that's an important thing that you stated was in that moment. When you have these tools and these ways to overcome and get you through, where you need some healing and some tenderness and some love. It's okay, to be on aisle nine in the soup aisle, really not feeling okay about what's going on. It's a part of the healing process, a part of that journey.

Adina: Yeah. And being okay with standing out I think is a really, really big one. I think in our society today the emphasis really is on blending in and not, not being an individual, and I think that's really hurting us. And my mission is to help women feel extremely comfortable in their body and in moving their body and then eventually maybe expressing their voice, so that we're okay being looked at and being witnessed in what we do.

Kimberly: Absolutely. It's about embracing that divine feminine that you are, and really stepping into your power and speaking your truth, that's why I call it Unleash Your Inner Goddess, because that's really what it is all about. Feeling into your brilliance and knowing it's okay to be you uniquely you, right? What have you done even with (maybe it's not always been the belly dancing or dance of any kind) but what have you done, that's helped you throughout your life in helping to overcome feeling invisible? Or having those moments where you're like, oh should I do that? Because I think a lot of women, not even where they've had to feel invisible, but they felt invisible anyway. Even in certain situations where they were trying to be invisible, as to not cause something to happen, that you helped.

Adina: Well, to be completely honest for most of my life, I totally numbed myself. I numbed out to all of it. I've been drinking since very, very, very young and I quit two years ago this April. April 1st, 2019, I was just done with it. And that was the first part of my life where I was bridging what I was learning all of these embodiment techniques and these kinds of somatic tools to use, also knowing about medicine and that sort of thing to use. And then bridging that until now. I think sobriety is incredibly magical, as a plug for sobriety here. When you get to that point where you can be with yourself without having to do something externally to make yourself feel a different way, I think that's really a beautiful place to get to.

And I know there's more, I'm excited for it. I think I've always been an individual person in this, or like kind of loner I would say. This might go back to that abandonment issue from before, right? I learned to be comfortable by myself, I think it has been important in my life to have people I could really count on to be supportive and to be there. My parents have been that at times, and my husband is incredibly wonderful at that. Just letting me be who I need to be and do what I need to do, without putting demands on me or external pressures. I think that's handy. And I will add, again, the power of dancing with women. It's just like you can be feeling any certain way and get into the room or the zoom room and it's like a whole different energy is formed. And if it's done right with the right people, a safe little bubble is there for you to kind of move everything through.

Kimberly: That's awesome. I love that. You said so many different things. Where did I want to start?

Again, that invisibility piece and that numbing, I think that's kind of our go-to knee jerk reaction in a lot of the things that we experience through life. It's that go numb because then you don't have to deal with it or think about it. And having a support system that can help you. And if you don't, there are a lot of groups out there even outside of dancing, there are a lot of different places that we can find our tribe of people to help us break through those limiting beliefs or that numbing and having something, especially dance. I'm right there with you, I absolutely love dance. It makes you feel incredible. It just does something to you and having that, as a go-to, even if you go into a room. Would you tell this to your clients, go into a room, shut the doors, nobody can see you, turn on some music that you love, and just let go, let loose? It totally changes your mindset, your perspective, your everything that's going on with you. Even if you feel like a fool dancing.

Adina: Yes. And I think that it really says something about the state of our whole society when a person feels intimidated just dancing by themselves, you know? I think getting used to that, just moving every day, many of us just go to work and that's all we do. Or maybe we work out, but it's structured and focused and it's hard, and we sweat and we're like, no pain no gain kind of thing. Even if we do yoga. Everything is wonderful movement, but I think there's something magical about dancing where you just, even if you look like a complete goon and you're like, trying to moonwalk and it's totally going wrong, or you're doing the robot or something, just moving your body. When we stay in our head, that's where all the anxiety and depression kind of come in, right? We ruminate, we stay stuck. When we move our body, it's powerful. I mean, people say it all the time that exercising is wonderful because it releases those, those emotions and creates those endorphins. Again, I'm just plugging dance because I think it's probably the most powerful thing out there as far as I'm concerned.

Kimberly: I'm all about dancing so I totally agree with you. There's something magical and powerful about just allowing yourself to, and I think what you were saying is because it's not structured, even though if you're doing a choreographed dance routine there's still freedom and flow and motion inside of that, that it's moving your body where you wouldn't otherwise. And even yoga, I do yoga, and dance is just a completely different animal itself. And it allows you that ability to just be free with no expectation. You can just be free to do whatever you want.

Adina: Yeah, exactly. And I love belly dance in particular. I mean, there's a structure to it and there's technique which is great. And I love that kind of dance as well, but there's also something magical about just doing whatever, whatever comes up.

Kimberly: Yes. There's emotion and when you attach it to dance, I mean, you can shake, you can add some hula in there (I grew up in Hawaii). There's so much that you can do inside of dancing. It doesn't matter. And I love that because it is a powerful technique to move through emotion and help overcome how you feel. It's an incredible thing to do. I love it.

Adina: Yeah. And really, I have had a love-hate relationship with it, as you do with anything, that's like super good for you. You get a taste and you're like, Ooh, that was fun. And then a part of you is like retreat, retreat, you know, it's too good. It's too good. Stay away, for years, the first few years, I would kind of come and go out of dance class.

Sometimes opting to stay home and watch Fear Factor and eat like a bag of Doritos instead of dancing, right? But now I'm fully committed, especially because now I teach. A little secret – I do it for others, but I mainly do it for me because it gets me dancing regularly.

Kimberly: What made you decide to go to belly dancing as opposed to any other type of dance?

Adina: Well, interestingly, I was in Romania in 1994 with my family and we went to this dinner thing, and they were having a show with different acts and one of them was a belly dance. I was mesmerized, years later, I mean, gosh, 2000, I was like early twenties, 22, 23, when I started dancing... I saw belly dancers at an earth day festival here in Columbia, Missouri. And I was like, Oh my gosh, it's here! Like I can do this now.

I started taking classes that next January that's really where that came from, oddly enough, back to the motherland.

Kimberly: I love it. I love that. It's always fascinating to me how we find whatever modality it is that we turn to. What intrigues us to use that in our healing and our journey on healing. I find it really fascinating. What would you tell your younger self if you had the opportunity to go back in time?

Adina: Oh, I would say, well goodness, darling Adina, you are so, so, sure that things are going to be this way, and that this is who you are and it would really be a good idea to stay open because you will be completely different. Stat open to surprising yourself. That is really what I wish I knew.

Kimberly: That was good. That gave me chills.

Adina: Yeah. I mean, I am completely not what I thought I would be, and I love it! I'm having fun in my life right now.

Kimberly: That's the truth though. I love what you said, because even some of the healing that we must go through, we have to forgive ourselves for not becoming the person we thought we were going to be. There's a lot of healing that goes around that. To really hone in and say, it's okay, you're going to just be this amazing person. It's your journey, your path. And to just be okay with where you end up. I love that.

Adina: Yeah. And be okay with wherever you are, you know If you're still drinking a bottle of wine every night, that's okay. That's where you are. And that's all right. You know, it's just like, I wish I could have given myself big hugs every night that I would do that, and just tell myself that it was okay, instead of beating myself up for it all the time, you know? Just ways that we sabotage ourselves. Little, little hug, and be like, it's okay.

Kimberly: It is. Especially as women, we always feel guilty about everything that we do and every way that we're trying to overcompensate, or even just compensate for what we're going through. Then we're bullying ourselves for a week later saying why were you doing that? It's just about loving yourself where you're at. It's ok, it's part of that life lesson, that journey that you're on and just embrace where you are, know that it's just a part of your story. It's adding character.

Adina: Definitely! Definitely! Yes. Love yourself. Apologize where you need to apologize and just move on.

Kimberly: Just forgive yourself. It's okay. It's totally okay to be, to go through what you're going through and how you're helping yourself in that moment. I love what you said. Be open, be open to who you're becoming. That's good. I love the conversation and I look forward to sharing your story everywhere. Thank you so much for being open and sharing all that you did.

Adina: My pleasure. Thank you for the opportunity. You know, some things came out of my mouth that I haven't thought about in years, or maybe I didn't even know were there.

Kimberly: It happens, and that's the power about these stories, is somebody needs to hear it. Thank you.

Adina: Yeah, my pleasure.

CHAPTER 2

Shot in the Dark

AnGele Cade

AnGele M. Cade is a consulting expert, who has dedicated the last twenty years to helping entrepreneurs develop effective corporate structures and implement managerial procedures while enforcing viable compliance measures. AnGele is recognized as the "Go-To" expert for structural, professional business needs. When AnGele is not consulting, you can find her speaking, teaching, and training on the best practices to set goals, create priorities and attain support for their vision. She is passionate about sharing down to earth, real world business experience to help solve problems and empower those around her.

Contact Info

Phone: (818) 886-4895

Email: acade@execonthego.com

Website: ExecOnTheGo.Com

The Universe kept calling for her to slow down; she didn't listen, then bam! It stopped her. ~KA

Kimberly: I am super excited to be here today with AnGele Cade. The founder owner of Executive on the Go.

AnGele: Thank you for having me. I am excited to be here with you, as always.

Kimberly: I adore you! Your story and your message are powerful. It just hits me on the inside of my soul. First, before we get into that, talk about what you do? What is an Executive on the Go?

AnGele: I consider myself a business consultant, I specialize in entity formation, structuring businesses, and making sure people have the right entities. Whether it's corporations, LLCs, nonprofit entities, no matter the structure, making sure that it makes sense for them. One thing that we do is we help people at startup, or a transition figure out what is going to be best for them. Digging into what options they have for the journey that they are going to be on. For example, their exit strategy, acquisition, succession, any of those things. Figuring out where they are on their path.

Another part of our business is helping professionals, attorneys, and accountants service their clients. We white label for them, do all the heavy lifting for dealing with the agencies. No one loves dealing with the state agencies, right? Somebody has got to go in, be able to speak that language and navigate those systems, especially as the world has changed where people are working remote, and more things are online. Everything is trying to be online Making sure that it's done the right way, hopefully the first time. That is why clients link to us to do that work, I've been doing it for 18 years. I love helping people and making sure that they are ready and able to receive money. It's great work to do.

Kimberly: Love that. So needed in the world for business, especially entrepreneurs, they need to find that.

AnGele: It's so funny, many people that I network with have said to me "where were you when I _____ or (fill in blank)" right! Because it's just such a missing conversation, it can be a blind spot. If it's not dealt with properly or didn't know that you had options and do the wrong. It's really nice to support people at the beginning or adjustment stages of their journey.

Kimberly: I would imagine that you coming in on the beginning saves a lot of time, money, effort, blood, sweat, and tears as well, though.

AnGele: It's true. If you can focus in on your zone of genius and superpower, you're going to make more money that way. Allowing us to do that work is going to relieve the tension, the stress of navigating waters that most people don't know what to do in.

Kimberly: Absolutely. I love it. Let's talk about you on a deeper level. We're here talking about what you've overcome. What has significantly happened in your life? Let's just dive into that. What would you say is the biggest obstacle you've overcome, granted, I know we go through a lot of different ones?

AnGele: When you pose the question, my mind goes to major, the high major events that happen on the timeline of our life. Really to even give something the title of the biggest obstacle. That was tough because like you said, we all go through so many things that kind of shape us, tool us.

My mind really settled on an enormous obstacle that I had to overcome that carried with me the longest. I would have to go back to the spaces that really sourced the idea of limited beliefs. I'm not enough, like where those things come from, when they were formed, how they shaped out in my life.

I want to say that the biggest obstacle that I had to overcome was when I was a teenager. When I felt like I didn't fit in. When I felt like I didn't fit in, I was looking to be loved; to have friends, to be liked. I was looking; Do you know what I mean? You want the validation; you want the accepted ness. I was hanging out with the wrong people, ditching school. Technically, I should have never graduated from high school. I was doing drugs, drinking; I was the one who would pay the person on the corner to go get the drinks. I lived that life so much so that I left. I ran away from home; I ended up joining a gang.

I was in a space where it just created this mindset for me that needed people to validate me. I needed to feel like I belong to something. You know, what I had wasn't enough, who I was wasn't enough. I needed these things, these markers, this acceptance, to speak into that. And it never filled it. What happened during that period in my life, we're talking about young, I mean, I was 13 and I was shot at in the upper right chest; it slowed me down. It was perfect that it happened. The trajectory that I was on I wouldn't have survived that phase of my life if I would've continued down that road. That moment where I was in a car, I wasn't where I was supposed to be.

I was on my way home. A car pulls up next to me, a few words are exchanged. The car slows down; they shoot into the car that I'm in and the bullet goes through the back window, through the seat that I'm sitting in, and it lodges in my chest. I heard the noise, but I didn't even know I got shot until I leaned back in the seat. My entire back was like filled with blood and the seat was wet. I did not know why. I put my hand around my back to see why is it wet... what's back there? And I pulled my hand out. I filled my hand with burnt tissue and blood. The whole car screamed. Everybody was like, what happened? Like it was quick, you heard it; you did. It sounded like a tire popping.

And I was... I was so in my head about where I was in that phase of my life that I demanded to be driven home, refused to go to the hospital. I remember going home. Everybody was like, you're crazy. I was like... I'm going home. Whatever it is, it is. I went in the house, took off my clothes, went in the bathroom, looked at the bullet wound, took some paper towel, wrapped it up, so I could just go to sleep.

My friend that was in the car with me, drove back to my house, knocked on the window. Mind you, I am 13. She was like, I'm going to wake your parents up. If you don't come outside and let us take you to the hospital, you need to go to the hospital.

I was like, oh, whatever, get dressed and go to the hospital and it was a wake-up call. Tried to give him a fake name. I tried to do this. They ended up calling my house, my dad answered the phone, they told him "Your daughters in the hospital." And he was just like, "no, she's home, we heard her come home, and saw the light go on and off. You got the wrong kid." I remember my dad telling me how, when he turned the light on in the hallway, he was so in shock. You could see the trail of blood of every place I had been in the house. I didn't even realize that I bled that much.

The bullet had lodged. I had surgery three months later to have it removed. But that was, that was at a time where I needed to slow down. It was huge the biggest issue was my mindset, my belief system, my value, my understanding who I was. It was during that period that I met a new group of friends, moved and changed schools. Everything that was going on with the gang. I had all F's and one D, and I had my D in PE, which is the running joke cause if you show up, you get it anyway. When I changed schools, when I changed friends, when I changed environment, when that shooting slowed me down and I changed my mindset, I literally went from those grades to all A's one B. My B was in PE because I still hated running the mile. I had good grades during that obstacle, during that transition, realizing that I already had, and I already was, enough. I just had to live that, to be that, walk in that. Graduated with honors and I ended up going to UCLA. I am who I am now, but I needed to go through that for my trajectory could change.

Kimberly: Wow. I'm taking all that in. All of this transpired at 13 years old. That is such a poignant time in our lives. Especially as little girls, everything changes for us, the way we perceive things, our bodies, the whole nine yards it's changing quickly. I find it really fascinating that you got shot, then went home. Like there was no pain? You were just completely in shock?

AnGele: I was completely in shock. I was more afraid of the repercussions of having to live the truth that happened. The hospital represented that it actually happened. And if I could cover my bullet wound with a Band-Aid, right? If I could make it, it wasn't a big deal; it didn't happen. Then I don't want to have to deal with the reality of the lifestyle I was living, people that it exposed me to, or the decisions that I made. It was an attempt to just go home with this idea that when I woke up, it would just go away. But the symbolism of it, that this friend cared enough in that moment to come back and threatened what I felt was safe, was enough to jar me, to get into action, go to the hospital, realize the seriousness of what had happened. I could have easily just bled to death in my bed.

Kimberly: That's what I was going to say next, even you moving around and doing all that could have lodged it into a different direction to where it could have instantly killed you. I mean, it's absolutely amazing. It's amazing that you're here. What age do you think it was at, I'm going to even start at 10, 12 before you hit 13, that you were seeking all this stuff outside of yourself? You went into the gangs and the drugs, leading up to that point why where you were seeking all this outside of you? What do you think caused you to go into that? What caused that feeling where you were felt unloved, valued, and appreciated.

AnGele: A lot of that stems from, I would have to say, it's learned behavior, it's triggered events. For me, it was from my mom. My mom represented just a lot of that; not enough, not pretty enough. You don't look the part, this is an issue, don't trust, people are just trying to take advantage of you.

It's funny because at the moment it just, she just seems so wrong and evil and just all the things that, as a little girl, you look at your mom and as I am now a mom, I just have so much grace for what it means to do the best with what you know in raising your children. Although, it didn't feel good when I was going through it for my experience. I recognize she was going through her own experience, trying to decide what was best. For a lot of years, it really kind of stemmed around this idea of mommy issues and things that I heard, things that were told to me.

All of it, culminates to this idea that, when you're not the popular girl, if you're not the pretty girl, if you're not the picture, model of what's considered, pretty, at the school or the kids tease you. And I was just, I was a different, I'm originally from St. Kitts born on a small Island. I grew up in Canada and Saint-Laurent, Quebec; I spoke French. When I came here, the black kids did not accept me. They would say, you talk funny; you act white. Why do you say your name like that to the white kids? You're not one of us. What are you doing over here?

So it was, where do I fit in? You reflect this, this other culture, you're trying to find yourself and find allies, people to love, just kind of realize where do I fit? Is it more about who I am and how to be fully expressed in that?

The moment I got clear on that part, as I was navigating, growing up into the authenticity of me, it just became clear that it wasn't from the outside, it's really coming from the inside. A lot of it had to do with my confidence, my determination, my focus, had to do a lot more with that than with how someone else treated me, or thought of me. Those things played a part into the wanting this to fit in. I think it speaks to what a lot of us look for as little girls. Which is why it's important for the inner child healing, allowing that little girl to have a voice.

Looking at the bigger picture is so important because those are the things that can scar you in a way that is painful, versus a scar being the evidence that healing was there, it's the scar that continues to re aggravate and hurt you. It's not supposed to do that. It's just supposed to be evidence of healing. And growing into that understanding.

Kimberly: I love your analogy about the scar, it's true. We think of them as, Oh, this happened to me. That happened to me. If you change your perspective, shift your mindset about it, look what I made it through, how strong I am, brave, I did this. It completely shifts you. Really it takes your power back. It's no longer the victim that went through something or experienced this trauma. You're able to own that was me, I did that, I can survive that. You survived that! Your story is just about your journey and your healing. In your healing process after you got shot, because you said you were doing drugs, you were in a gang and you were drinking. With all these other people that weren't healthy for you, then you got shot and you said it slowed you down.

AnGele: It got my attention. I think a lot of times when things happen; it gets your attention. For me, I think about every car accident, everything that happens and really, leaning into... do things just happen and it just happens. And it is what it is. I have a thing that happens to me where for years, in terms of my stress and how I work, I would get sick. So eventually I would build up, I would get stress, stress, stress, work, work, work, work, work, and then it will culminate in me getting sick. And so it would occur in my body. And so how am I going to pay attention to it?

There's always something that happens that there is a sign that says, pay attention to this. You have a choice; you make a change. That opportunity for change was real, was the first major one that happened in my life. Ok, you got shot. You're not mobile, not going anywhere, in the hospital and alone in your head. No one else is talking to you, no distraction, no drugs. There're no seeds between your teeth, no weeds, no roach clip, no Kool-Aid, no Thunderbird. No doubt that it's just you and this bed. Now what, right? Being able to really process through what is the rest of my life going to look like if I continue on this path. Being able to see it from a place that says, I have a choice in the matter, what am I going to choose next? Slowing down gave me enough pause for thoughts, gave me enough pause to, to re-adjust to dream, gave me enough space to make some decisions. And all of that happened in that time period that allowed for a shift in how I was going to live the rest of my life. Those are the things that I could do in that space of pause.

Kimberly: I want to touch on something that you were just describing. You took this experience, you now know that when something happens to you, it's the universe calling out, you need to stop. You need to slow down and take a moment, breathe, pause, and re-adjust. I find it really fascinating; I want people to understand what you're saying that massive trauma that you went through, taught you as you were growing up into this beautiful adult woman, that you now know and recognize when something's too much, and you need to have a course correct or pause in those moments. What I really love about what you were talking about is understanding how you can take the trauma or an experience, mind shift, beliefs, and recognize how they come up in your life. Taking those moments to switch gears or whatever it is. I think that's so powerful how you explain that.

AnGele: Thank you. Listening to you say it, I am awake to the fact, or awakening, that there are many things that I'm hard-headed about that present itself repeatedly in different way. It doesn't have to take all of that. If there are things we would just get sooner, right? The things that we would understand or shift, these conversations are important because in your listening of someone else, hopefully you could see yourself so that you can collapse the time to speed up your own learning. You don't have to get... don't have to get... slowed down by a bullet or get into the accident.

My body was a sign. It would constantly tell me, like AnGele, it's too much. I would go days without sleeping and just working. It was a lot. My body would talk back to me and say, you can't keep doing this. I would end up in the hospital every year. And it was. It was getting to a point where one day I might go and not recover. Like, I can't keep doing this to my body. The final straw was that I was driving one night suddenly the lights look blurry; I already wear glasses. I was like; they blurred like, what's this?

I closed my eye; it was fine. I closed my other eye, I couldn't see. What's going on? I've been having a little headache, working a lot, not a big deal. I'll take some stuff, it'll go away, ignored it for a couple of days. I decide I'm uncomfortable driving because now I'm seeing double, like what's going on. The moment I told my husband, I was going to ride into the office with him. He was like, oh no, something is wrong. Cause I'm usually out in the street. He was like, something's really wrong.

I go to the doctor, explained to her what happened, and I was having these headaches, then my vision. She was like; you go to the hospital right now. She wrote a note, looked at me like I was crazy, told my husband, take me to the hospital. I figure maybe I'm going to get injections for migraines; I was thinking maybe I have migraines or if they're going to give me like something to release that. Waiting, I go in there, I'm doing MRIs, on steroids drips, had optical neuritis. I had many strokes that were happening, they could see the clot. It was insane. I was in the hospital for eight days. Your body is going to give you the feedback that you are out of sync, something that you cannot continue at that level. If you don't listen to it and take those pauses, it is going to take it for you. When it takes the break for you, as I got older, I realized I'm not recovering as fast. Since I'm not recovering as fast, I probably don't want to take the risk of pushing it to this level. What point do I get the lesson that says, know what I'm going to listen? My 45th year around this here sun, that I was like, hmm, you know what? I'm going to bed.

Kimberly: It came to my mind when you were talking, is that you kept winding up in the hospital, the one place you did not want to go, even when you had a bullet in your chest. After you kept going back every year, like how significant is that? To sit back and go, okay, wait a minute. I can't wait that long. I need to act now for my health, for myself, in those moments.

AnGele: That's huge! I actually never even put that together. That's going in the book, that's huge because the thing is, and that's the thing! We're running from this place and it's where you're going to end up if you do that. You're going to end up in that place if you don't get it. Right! You keep running, it's going to keep showing up because you keep making the same decisions in different ways, in different lanes. The same thought pattern that says, you know what? I'm not enough don't have enough time. There's plenty of time. It's just, what am I choosing to do with it? Getting those things clear, but I love that. Oh, you get all the coaching dollars. Yes. That's good.

Kimberly: What would you tell your younger self if you could go back and tell her?

AnGele: Oh my gosh, I would tell her. She is amazing, powerful, and beautiful. You got this. Trust it, trust you, you got this. You don't need anything that doesn't make you feel good and if they do not align with all the goodness that you already are. Just bet on you. Trust you. You don't need someone else to validate your amazingness. That is what I would tell her. I would want to hug her, just love on her and just let her know she is always, has always been, will always be more than enough.

Kimberly: Amen to that. I love it. Your story is so powerful. There are so many lessons and inspiration within all of it, the whole weaving of every piece. We only touched on a bit because I know your story. By taking those lessons, that trauma, what you went through as a little girl at 13 years old, which still baffles my mind, taking those lessons, using them to better yourself to becoming this amazing woman that you are today. I'm just honored that you're here with me sharing your story. It's such a powerful story and message that you have to share with the world.

AnGele: Thank you. You are a gift too many of us. I appreciate the flow of what it means to know you, experience you, and be able to be on this journey with you. Thank you for inviting me to be a part of this community and the work that you're doing. I applaud you and I support you in whatever you need.

Kimberly: You're amazing. Thank you so much.

CHAPTER 3

The Little Voice That Save Me

Antisk Atma

Antisk Atma is the owner/ facilitator of Taoist/Tantric Temples in SE Qld Australia. As a Tantric educator, Tao instructor, and Yoga teacher, her mission and passion are to share these Sacred Practices and Therapies with others. Through her story of trauma and struggles to survive, she desires to enlighten others that happiness after trauma is possible. She traveled to the world for 12yrs studying, going to workshops, under many Masters and teachers in search of ways to Heal. Her mission in life is to be an advocate to show that she walks her talk, and practices what she teaches.

antisk@rocketmail.com.

https://www.facebook.com/antiska.

Listening to the little voice inside that saved her. ~KA

Kimberly: I am with Antisk Atma. I am so excited you're here. Why don't you first share with the world what you do?

Antisk: Okay! I founded a Taoist Temple, Temple of Golden healing and I'm a Taoist instructor of Tai chi, Chi gong. I also teach emotional release, post sexual healing. Trained with the grandmaster Mantak Chia, I found my way into Taoism and tantra and found my healing. Trained through the source school of tantra in the USA and at The Temple Lotus and Temple Kamala, it's a small temple that I've really set up for sexually traumatized women. It's my absolute passion to work with those women. I hear a lot of stories as the people are going through their trauma and triggers that come up and things like this, and to do that work now, I really need to make sure that I am healed from my trauma. So, it's an ongoing thing to make sure that I'm looking after myself as well, because when I've worked with them, it's not like what we're doing now, where I share my story with them. I'm just hearing their story. So for me just to do this series, it's absolutely a great honor, because actually, this is the first time that I've been able to share my entire story.

Kimberly: Well, I am so honored that you're here with me. Let's talk about your story. What would you say is the biggest obstacle or trauma you've had to overcome? What is your story?

Antisk: Okay, well, I was 15. I was an innocent Virgin, and I was a random pick by a rapist on the way home from my very first job. I was on a remote road with no streetlights or anything; it used to take me an hour to walk home. I'd walked it since I was seven. So now I'm 15. I got strangled from behind, dragged into the Bush, strangled to unconsciousness, and then I was buried alive. I woke up with him trying to light a cigarette and burn me with all the twigs that he'd put on the top of me in that grave, on the side of the road. He dragged me by my hair and the stockings tied around my neck for over 1 hr. On the lonely country road in the dark. He was holding me hostage, but I managed to get free. I ran in front of a car on the highway desperate the car came to a screaming halt in the dark on the side of the road. It was cold, don't know how long they held me hostage for. The car drove off, saying that they didn't want to be involved. That was really traumatic for me. Then another car come along, and I'd did the same thing; ran in front of this car. Being traumatized, I really didn't want to be alive. Hurt and bleeding with a broken nose, I had lots of things wrong with me. I just had words in me telling me I need to do what I'm doing and try to get some help.

The car came and again, they said, no, they said, we don't want to get involved. So they told me to run to a farmhouse that was on the side of the road. I went to the farmhouse, bashed on the door. I could hear a TV on and nobody came to the door. Desperate at that stage, so I broke the window and dove through the farmhouse. Had a shotgun put to my head, and he realized that I always hurt and naked. I still had the stockings tied around my throat that he'd strangled me with. I told him and he rang the police. So I went to the police station. I had no support from my family at all. My mother and father didn't really want to have anything to do with it. My sister is married to a police officer, he came and told me, "You're making a fool out of yourself, pull it out of the court."

I was 15 I ran away, and I lived in the park. I used to watch people come to the park, eat food and put it in the garbage. That's how I survived. I had nothing, and I walked off with nothing. Didn't have money, no jacket, no blanket, I had nothing. I went to the Supreme court of Sydney all on my own. With no support, didn't get a solicitor, only the police prosecutor. I survived that.

I met my magnificent husband that I'm married to now for 7 years tomorrow. We met at school when he was 11, so we knew each other before this time. We got together, got married and had a son. My life was very different, and he knew me before that... when I was a happy kid. Suddenly I was this person who didn't feel like I fit it into the world. So I felt alienated, always victimized by community and neighborhood, that's what made me run away.

I didn't realize that I was so traumatized, hadn't cried because I didn't have any support to do that. Had to think, I just kept thinking all the time. I spent the rest of my 44 years after in post-traumatic stress disorder, and I didn't realize that. My husband and I have a talk about it. I say to him, you know, like I couldn't talk about it. And he states now I didn't know what to do to help you. So, I'm getting a little emotional now. It was one of those times in my life that I used to get brief messages with insights saying different things. When I was 40, a lady that was doing a stripper-gram inspired me. She came and asked me if I want to do her music for her? I said, well yes, I would. And I went, and I saw the happiness in that. I become one of them, a stripper-gram. My 40th birthday, my husband said, what would you like to do for your birthday? And I said, I want to strip in King's cross in Sydney. So, I did at 40; I went on stage out there naked in the dark drug city (I never took alcohol or drugs). It's a pretty rough place in Sydney. And all I could hear is "they can look, but they can't touch you" that's what held me together. I was great on stage; I wasn't great inside. Stayed with that career for 10 years; It made me who I am. I won a contract to striptease in Japan on my 50th birthday, doing wonderful things, then I retired, after I just fell into a big heap. I couldn't cope. Still hadn't cried, lost all self-esteem. I felt alienated. One of my yoga students inspired me - she broke down and triggered me in one of my yoga classes. She was a rape victim as well. She shared with me she was going through victim services. I went home, picked the phone up, and I contacted them and they said, what? After 44 years, it's too long, we can't help you. And I say: I was too traumatized. I didn't know. I hadn't been told, and I really need to do this for myself.

It was about just being acknowledged. I did, I pushed it through; it took me five years. It wasn't easy, and I was suicidal. Coming across a lot of blocks, I couldn't get through the blocks. They raped me in 69, in 1970, all the files before 1970, they'd burned them. So, they burned my file in the courts and the police stations, the records. They went trying to look for the rapist, and I didn't know the rapist. I was just a random pick. Luckily, they found the entrance to the jail, his name in the jail records. So that helped me. So, I started feeling more inspired through those five years of trying to do that. Victim services told me it would be one of the hardest things that I'm going to do is go back into the story, just like I am now.

I wrote a book I didn't get published. 90,000 handwritten words over five years, whatever came up. I tried to heal myself I took a home study course for counseling. Tried to see myself and I still wasn't there. I had become really traumatized. It broke my marriage, John and I broke up for 10 years and we went our own ways, and I just tried to find myself. That's when I found the tantra and Taoism, when I went and watched the live demonstration. That was the first time that I actually got triggered, to realize how bad I was. So, I went, got some healing, I searched for it and that was 2014.

It took me all that time to find my way from 2014 I've just been ongoing. I've been now to America, and I went also to India to study Eastern tantra. I asked to be triggered I said – "if there's anything left in me now, I want to be triggered. I want to see it. I want to be healed" ... but nothing came up. So nothing came up.

They've told me that, like my DNA, healing attachment to my trauma has been healed. I totally feel that. And that's what I do in my work now. So, it's just such an honor to be here, Kimberly, to talk like this. I thought to myself, okay, I'm going back into my story. Biggest things that I had to learn, to be where I'm now, I had to learn forgiveness.

That was really hard to forgive my mother that didn't see me, that never gave me that cuddle, that I had to forgive my father that smashed me across my broken nose didn't believe that my story was real. I had to forgive communities that called me bad names and victimized me. Today I'm really, really happy. I've got my beautiful husband sitting beside me here. He's my support person. We have a fantastic marriage now, we've repaired everything.

Kimberly: That's incredible! Wow! In all of that, I would imagine that going through your life, all of those things kept coming up for you. Like the abandonment, I found it really interesting too, that you said, you realized you had never cried. There was this whole numbing thing that came over you. This mechanism that we have, our brains have to remove it, forget about it, there's a lot to be said about healing through it, so you can move beyond it.

Antisk: Yes. The time that I cried was that time in Thailand. That was the meeting of the two masters, with Mantak Chia and Charles Muir. The first one that Charles did in Thailand and Mantak Chia wound up as my partner at that workshop. All he had done was put his hand on me. One hand on my heart, other hand on my stomach. It was quite amazing. I keep going back through this all the time. It is one thing that inspired me. The moment that he put his hand on my heart, I immediately started an emotional release. It wasn't because of the rape. I was brokenhearted from never being held or seen, acknowledged, or supported. That I held in me more than the actual rape, because of so many things. The two cars that didn't allow me to be helped, and the communities that turned away from help every time, my sister's husband had told me to pull it out of the court, and that is what I held.

I never heard myself whimper that ever again. I was a mess, having convulsions. I know I have seen a lot of the trauma come out in the workshops, but I've never seen one that like what I'd done. I went home terrified of that from Thailand. I said to my husband, don't even put a hand on me because you won't know what to do to help me. We didn't have any experience then, but I have training now.

Kimberly: There's a lot of power in that, and I can imagine it hurt you on so many levels. So many points after the fact, like you said, the cars that passed you by. You were a child, and nobody was helping you. You were beat up, naked, and still had the stockings tied around your neck. My God! And to think that people drove past you, I can't even imagine how that just made you feel, just defeated.

Antisk: Yeah. I've given it a lot of thought as well. My family that didn't support me, they've still never supported me. I just sort of come up to the point to think that it was just too much for people to handle. I've had to look at it a different way, not just look at the bad parts. I've just had to think, oh my God, that poor old lady that sat in that car, that saw me, and I could have been like her daughter. One thing that I asked, and I never got to know, I always wanted to know who took the stockings off? When I went into that farmhouse, I still had them on and I still had it tied around my neck.

I just like to point out, one thing about me is, because of the 44 years of trauma that I went through, there is no way that

I could have done what I am doing right now. I look at myself and go, my God! I could not have done this! Which is to have my book chapter on this, right? To have my hair down. I couldn't do that because of how I was grabbed and strangled from behind. Couldn't wear a scarf, couldn't have anything wrapped around my neck, but today, I've got a scarf on. I can do that today, which I couldn't do before, after 44 years. I've taken a lot away. Now I can help people because I understand it. I understand you need to be triggered to be helped. So, coming through with my story, hopefully people can see that, even if it triggers them, to do some healing because that's what we all need. I do as well in my work. When I get triggered, I will not work. I can't work with them if I'm triggered. I hear some pretty horrific stories as well; they've remained personal of course. Wow, Kimberly, this is just, I'm still overwhelmed! You know, when you contacted me for what I put up on Facebook, I was just like, oh my God, look at this, I said to my husband. I'm doing it. He said, what are you doing? I said, I've got to answer first. And then I told him.

Kimberly: These stories are so powerful because we all go through something, and you can have 10 different stories. I'll just use domestic violence, because that's my background. You can have 10 women talking about domestic violence, every one of those stories is different. That's why I think it's so important to bring all of us together as women and share our stories because there's so much power in the release, and us healing, as we share it. Also, because it helps women on the other side, knowing that they can get through it. Your story is so incredible, especially knowing now that you held on to all of that for 44 years. That's a lot of time to hold on to that, and all those little details of your story, even getting buried. I didn't know that. Incredible to even have to get out of that... You were fighting for your life the entire time.

Antisk: Yes.

Kimberly: I don't know if you really recognize that, but you were fighting to survive the entire time. You are the epitome of a survivor.

Antisk: Yes, yes. What I found at first is, when I started screaming at first, I was just getting bashed, and every time I tried to use my voice, I would be worse off. So what I had done is listened to my inner self, and I was just, okay, you got to be quiet to think, and that's actually what I had done. That's I think how I survived. I feel have a few traits of being buried alive. I try to work through them. I have a lot of trouble laying on my back for too long, I sort of have a bit of anxiety. I'm not afraid of the dark because I grew up in the country in the dark and I actually live with no power now. I don't have a phobia with that. I have nothing with my throat anymore, but I did. At one time I got thyroid problems because of it. I also couldn't speak; it's not like I didn't have a voice. I couldn't speak. I felt alienated. I felt left out and terribly alone in this world. I've come such a long way. I really am proud of myself. I'm really amazed at what I've done. To see today how I am. How I can talk about it, just amazing. It's really amazing.

Kimberly: You gave me goosebumps.

Antisk: Right?

Kimberly: I'm proud of you. This is incredible. You've come so far, you've turned around, and you're using that to help other women and helping men. To really move through that pain, that period where we hold it. We don't even realize; I think most of the time that we hold on to it in lots of different parts of our bodies, right? I love the work that you do. I think it's absolutely incredible to help people move through that. I like how you said that you're able to help them release it, that's another thing I really wanted to say.

You recognize that even if you get triggered; you don't work. That's important because I want people to realize that it can still come up. It still comes up for us. Like you said, even laying on your back, you can't do that for so long. You have anxiety. There are lots of different ways that it will still manifest, but we have learned different ways that we can get through that emotional trauma much faster.

Antisk: Yeah. what I've found is just by being, acknowledge I can do something about it, but for those 44 years when I was in a post-traumatic stress disorder, I didn't even know that I was in it. I just felt really victimized, alone, suicidal, and I just didn't have any happiness in me. Even though I'd done all of those inspiring things, stripping in King's cross and Japan. Inside me, I was still a really hurt person, like the clown taking off the mask when you have got nothing there. It was all part of who I'd become.

I didn't recognize that in that time, when I saw the live demonstration of the sexual trauma in the tantric practice, I kept on saying, no; I don't need to have a practice. I'm OK. I'm fine. And somebody said, I think you need to have a practice. Then I started thinking, well, yeah. I was hesitant to go to the workshop that evening. I didn't want to go. And then when I walked in there, there were many people that didn't want to go because we were all triggered by that demonstration. But I went, that's where I got that release from. I look back now and think, oh my God, I'm so glad that I was in that place to receive that blessing. It was a blessing.

Kimberly: Absolutely. What would you tell your younger self now, if you could go back in time?

Antisk: Oh, well, that was one of the hardest questions you gave me. I thought about it for two entire days trying to think. If I could go back in time and talk to my younger self. I just have to say to myself how proud I am of my younger self. For listening to that inner guidance, to still my mind, and to find that way. And even though I was coming across all those barriers even, in the police station. There I was, all battered and bruised, and they kept coming in and telling me I do know the person who had done this. Asking me, were you protecting him? I didn't know him at all. I was really trying to hold myself together without losing the plot, is what I was doing. I kept hearing this word inside, justice, the word that I heard, justice. Justice will be done, and that's what held me together. So, I have to say to my inner self, you know, thanks for letting me hear from you.

Kimberly: I love that. You are truly a survivor. I love you, said your intuition and you recognized it. Even in the moment of all that chaos, having the wherewithal to say, okay, I have to be quiet so I can hear myself think. Getting yourself to that next step, to that next step over and over. Incredible. Absolutely incredible. You're more than a survivor. You're thriving.

Antisk: And now I am a Goddess!

Kimberly: Absolutely. you are a Goddess! I just thank you so much for being on here and sharing your story. You've come so far to know that you're still moving, still helping, not only yourself but others heal from all of this. It's incredible.

Antisk: It's an absolute honor. My passion is to reach out, and let people know that there's something available. I didn't know that there was anything available. That's where my passion comes from.

And thank you, Kimberly. Thank you very much for the offer, it's just a privilege. It's a godsend. That's what it is. I love it. Thank you so much!

CHAPTER 4

Progress Over Perfection

Barbie Ray

Barbie Ray is the CEO and Creative Director of Barbie Ray Designs, Inc., an award-winning graphic design company dedicated to helping small businesses attract their ideal client through strategic design.

With over 14 years of experience in design, marketing, and brand development, Barbie believes design has the power to influence change. She uses design strategy to help.

purpose-driven entrepreneurs grow their business, gain confidence and clarity in their visual brand. She thrives on helping her clients make the RIGHT first impression.

Besides bringing brands to life, Barbie's other passions include soccer, baking, exploring new foods at local restaurants and enjoying the outdoors with her family. Her husband and toddler son are the joys of her life!

Contact info:

Phone: (951) 595-7840

info@barbieraydesigns.com

https://barbieraydesigns.com/

https://www.facebook.com/barbieraydesigns/

https://www.instagram.com/barbieraydesigns/

She had it all, then she didn't. Having to breakthrough her barrier to the other side, she found success. ~KA

Kimberly: I am excited today to talk with Barbie Ray, Barbie is the CEO and creative designer of Barbie Ray designs incorporated. Thank you for being here.

Barbie: Thanks for having me.

Kimberly: Share with us a little more about what it is you do in your business.

Barbie: Sure. I am the CEO and Creative Director for Barbie Ray Designs, a graphic design company, specializing in logo design, branding, and print design. I help small businesses; especially female entrepreneurs gain confidence and clarity in their visual brand through strategic design.

Kimberly: Love it, definitely needed for businesses. Well, let's get into it. What would you say is one of the biggest obstacles you've gone through or had to overcome?

Barbie: Probably in life and professionally, it's a limiting belief in myself, having confidence that I am capable and that I have the talents; the skills, and know-how to pursue my passion. For me, that was graphic design.

I'm sure many people out there could probably relate to this, but me I definitely had imposter syndrome. Not believing in myself and thinking, "Am I good enough? Can I, do it? No, they won't like it. There's no way!" It was having to overcome that hurdle. Understanding, "No! Own it, move forward. What's the worse that's going to happen, really"? You end up being your own worst critic and your own worst enemy in that way.

Kimberly: Definitely. I always say we are our own worst enemies. We've got to snap out of that thought process, the limiting beliefs. That is huge. I think it doesn't matter what you've ever gone through in life. That seems to always surface up for everyone, especially women. How did you recognize that what you were battling against was yourself?

Barbie: Income, honestly, from an outside source – from my husband. He might be biased, but he really saw the talent in me and saw my passion for graphic design.

Maybe I should go back. To how I started my business. I had my dream job working as a designer for a local marketing agency. I was there for a few years. We were building brands for these amazing clients from all over the world, building all these great marketing campaigns. I had an amazing team, and we were like a seamless machine – things were happening. Life was good. Then one day, we had a staff meeting, and the owner said, "Hey guys, we're shutting our doors." What?! That was shocking for me, it devastated me.

I didn't know what to do because my husband and I bought a new house. We were talking about starting a family. Suddenly be halted in our tracks was very shocking. I had to take a moment to figure out, "okay, well, what are we going to do here?" I did the whole job search. I was looking around and actually got a few offers. The more I thought about it, I was like, "you know, something doesn't feel right." I had to do some soul searching.

I sat down with my husband and did list of pros and cons. Do I pursue this or not? My husband simply asked, "Why don't you start your own business?"

It never occurred to me that was a possibility. I focused on, "get another job; keep moving forward" That made me take a step back, I was like, "you know what, why not? I probably could do that." Luckily enough, I had built some great rapport with the clientele from the marketing agency I was laid off from. Some of them even called me personally to say, "Barbie, we are so sorry to hear what happened. But wherever you go, we'll follow." Having that, also my husband's support and him saying, "Babe, do it. I know this is what you love to do. I will be there with you 100% whatever obstacles come up; I will always be there. So, don't worry about what's going on."

I said, "Okay, I'm going to do it! I'm going to take a leap of faith." And I did it. Four years later, I'm here still running my business and working with some amazing clients. Having that outside perspective to believe in me and further light that fire in myself made me realize, "You know what? Yes, I can do it. I appreciate the support and yes, I am great! I can really do some great work to help serve others. "That was the catalyst really, that helped push me forward and got me thinking, "Own it. Step in my belief, in myself, the world's my oyster."

Kimberly: Absolutely. It makes a vast difference on support systems. Especially when we're struggling with limiting belief. If I'm good enough, if I'm worthy, will it be successful, can I even possibly do this? Then, of course, the imposter syndrome on top, there's all those things that constantly stop us as we keep moving along. Even after four years, I would imagine every once in a while, it bubbles up.

Barbie: That little voice, that's when you have to be like; "hold on. It's okay." I guess it is a good, a reality check because I know

I don't know everything. I'm constantly learning as I go. I always feel like I'm a perpetual student. If you're not learning, you're not growing, right? If there aren't any challenges, there aren't any opportunities. You roll with it; you learn that it's ok. It might be a little roadblock or a minor speed bump, but you'll overcome it. "Well, what's the worst that can happen? It's fine. It's fine."

Kimberly: It's actually a great attitude to take. I love you said that. If you look at it from that perspective, well, what's the worst that can happen. You keep falling forward, getting up again and keep going at it. The success will follow, right?

Barbie: Exactly. Exactly. You keep trying and then that one time, you know. You might do it 99 times, then that 100th time - BOOM - you hit it and you're good. Don't have to worry about that again.

Kimberly: That's for sure. Have you always been able to shift your mindset when those kinds of things came up, those thoughts, those limiting beliefs? Was that something that you learned as a child?

Barbie: My dad, my parents were an enormous influence on that. My dad came here from the Philippines with $50 in his pocket, had to make things work. He worked a few jobs, moving his way up, becoming CFO of some businesses and eventually became his own boss. Now, he is running his own business as a real estate broker. I think seeing him as I was growing up, seeing him doing what he needed to for his family, not letting anything get in his way. He would always give us, my sister and I, like little tidbits of life lessons and business lessons. Seeing how he was the owner and the driver of his own life - that he can do what he wanted for himself, for his family.

A challenge was more of an opportunity. Having that positive mindset and having that positive influence affected me to know that. It's been great to have that mindset because mindset is everything. We were saying earlier, right? I want to say it was

Henry Ford that said, "Whether you think you can or think you can't, you're right." That goes to show that whatever it goes in your mind is going to follow through to your body, your actions. It's really best for you mentally, emotionally, and physically to have that positive mindset.

Kimberly: Absolutely. So, you had a really positive role model in your life. Who was your dad, and watching him do all that he could do? What I really want to point out too, is that you have this outstanding role model, you landed your dream job. All that came crashing down with your dream job, then stepping into entrepreneurial ship, which a lot of women do. We're seeing a lot of that happening where we're going from corporate to our own businesses. Many things come up, even though you watched your dad do well in his life. And then you did well, starting off here you were again. I think it's important for women to realize that these things happen all the time. It doesn't matter if you have what you think or perceive, or what the outside world perceives as your perfect life or not, it's how you embrace those. Would you agree?

Barbie: I agree with that, that's spot on. We all go through this, all have our own experiences, but more or less, that common thread right there. We all have some type of limiting beliefs or those mindsets that we all go through.

Kimberly: When you have a belief or a mindset moment, we'll call it reset. What do you do? How can you help other women really understand from your perspective how you get out of that? Sometimes it can keep us in bed all day, and we're never getting out of our pajamas, or we're going to binge watch Netflix, and those days are great. Take them, don't feel guilty about it. But what's really helped when you have those moments?

Barbie: Sometimes it helps to cry it out depending on how emotional or how big the challenge is. I know I have those moments. Sometimes you're like, "Ugh, I got to let it out!" it's okay to feel those emotions, let it be, take a moment. I need to actually physically get out of the space that I'm in, that I feel it's marinating where maybe that negative energy or those beliefs I'm having. If I'm sitting in front of my computer and I'm feeling like, "Okay, I can't do this right now!" I step away. I like to take a walk, go out to the park, be one with nature, and take my mind off of it.

Sometimes, what helps for me too is then to refocus on, "Okay, what is it? What's the actual task at hand? What is it I'm struggling with?" Sometimes, I have to write it down. Everywhere I go, I always have like a pad of paper. Because sometimes I feel like if it gets all stuck in here (my mind) and I can write it down, that helps offload things and I can think with clearer. I'll make pros and cons lists, take some deep breaths, refocus. I'll even get my husband; we get that third party and to help offload things too. And sometimes talking out loud because as a solo entrepreneur, it can become a little isolating sometimes. Having that other person to talk to is extremely helpful. I also have a great support network through other business professionals that I can lean on and stuff like that. It's having the right network and daily routines that you can do to kind of help. Keep yourself moving forward in whatever you can to help clear your mind.

Kimberly: I want to go back to what you said about crying it out. We think it happens all the time, but we feel guilty about that, often we're labeled as emotional. Embrace that we're women, we're supposed to be emotional. It already comes standard in the book. Embrace it. I love you said that we don't talk about it. Have a full ugly snot cry, let it out, let it go. And it helps.

Barbie: It's terrible because what I do, I think it's because I have a toddler son (he's about two-and-a-half years old) and we are teaching him it's okay to feel whatever he's feeling. He might get upset because we took a toy away from him, but I always acknowledge him and say something like, "I see you're upset, it's okay to be upset. But right now, we have to do X, Y, Z,". I do the same thing for myself and for others, empathy that it's okay. We are human beings; we are emotional creatures. Feel all the feels that you want. But then, you regroup, right? Because if not, then it gets built up. You're pushing out the inevitable, I say, feel it all.

Kimberly: And that's such a powerful tip because when you allow yourself to feel, it helps move that energy, that emotion through you, where you're saying, it gets stuck; bottled up and eventually, like a volcano we're going to blow. And who knows, who's going to get it, that could be your kids, could be your family, could be whoever, understanding that it's okay. And you're going to be okay, let it happen. I really love that you talked about that because it's important! And then the other thing, taking a walk, getting out in nature, getting away from where you feel like it's marinating.

Barbie: That is huge. Or even like something fun and random. A little dance party in the kitchen, get the wiggles out or whatever, shake it off Whatever you need to do to shake off the bad vibes tell yourself, "Deep breath. Reset. Okay. Here we go."

Kimberly: I love it. Yes! Yes! It's so good. Taking a walk, it's about really stepping into that. People need to understand; most of the time, our limiting beliefs are not even our own beliefs. They are other people's perceptions that have been put on us and reinforced along the way. Realizing you can break free from those is a good step forward. That it's all in your mindset, change your mindset, you can change your life, literally.

Barbie: Definitely! My personal mantra has been "progress over perfection." It's taking those little steps. I'll say it, I'm a recovering perfectionist. Who else is guilty of that? When you can that, it's okay to take those baby steps. You're falling forward, do what you can to keep moving. If you focus on that versus having everything perfect.

Kimberly: I have always said there's no such thing as perfection. It's all progress and progress is perfection because eventually you keep going. Yoga is a practice. Guess what? Doctors have a practice. They don't go in and say, I have a perfection. This is my doctor's office perfect. It's a doctor's practice, its mind blowing when you realize that. You can always keep moving forward and keep going. Practice makes perfection, and it keeps getting better and ultimately easier. You are also switching out of your mindset to release the negative.

I love how you call it the wiggles. If we remember to do that, and I would say, we sometimes forget these simple fun tips when our kids get older. Kids can snap in and out of things fast, and if we can mimic that, it can help.

Barbie: There are those moments on the other side of the tantrum, but then it suddenly switches, and he's having fun playing with his fire truck. I'm like, "all right, cool dude. You're good?" Having those moments to snap out of it is helpful and necessary.

Kimberly: If we look at it like those are our tantrums or meltdowns, moments where we need to cry it out and let it go then we can switch and change into that new. That new mindset, that new belief in ourselves. We can do it faster If you accept that you need to go in your room and shut the door and get on the floor and tantrum it out.

Barbie: Yes! I have walked into my closet before cried, hit the clothes that were hanging because I needed to get that energy out. I'm like, "all right, dresses, here we go!".

Kimberly: I used to have a punching bag hanging in my garage. All those things help, and all those things are okay. It really helps put you in a different mindset. That's the biggest thing is it's the release and letting go, right?

Barbie: Definitely. Like you said, and also that transfer of energy, let that out. Get the good energy in.

Kimberly: Yeah. I love it! What would you say has propelled you into business? I'm curious, knowing that you've had an outstanding role model going back to your dad. Even for yourself, having that success and having that torn away because that's crushing. What was the one thing you say has propelled you the most?

Barbie: My biggest supporter has been my husband. Having him, building out my network and building relationships because for me, that's what business is about, right? Relationships, understanding who you're working with and what is going on with them.

What I do with my clients too, is I don't approach them as a client, but more in, "Hey, how can we help each other? I want to get to know you. Why did you start your business? Having those connections, having those real heart-to-heart moments for me is everything. That's kiI was 15 I ran away, and I lived in the park. nd of why I love to help others, serve others is to kind of help them pursue their mission and pursue their passion. Paying it forward, I really want to help people be seen the way they deserve to be seen. A lot of times, they're stuck in the day-to-day and not focusing on what they need to do to help grow themselves or their businesses.

Kimberly: I love that because, what you're saying is we get stagnant in our life?

Barbie: Yeah, it's easy to get comfortable.

Kimberly: Stop growing and you stop excelling. It's important to always be a student of life. We're always growing, always expanding. Sometimes it's not great, we come back again, and try it again.

Barbie: Yeah. You're like, "Okay, I didn't like that road. Let's go this way."

Kimberly: You tried, you have the option, the choice to move forward to change your mind. It's all good. I think as women;

we beat ourselves up too many times and feel guilty over what decisions we've made.

Barbie: Thinking to yourself, is this the right one? And then sometimes you get in that whole analysis paralysis. Too stuck in thinking, what's the right choice, what do I do? Do I do this or that? You never decide. Indecision keeps you from doing anything. That's when you've got to make that decision and move forward. If it works out, awesome! If it doesn't, that's okay. Take a step back, reevaluate, go a different route. It's okay to fail.

Kimberly: That is true. We could have an entire class on that.

We're afraid as women, talking about intuition, we second, third, fourth, fifth guess our first initial gut instinct. When we decide, have clarity, decide, move forward, then you're like, okay. Like you said, if it doesn't work out, let's take a step back, regroup, evaluate, move, go to the next, or try it again. Makes a big difference, so you're not stuck in stagnant. I love that. If you could go back and tell your younger self one thing, what would it be?

Barbie: I would say don't be afraid to be you. Own you, every ounce of you. Whatever this weirdness quirkiness, you know, anything that happens. That's what I would tell myself is that it's okay, you are you. God made you the way you were, own it. If people don't love it, that's okay. You're not for everybody, but you are for somebody. For me, that would be the biggest that it's okay to be you, do what you want to do.

Kimberly: Yes, yes, yes! All day long, yes! I love that question because if we could go back and tell ourselves something; we don't know that we're going to make it through to the other side sometimes, to really embrace you, all the quirky, the crazy, the awesome.

Barbie: Right! Until we love ourselves, then how are you going to love anybody else? Nothing else in the world is going to matter.

Take care of numero uno, yourself, then the rest is going to be a ripple effect. You're going to radiate this light, that's going to attract what you want.

Kimberly: Do you use that mindset now in your business?

Barbie: I definitely do. I know I'm not for everybody, but I am me. I'm very transparent in who I am, clear in my communication, I let it all shine. Then that's definitely who I attract, the people that I want to work with, be friends with, let into my inner circle. I own that, lead with that - lead with my light.

Kimberly: Lead with your own light. That's so good. I hope that really sinks in for everyone, that's going to watch this and read it in the future because when you own your own light, you allow others to own theirs and shine bright as well.

These conversations, I love them because they're transparent. We allow ourselves to be vulnerable, have these conversations. My passion for it is to really to share stories, all different stories to help women all over the world (this could wind up in a man's lap too). Be inspired, impacted, able to change their lives and collapsed time, find that success, find that happiness, joy and shift their mindset faster. It's been amazing. Thank you for sharing your stories and your wisdom.

Barbie: It's been so much fun. Thank you for the opportunity, Kimberly. This has been fantastic! I look forward to connecting with more women out there and would love to help to anybody as much as I can. I'll be that shoulder to cry on. You can ugly snot cry all you want. I've been there, I totally get it.

Kimberly: We've got Kleenex. We can do the laundry. It's okay. I love it.

Thank you so much.

Barbie: Thank you, Kimberly.

CHAPTER 5

Push On to Your Goals

Bridgette Moore

Bridgette and her husband, Stewart Moore, have called Wildomar their home for the past 23 years. They have one son, Jake. She, also, has a bonus daughter, Catherine, and two grandsons, Emmet and Sam.

A year after they moved to Wildomar, the local parks were closed. Bridgette started volunteering and assisted in the parks being reopened. Later, Wildomar became a city, and Bridgette was elected to the inaugural city council in 2008. Councilwoman Moore was the first woman to serve as Mayor in 2010 in the city of Wildomar. She was appointed Mayor, again, in 2016.

As a public servant, she has the reputation of being committed to bettering the lives of our citizens. Actively involved in the community and volunteers her time with organizations such as VFW Auxiliary, Wildomar Rotary Club, Caring Hearts for Veterans and Community, Cops for Kids, Operation Prom Girl/Dresses & Dreams Project.

Contact info:

Bmoore@cityofwildomar.org

Www.cityofwildomar.org

She is goal driven, getting in as much as she can to live life to the fullest. ~KA

Kimberly: I am here today with Bridgette Moore. I'm excited to talk to you today. You are the city councilwoman for Wildomar, Ca. I love this. How did you wind up going down that route?

Bridgette: Hi, Kimberly. I thank you for having me. I didn't start out thinking that I would be on city council one day. I was not involved with anything like that in high school. I was not on the debate team or anything. We moved to Wildomar in 1998 and Wildomar wasn't a city yet. There were obstacles and things happening to our area. Then I joined the Wildomar Incorporation Now (WIN) committee, to help Wildomar become a city. And so when I was on that, it was deciding who was actually going to run for the first city council. 18 people ran for that first city council. I was one of them, and I was the second top vote getter. I became Mayor Pro Tem in 2008 and 2009. Then 2010, I was the first woman mayor of the city of Wildomar.

Kimberly: Wow. That is awesome. Congratulations on that. And do you also do something else? Cause you know, that doesn't take enough of your time?

Bridgette: Well, being on city council, it really is just giving back to your community as we just receive a stipend of $400 a month.

So I work a full-time job. Many of us do. I'm the manager of treasury for Impact Mortgage.

Kimberly: Very nice. Well, let's just dive right into this. We're here talking about overcoming beliefs, traumas, obstacles. I know we go through many of them in our lifetime. What would you say is one of your biggest obstacles that you've overcome?

Bridgette: As a child, I actually had asthma and allergies very severe. I'm actually still labeled a severe asthmatic. So if you follow me on social media, you might not think that, because it is controlled now, but as a child, it was not controlled. I was sick all the time and in the hospital and in urgent care. The age of one, is when my asthmas actually started. My parents were young, 18 and 21, and my mom worked the night shift. She came home and usually I'd be up by then. And she said, to my dad, "is the baby still asleep?" And he said, yeah. So she went to check on me. Well, what had happened was I had thrown up, and so I had choked on my vomit. This was a long time ago, before 911. They put me in the car and drove me to the hospital. I was turning blue. So it's really a miracle that I didn't have any brain damage, which was amazing. I still have a scar from when they had to cut me. From then on my lungs were damaged. To this day I don't operate on a full lung set. It's controlled now. I take medication in the morning and at night. I have my long acting inhalers. Then I have my short, fast acting inhalers I keep at my desk, one is in my purse and one is by my bed. Whenever I need it, it's there.

Growing up, like I said, I was sick all the time, missed school, they wanted to hold me back. My mom would always say no, because I could still get good grades, still able to pass, but I had the attendance issue. As I grew up, I was blessed to have really great friends. I wouldn't say I had a lot of friends because I was the kid that was always sneezing. This is before real inclusion, which now, people are much more accepting, but back then I was the sneezing, running nose kid all the time. It was really embarrassing. I carried tissues with me wherever I went because the allergies were so bad.

I had great friends that stuck with me. They understood, -we're still friends today. So on top of being sick, my mom was a single mom. It was very difficult. Even going through teenage years, I was always in and out of urgent care at this point. So I grew up early. I grew up with having a single mom and then being sick all the time. I really learned to grow up early. Even in sixth grade, I would go get my allergy shots. I did allergy shots for years and they worked. I can be around a dog now, and not go into an asthma attack. In sixth grade I was riding the bus, riding public transportation from my house to the doctor's office. My mom wouldn't be able to get off work at the time before they closed. I would arrive at the doctor's office and get my shots, then you have to wait 20 minutes to see if you have a reaction. So by that time, my mom could get off work and come pick me up. Literally sixth grade, I'm taking care of myself, getting on the bus to another city to get my allergy shots. And so I just grew up really fast, and mature, because I had to take care of myself and even into the teen years when I could actually drive, I'd be driving myself to urgent care. My mom even dropped me off; as a teenager I had an asthma attack, we were having the carpets cleaned. So, she had to be there to let the carpet cleaners in. But also, I need to get to urgent care. She literally pulls up and I walk myself in. I'm turning blue. I remember that receptionist because she was just panicking, and I was fine. I was, I knew what I needed. Give me a shot of Decadron, give me some oxygen, give me a lot of prednisones to go home. I knew the drill. Luckily, as I got older, medicine had improved, so now it's controlled. I'm able to do a lot more things, you know, not so much exercise, even though you see an exercise bike, I need exercise because I still need to exercise my lungs to keep them going so I can live longer.

Kimberly: Wow. It's interesting to hear you talk, because I'm thinking, that literally affected your whole life. I mean, you just said you have your medicine everywhere with you at all times because you never know.

Bridgette: It did. Yes. Right. And so when it was uncontrolled, I'd have a breathing machine, so that I could do the breathing treatments at home, and we'd have to take it on vacations, take it going away just for the weekend, wherever you went. I had to tote along this big breathing machine with me. You never know when you're going to have an asthma attack. I haven't been in urgent care since last February, now that it's controlled. But between that and growing up with a single mom, it made me determined. Because I missed a lot, because we didn't have money, or because I was always sick. I knew when I wanted a family; I wanted to have a home; we moved a lot. Whenever someone raised the rent, we moved.

Wildomar is the 23rd place I've lived. If you're in the military, then you move a lot that way, but this was just a single mom trying to get by, which is why we always need affordable housing. So this is my 23rd home. I married my husband, Stewart, in 1994 and we adopted our son in 1997. I really wanted to make a home, somewhere to stay and put down our roots. I wanted to get involved because I just wanted that whole feeling of that I had always wanted to be part of the community. I first started volunteering, and I helped bring parks back because the parks were open and then they closed. Then they opened, and that led to being on Wildomar Incorporation Now committed, which led to being on the city council. So that's just kind of how I got to that point.

Kimberly: It was a need that you saw and wanted for yourself and then your community.

Bridgette: Right. And for my son, I really did. I didn't want him moving like I did, so he's lived in two places. Well, technically he moved out, then moved back. I didn't want him to have to move all those times and change all those schools. I really wanted him to live in one place to grow up. It is a community, and everyone knows your name. Wildomar is a small town community and you can go to the store or the grocery store and you see neighbors and friends.

Kimberly: I'm curious. How did that affect you growing up with your mindset and your belief about always having to have medicine and at sixth grade taking yourself to the doctor, did you feel like it was going to hinder you in your life?

Bridgette: I knew it was just something I'd always have to live with because sometimes people grow out of asthma. I knew my grandmother had it and she was born in Mexico. They immigrated, and she had asthma. I don't know how much further back from her, but she still had the asthma still as an adult until she died. My dad had asthma until he died. I knew that this was the type of asthma I'm going to have my whole life. And then it even affected, how I said, we adopted our son, because I have been on medicine since a year old, I can't be off of them. A lot of times, you're talking to your doctor and they say, well, you know, during pregnancy, we like you to be off your medication, I can't miss a dose.

I literally can feel it. I have my long acting inhaler, and if I miss the morning dose or the night dose, I know I can feel it. So there's no way I could be off for nine months. And we don't know what all that medicine would do to the baby. I mean, I know it's a lot better now. But my husband and I felt like why change it, you know? And there were so many children that needed a home. And so we were lucky. It was kind of a friend of a friend situation. And so we adopted our son. He was only five days old the first time I held him. Having asthma has affected my whole life.

Kimberly: I keep hearing it's a mindset. So what would you say is one of the biggest mindset beliefs that you've really embraced to move you through each stage? Because knowing that it was a lifetime thing that it has affected you, even in your decision to be a parent, what have you embraced? It will not matter. Like, what is that one thing?

Bridgette: I guess my mindset is I always want to try to see what I can do. I know my limitations though; I know when my body is saying, Oh, you've pushed it, because I'll go to bed late, get up early. I'm working two full-time jobs. So I know when I've pushed it and I'm not taking time for self-care, my body will let me know. I try not to let it stop me. I want to live as much as I can.

I'm not trying to be morbid, but I have a lung disease and that's what it is, is lung disease. I don't operate on full capacity lungs as it is. My grandparents passed away early, my parents, my dad passed away early. So, you know, just looking at all that I might not live a long life, 80 years old or something. So I do want to get as much as I can and I missed it a lot in childhood. I do want to get as much out of it, and live life. So I guess one thing I say is work hard, play hard. And so I work hard. I have these jobs, I'm very committed. I love helping the residents of Wildomar. So very committed to my public service. But on the weekends, I want to play hard. I want to enjoy my time, and we just never know.

Kimberly: Right. I love that. Do it anyway, try hard, just keep going.

Bridgette: Right. But know yourself, my body will let me know. Hey you, you've got to get some sleep and you've got to take a break here.

Kimberly: I think it's given you a powerful lesson, most people don't know their limitations. For you to say that, that's a pretty big thing to recognize. We just exert ourselves until we're burnt out. You don't have that. You don't have that luxury, but you also understand the importance of like you said, self-care.

Bridgette: Right. So I need to work out more. That's one self-care, I did little in 2020, so I was working in Irvine and then,

March 30th, 2020, we went home to work remotely for two weeks now I'm still working from home and I love it. Here is one caveat, I haven't been exercising as much because when you went to work you parked in a parking building that was far away and you had to walk across campus to get to your building. And then, even the restroom was a half a building away or the break room. And now it's just right out the door. I need to get back to walking and exercising to exercise my lungs.

Kimberly: Do you think knowing that this was something that you had to deal with lifelong, it kind of gave you that attitude that I'm going to push forward no matter what, instead of it coming on more when you're older, does that make sense?

Bridgette: Yeah, I'm very goal driven. I asked a couple of friends about my life or what I had to overcome or obstacles. And, my one girlfriend said you're so goal driven. You're so about accomplishments.

Sometimes my family or friends might think I am a little too driven, but you know, if I come up with an idea I go for it. We just started this litter pickup program last July in our city, we're doing litter pickup every Saturday. We're going to clean up the city. I have these goals. I don't want you to get in my way. I'm very driven. And I think it was the asthma that has shaped me.

Kimberly: Definitely. I think that's a great way to put it, to all these experiences, traumas and obstacles that we go through. Every one of us shapes us on some level. And for the better, I mean, if you don't go through those things, you don't know your full potential; you don't know what's going to cause you to really step into your brilliance. I love that you just said that, that is awesome.

Bridgette: I agree that everything in our life has shaped us and there are always pros and cons. And you take what it dealt you with. You 're given how you're born, what happens in your life and what are you going to do? So I often have a goal. I wanted to get parks open. I'm going to get the parks open. We're going to do this, and we need a fundraiser to do this. People are like, Oh, well, what are you going to do about this? I am just going forward, going forward. Oh, they tried to derail me. "Oh, what about this? You're not really going to get all those volunteers. You're not able to raise the money. And I don't know how we're going to get a goal." All these people are trying to say, "Oh, this will not happen", but it's like, no, we're going to get parks opened, and we did.

Kimberly: You said a great metaphor for life actually, because that is our mindset. If you think about it, you're going through, you have this goal, very driven. You're up against people saying you can't get this; you can't do that. All those outside people are telling you, you can't, our mindset does the same thing especially as entrepreneurs and you just keep going forward. What a great metaphor. I love that.

Bridgette: My girlfriend gave me a pillow for my birthday last year. And it says, underestimate me, that'll be fun. I was like, this is perfect. I want everyone to succeed. You know whoever is in my circle, whoever I'm speaking with, I want everyone to succeed. I'm your cheerleader rooting you on. I'm helping you.

One of my pet peeves is if I see someone who I can see there's potential, they have all this potential that they could do and they're not doing. I'm like "why? you can do this!"

They tell me their goal, what they want to do. And it's like, okay, well, here's your first step. You don't need to know all the steps, but here's your first step you have to do in order to get that.

Kimberly: Absolutely. And that's such a big thing. You don't need to know the how, you just need to take one step at a time.

Bridgette: Know your why. We just did a book club, that was one of them is, know your why. What is your purpose? Sometimes you don't know. I didn't know when I was taking the bus to my shots that one day I would be on city council helping people. But I felt that this is my purpose. I love being on council; I do not consider myself a politician. I'm a public servant. I have no aspirations to go higher. I'm just here serving our community. I love helping people. That turned out to be my purpose. I didn't know that then; you evolve.

Kimberly: Yes, absolutely. And it's important too. What did you want to be when you were little? Do you have any ideas?

Bridgette: I wanted to be Julie on the Love Boat. I love planning the events for this city, and I love planning the event that I've gone back to school. So that's on top of working full time and city council. I am a student at Northern Arizona university and I went back and get my parks and rec degree because I love doing the parks and rec for the city. And I did not know that I would do that. But my son, we came here; the parks were open. My son was one. I'd take him in the stroller down to the park. And then a year later they closed. I was like, what? I want these parks open. How do I help? Well, if you ask, how can you get them open? You're put on a committee. So it put me on the Wildomar Parks Formation Committee and that's how it all started.

Kimberly: Wow. That's awesome. I like how you incorporated your childhood dream to some level into what you're doing now.

Bridgette: Yeah. And I love to travel. I always wanted to be Julie on the Love Boat.

Kimberly: That's so cute. If you could go back and tell your younger self one thing, what would it be?

Bridgette: Be more confident. I was not confident as a child. I don't know why that just made me tear up. Just to be sick and you know, like I said, it was embarrassing to sneeze all the time. Even though I still sneeze now, I still hate it. It is so embarrassing. Even going to your friend's house, First I'd have to ask, do you have animals in the house? If they had animals in the house, I couldn't go play with them because I'd get sick. Then if they didn't, their parents would ask, are you sick? Why is your friend sneezing? And snotty nose, they don't want their child to get sick. So I was always constantly explaining it, I just wasn't confident. So to be more confident and believe in yourself.

Kimberly: Yes, always and still today, right? It's interesting because I don't think as parents, you recognize, okay, you want your kid to always be healthy and well and happy. But for you having to ask, do you have pets? Do you have this? Can I even go in there because I could get sick? That has affected your beliefs and how you feel. I can see how that would completely just make you constantly wonder. Do you find that you still have moments of that as an adult or as you were growing up?

Bridgette: Oh, definitely. Yes. If friends invite us over for a dinner party or something, I would ask if you have a dog inside. I am much better. I could be around the animal now, longer, and it might just be sneezing. It won't turn into an asthma attack. My asthma is allergy induced. So my aunt Verna, she had a dog; she would clean the house and clean the house and that still ended up getting sick. She tried so hard.

Here's an example. If we rented an RV from a person to go to the Rose parade and I was like, do you have animals? Because if there are animals inside the RV, I knew I would fall asleep, and I'd just be sick. So just have to think ahead.

Kimberly: Definitely a lifelong thing that you have to be so conscious of.

Bridgette: Right. We were at the park event and a gentleman that lives close by has a large dog, it's a gorgeous dog. It's a big, gorgeous dog. Even now, the dog will come up to me and I'm like, oh please, I don't want it close, because if it touches me, or gets on my pants or too close, I just could start sneezing. Obviously I don't want that when I am on stage, you know? Thanking our sponsors or something. So, please, I just don't want animals near me. I like your animal. That's a pretty dog. I love animals. We have a tortoise. It doesn't make me sick.

Kimberly: Wow That's something else just to know that you have to constantly think about, even in an outside environment, and have to be so cautious and aware.

Bridgette: Yeah. We tried. Because my son really wanted a dog, and we kept it outside, but you know he goes out and hugs the dog and then he comes inside, sits on the couch. Then I sat on the couch, and so we had the dog for maybe a year and then we had to adopt it out. We tried, it's not just me, it affects my family. My husband would like to have a cat; my son would like to have a dog. Real Christmas tree; we haven't ever been able to have a real Christmas tree. My husband really wanted a real Christmas tree. It affects not just me, the entire family.

Kimberly: But it's okay. There are things that we have to deal with knowing its lifelong.

Bridgette: And they understand. My husband's been great because he's had to drive me to the hospital and stuff, you know, not recently, but in the past.

Kimberly: What advice would you give somebody who is struggling with that situation or any situation? Something that's a lifelong condition or situation. Not necessarily asthma, but anything because there are lots of things that affect us. Long-term, how have you really been able to cope?

Bridgette: I would say learn about it. Not that I know everything about asthma, I learn about it and really you need to be your own advocate. In that situation when I walked in, I turned blue and the nurses were upset. I was like, "Oh no, I know". Just give me a shot of a Decadron and give me some prednisone. Give me some oxygen. You really become your own advocate because you know what works for your body. Even then, just a couple of years ago, my doctor wanted to change my medicine. I'm like, no, this medicine regimen that I'm on right now works for me. I live a full life, I sleep well. Because that's another thing is, as a child, I literally slept almost sitting up. My stepdad had to make a bed. I could not lay down. Now I can lie down, I can sleep laying down so it has really gotten better. You'd really have to just be your own advocate. Like I said, think outside your box, do things, do what you want to do. You just know your body will let you know when you need to take a step back, but live your life because that's the only life we have.

Kimberly: I love that. What you're allowing people to understand is that you take back your power when you learn about it and know how far you can get. Know your limitations and all of that, that really suits you in that power seat and not just letting life drag you around.

Bridgette: Right. Surround yourself with substantial support. My husband, my son, my friends, and they all know that if we go for a walk or we go hiking, I'm a heavy breather. My lungs are just working. If that's something that would irritate you, maybe you don't want to hear me breathing that hard. You know we don't go hiking together, but my friends understand that they've always understood.

Kimberly: You are absolutely incredible. I love your strength. You are so strong, so brave. Thank you for sharing your story because so many people go through something. And it doesn't need to be asthma, we bring with us lots of different things and you just shared so many wonderful, powerful things to help other people. Thank you so much.

Bridgette: Yes. I just say, push onto your goals, whatever goals you have. I'm a list person. So every day I'm writing my list and cross them off. The best thing is crossing something off the list. Just very goal-driven, whatever you have, whatever disease you have or whatever obstacle you have in your life, write those next few steps and then go for your goal.

Kimberly: I love it. Yes, my notes have notes, and it feels so good to cross off that line.

Bridgette: I love it. Unfortunately, it's like two more things get added, but I just love it. I just have to make my list every single day. I also have another book that has my appointments and people are like, you don't use your phone calendar? I still use a paper calendar. I just want to see it all, how it feels. Then, your life changes and especially during this pandemic, I started gardening and so I never did that before. And so you just evolve, you keep changing in your life and you just keep going.

Kimberly: I love it. Thank you so much.

CHAPTER 6

More Than This Moment

Cherie Miracle

My name is Cherie Miracle of C. Miracle Photography. I have always been artistic – I sing, play guitar and hand drums, dabble in painting and writing. It wasn't until I discovered my passion for photography that I found my true voice and expressive spirit. I discovered passion doesn't always equal instant success. I instinctively had an artistic eye and understood what it took to capture a beautiful moment. The steep learning curve I faced was the technical side of photography. It was a true investment of time to develop my style in the post processing phase of photography and it is constantly evolving. I started out undervaluing my ability and lacked the confidence necessary to allow my business to flourish. Only in the last 2 years have I found my true worth. I am still shocked and embarrassed when I hear people gush over my work. I am truly blessed.

Contact Info:

www.cmiraclephotography.mypixieset.com

www.instagram.com/cmiraclephotography

www.facebook.com/miraclephotography1

She is determined to not let her past define her future. ~KA

Kimberly: I am super excited to be here today with Cherie Miracle. Thank you so much for being here and having this conversation with me. I've been looking forward to it.

Cherie: Me too. Thank you so much for having me.

Kimberly: Let's just talk about what you do first, because you're an amazing photographer.

Cherie: Thank you. I appreciate that. so I've been a professional photographer for just under seven years. I've stepped back from managing a coffee shop, full-time about a year and a half ago to focus on my business. And, I'm so glad that I did. It was the best thing that I could have done for my small business and even with, the year of COVID 2020, I had the best year that I've ever had in my business. I'm continually learning and, striving to be the best that I can be here in Southern Arizona. I was chosen as one of the top three local photographers for Sierra Vista, so that was exciting. I've been in a couple of magazines and things like that, so yeah it's kind of weird the way that my business has grown and how blessed I've been. I'm really excited to be on this journey with you as well.

Kimberly: Thank you. I saw your picture that went into one of the magazines with the woman and the horse.

Cherie: Yes.

Kimberly: Gorgeous. And say the name of your company. I love it.

Cherie: So my name is Cherie Miracle, but it is spelled French. So, when I decided to name my business, I love my last name. You can't beat the last name miracle. So miracle photography was already taken. So with the first letter of my name C, it's C miracle photography.

Kimberly: I love it. It's so awesome. Well, let's just dive into the meat of this conversation. What would you say is the biggest obstacle you've ever had to overcome?

Cherie: A little bit of backstory because, I had childhood trauma that I have had to overcome throughout years into my adult life. I was sexually molested by a family friend from the time that I was nine years old till I was 13. So that was definitely the biggest thing that I've ever had to overcome in my life. I was afraid to bring it up because I thought that I would get in trouble and that's, a typical response to someone who's being abused. I didn't want this person to not like me anymore and things like that. So that was really hard to act normal, which I guess I did a good job because no one knew that it was going on until I told my parents when I was 13. They were like, wait, what?

They were shocked that they hadn't noticed, the small things, maybe that would have given them some insight that was going on. And, I don't know what that means if I was really good at hiding things or what, and I've always had a really close knit family, really close with my parents. They actually live with us now. Both of my brothers, we're just a really good close family, but I was able to hide that from them. And that trauma followed me throughout my teenage years, into my marriage, and has made some big issues for my husband and I, and we just celebrated our 21st anniversary in December, thank God that we've made it that far. Especially having to overcome these kinds of things that have risen to the surface in the last couple of years. I've gone to counseling, I've tried to unpack those battles. So as my counselors have said, to really find kind of the root of that trauma and to overcome it. So I would say that that is definitely the biggest thing that has kind of shaped my life, but has also, I think made me resilient in my adult life now, despite everything that happened to me when I was young.

Kimberly: That is a giant thing to have to deal with and the impact psychologically on a child. And I can't even imagine how you finally decided to tell your parents, how did that go?

Cherie: It was actually at my 13th birthday party because, this person was a family friend. One of my oldest brother's friends. So at the time he was legally an adult and this was still going on and he was there at the party and it was just, just this weight on me seeing him there, and pretending like everything was fine. And I don't even remember what it was exactly that straw that broke the camel's back kind of thing, that made me need to tell them this because this is a big deal. And so something though, that I wish had changed, is that nothing was ever done to him, because of what he had done to me. And, in 2018, when all of these, other things because of this trauma came up, my parents were like we should try and prosecute him.

It's still within the timeframe that we could, legally do that. And I was like, what is that going to do? I mean, I'm, I'm not technically over it, but I'm working through it and it's not worth, ruining him and his family in order to just make me feel better. So I chose not to pursue anything legally. I think that was the right choice. I wrote him a letter and got basically like a form letter back that said, Oh, I don't remember that ever happening. And I'm like, okay. So what happened for four years? That really made an impact on my psyche and my life. It hurt even more that he couldn't remember that he did that to me, you know, like I should've felt justified for him to be like, Oh, wow. Yeah, I did that. I'm so sorry. And some sort of repentance and there wasn't that sort of thing there.

Kimberly: Well, I'm sure he remembers it. He just didn't want to admit to it.

Cherie: Probably

Kimberly: Embarrassment and the fear of that and all, but it's unfortunate that he didn't come out and say, I am sorry, and I was very wrong. That helps that healing process a little bit more. I Want to point out something that you said about going through it, because one of the things I always talk about is we overcome, but it's not necessarily an overcoming of our experience. It's, we're working through it. We're, learning how to cope and deal and heal from it. And I've said it a bunch of times, we can be walking down the grocery store aisle and all of a sudden have a meltdown because it comes up again and it's like, here we go again, let's peel this next layer off, but it's about that journey of healing. And for you having to even deal with that, becoming an adult and going into a relationship with your husband now, there's a lot of things that you're constantly having to deal with.

Cherie: Yeah, absolutely. And that in turn makes him have to deal with it too. And thankfully, I married a wonderful man and he's always been supportive and trying to help me through things and understanding, because the intimate side of me I think is broken because of it.

Kimberly: That's a lot of communication and trust you have to work at often, I would imagine. And bless his heart for being so gentle, I guess would be the word I would say with you.

Cherie: Yeah, absolutely.

Kimberly: What astounds me is people don't realize the reality of abuse, all abuse affects everyone. It's not just the victim. It's literally everyone. And do you have children?

Cherie: I do. And I was just about to say that so my daughter will be 20 this year. My son will be 18. And I remember when Gabi was kind of hitting puberty. I told her my story kind of as a cautionary tale, because I didn't want to be on the other end as the parent and look back and see something that I had completely missed. Especially when I've already been through something like that. So, I think I told my son about it too, actually, because, you know, as a young man, I want him to be respecting of young ladies that he may date and eventually marry. And so, I'm hoping that my hard circumstances from my childhood can help them in some way lead a more, eyes wide open kind of life and not get sucked into something that they feel like they have no escape from, which is what I felt like.

Kimberly: Oh yeah. I would imagine that affects you. but that's smart of you to even bring it up to your children. A lot of people are terrified to have that conversation and then they're paranoid. My mom was abused as a child and she was paranoid, at seven years old she had me terrified something would happen to me. So it affects people differently. And I think having that conversation is very wise to have with your kids, to just make them aware, not terrified but aware of their circumstances and even for your son to just know that things happen, and he might wind up in a relationship with someone. You mentioned that you felt like you didn't understand how your parents didn't notice the signs, or were thinking that you were so good at hiding it. What do you think just for the sake of this conversation? Because I think it would be interesting for people to hear that perspective. What do you think your parents were missing? Where do you think you were really that good at hiding it? Or do you think it's possible that, sometimes parents don't want to believe something like that as well. Or, do you think they just truly had no idea.

Cherie: Yeah. I feel like I wasn't that good at hiding things. I mean, I was nine years old when it started. But I remember, basically my mom walking in and like catching some of the abuse happening and it was just kind of like, what are you doing in here? He ran out and I was just kinda like, Oh, I don't know what was happening. And it didn't really click that. Oh, maybe something else is going on. So I don't know if it's because they wanted to turn a blind eye and not think that something like that was happening to their daughter, their youngest, their baby. I've been raised in the church. I have a very strong relationship with the Lord. I don't know if maybe that kind of relationship, my parents were thinking, he's a church kid, so of course he's not going to do anything bad, you know, just kids being kid's kind of thing. So, I think it's between me being able to hide things well enough, and then them maybe just choosing not to open their eyes to it. So that would mean that they failed in a way. So that's a big deal for a parent to accept that of themselves. Like, oh my gosh, I failed my child, you know? So I think that that might have something to do with it. I've never actually talked to my mom about it. It's not something that I really want to, I don't know really their reasoning or if it just wasn't obvious to them.

Kimberly: You said something about them thinking, because he's a church boy that nothing happens. And I think that puts a lot of blinders on many people, because you never know.

Cherie: Yeah. You know, about abuses and affairs and things like that in the church because this world is fallen, just because you believe in Christ doesn't mean that you're not going to come up against things that, test you and tempt you and things like that. So many times you see people falling from grace as it were, that are church leadership or, evangelists, things like that. So I think that people that don't go to church, kind of lump that side of church, everybody into that side, like, Oh, well, they're hypocrites. Why would I want to go? And, you know, be a part of that when that's the exception, not the rule.

Kimberly: Definitely. And I want to go back again to abuse really hits everyone. It affects everyone because again, going back to your parents, not knowing, and then obviously not thinking because he's a church boy, but then having to deal with that as parents and failing that's, a huge thing. Like you were saying, I can't even imagine feeling that way with my daughter, or even my sons and it affects everybody. That's why I have these conversations because abuse hits everyone. It's not just the victim.

Cherie: Yeah. And it doesn't care, how much money your family makes or, you know, it doesn't care about those types of things.

Kimberly: It is completely unbiased. It does not matter who you are, where you came from, what your skin color is, what you believe in, where you are in life or in the world. It's everywhere. And it's, shocking. I remember being 18 years old and walking into a domestic violence women's group. And literally there was a group of women of every age, every color, every status, everything, I was floored, I was completely blown away.

Cherie: And you have to come back from that, you know?

Kimberly: Having gone through that experience, has that changed the way you have relationships with people as you've grown up. Did it cause you to have an instant trust issues or did you kind of compartmentalized that, and how were you able to deal with that as you were growing up?

Cherie: So I know that as a teenager, I was kind of boy crazy because I think I was searching for, I guess the love that I thought I was supposed to feel during that abuse. So it was me running towards trying to get that affection that I wasn't given in those situations when someone else was getting something for himself. I think that, in that respect, that was a big problem. I did tell my husband before we got married, that it happened so that he was, fully aware of my background and things like that. and as for like friendships and things like that, I think I'm more trusting because, I have mostly girlfriends. I don't be friend men because that's inappropriate.

I love my husband. I don't want to be tempted in that way. but for girlfriends, I tend to be kind of a mother hen, I feel like, so I don't know if that stems from anything that, came from my past. I do trust women more. And, I ran towards relationships as I was going through those more informative, puberty years. So kind of a flip flop, I guess, in that way, between, men and women, girls and boy's kind of thing.

Kimberly: You hear that a lot, though, with abused kids, girls that run towards it in their teenage years. You said something so powerful there, you were looking for the love that you thought you should have felt. I want people to really understand the gravity of that because that's huge, as this child, you're thinking it's supposed to be love, which it's supposed to be, not in that case. And so, for you to think that you're trying to now go find it is interesting in the psychology of how that played out. What would you tell your younger self, if you could go back?

Cherie: I would say to not let my past determine my future. I was in a Bible study years ago. It was probably 2006. It was shortly after my husband had joined the army and it was our first station in upstate New York. And we found a really good church and I befriended some ladies and I was at a Bible study, and I just brought up that up, that I was abused from nine to 13 and one of the ladies there was like, why aren't you broken up about this? I was like, what do you mean? She said, I can't imagine having lived through that. I don't think she said like flippantly, like I used the term flippantly or whatever. It was just kind of like, well, this is my past, and I'm not going to let that determine how my future plays out for myself. I don't want to be the victim anymore. And I think that is a huge one. I know that a lot of people that are more severely abused than I was, might have that victim mentality, but I don't know when it was that kind of my mind shifted. I decided that no, I'm not going to let this color my whole life. And, me just be the victim and woe is me, feel sorry for me because of this. I've only recently, there was that time at the Bible study. And then, probably three or four years ago at a different Bible study here in Arizona, I brought it up and, had had an older lady that I really respected, kind of walk me through a little bit more healing for it.

I love when you can find those kinds of mentors that say, okay, this happened to you and it sucked, but you know, this is not who you are. You know, you are someone more than this. And so I think that that is, something that we, especially as women. And we

deal with hurts every single day. We deal with friendships that have gone bad, or a family that has turned their backs on you, or kids that don't like you anymore because they're teenagers. My kids are great. I love them. I actually love these teenage years. We go through little almost micro traumas throughout even our daily lives. And I think it's a mindset that we need to keep that we are more than this moment.

We can't let our past determine our future. So I think that maybe the mindset that has helped me and my business thrive, I treat every client like a friend and as so many people, so many clients turn into my friends and it's big, cause of that kind of relationship thing that I try to, try to foster them. And, a lot of times they'll leave, a session and be like, well, this is the easiest thing I've ever done. I feel like mentality, I guess, that I want to, evoke in people that meet me. So, yeah.

Kimberly: That's awesome. You make them feel very comfortable so you can take these amazing pictures of them. I love what you said about your past doesn't define your future. I Talk about that a lot. I think that's such a powerful statement, because it's just something, when you can stand outside of it, no matter how awful the trauma was and look at it as a lesson, okay, what did I learn from this? How can I use this and move forward? I gently say it adds character, because now you have an entire new perspective of things that are of this world. And you can, even as a photographer, I would imagine that you come across this, there's a lot of self-doubt, confidence issues, worth. And am I good enough to even be in front of this camera, can stem hugely from all of our experiences we've had in life? And so you're helping them. That's another way of healing is through that lens.

Cherie: Absolutely. And you know, most of my sessions tend to be family, couples, weddings, things like that. But I have recently redone my home studio and so I felt more comfortable doing a boudoir sessions and I love how like someone will come in and they're nervous and they might even be like shaky because it's not normal to take off, most of your clothes in front of a stranger. I try and make them as relaxed as possible and we talk and we laugh. And, I just like how empowering it is for these ladies and throughout the sessions, I'll show them the back of the camera to be like, look how amazing you look, this is all you.

So, I haven't edited anything, and it really boosts their self-confidence. And by the end of the session, you can tell that they sit up a little bit taller. They, bring out the smolder a little bit more in front of the camera and things like that. And I think that is so important too, to build up our fellow women. Nobody's two stories are ever going to be alike. So you don't know how horrible of a day they've had. As soon as they step in front of my camera, I try to bring them peace and keep them relaxed and make it enjoyable for them. I would say every single time they've left and they say, first of all, that was so easy. Like they were so scared that it was going to be really scary being in front of the camera like that. But they're like, Oh, that was so easy. Oh my gosh. And you know, I can't wait to see the pictures. so many times, they'll message me like, oh my gosh I can't believe that's me.

So that's something that I've been trying to focus a little bit more on in my studio so that I can bring that empowerment to local ladies here and let them know that they are good enough and they are special. And they're beautiful, no matter the size, no matter if you, had a baby five months ago, embrace those, curves, those imperfections, because that is what makes you, you, and I think that we tend to forget that because everything that we see is airbrushed and tweaked a little bit, I've had lots of ladies say okay, can you take 10 pounds off, for the photos? And I'm like, you don't need that. You are beautiful just the way you are. And, and I think that we need to be told that way more than, we actually are. so yeah, I think that is one of my favorite things here lately.

Kimberly: I love it. That is so empowering. And having helped on that side of the camera and been on the other side of the camera, it's a game changer. I hope as many women can get in front of your lens as possible. That would be amazing because you're changing and transforming lives just by using your camera. It's awesome. I have absolutely loved this conversation. I think this conversation could go on for weeks because of what it is. I want to just thank you so much for stepping into your power and bringing, truth around your story and sharing it like this. And then again, using your lens to help other women step into their power. I think it's amazing.

Cherie: Thank you so much. I appreciate being here and being able to get that out to other ladies.

CHAPTER 7

An Encounter with God

Di Carter

Di Carter is a Founder of No-Profit Christfest PC 503c (Christian concert since 2014), founder of Social Entrepreneur Leaders, and CEO of a successful international distribution center. 1st Runner up 2019 Mrs. Indiana woman of achievement. #1 International bestseller and #1 National Amazon best seller in the world She is deeply passionate about online home-based business, social media sales, and authentic branding.

Recently, Di started helping moms on their journey quitting smoking to find happiness and live healthier. She believes "you are made for more." and God has a purpose for you to discover.

When Di isn't running her businesses, you can find her spending time with her husband, her two beautiful twin girls and helping many of the less fortunate in mission trips.

Contact info

Www.dicarter.com

Dicartertv@gmail.com

Her past didn't become her present.
She kept going. ~KA

Kimberly: I am thrilled today to talk with Di Carter who is the founder of a nonprofit Christfest PC, and a Network Marketing Top Leader Let's talk about that. And first, thank you for being here.

Di: I am super, super excited to be here. I just want to say thank you so much for the opportunity and It's an honor to be a part of this amazing project and this summit, it takes a lot to organize an event like this. And I just wanted to say that I adore you to pieces and I feel super grateful. So my name is Di Carter. I am a social Media entrepreneur. I simplify building business online. I'm a mom of twins. My husband is a pilot. My entrepreneurial journey started seven years ago.

In 2014, I found Christfestpc for my community. It's a Christian concert where it brings the community together. We already had 4 successful concerts. It was just like this stress that you have in yourself whenever you are an entrepreneur because you never know whenever you come up with an idea or God brings that to you in your life. And it's like, are people going to understand what I'm doing? And I had that in the beginning. I wasn't sure. And I just say, yes, I say yes to the adventure. I say, yes, the journey I say yes, that the universe and God will bring the right people to help me and place the right people by my side to do what they can do the best with their own gifts.

And our first year we had 500 people. They came to this beautiful auditorium right here in Greencastle, Indiana, and DePauw university. And then we had 500 people worship. So it was super successful. The second year we had the concert again. And once again, you have this things in your head, like, is that going to work? Are people going to come, do they love it? And guess what they did, the second year, we pretty much doubled the number. We have 900 people that came around. So that is a little bit of the beginning of my story when it comes to being an entrepreneur.

Kimberly: That's amazing. I love how you put in there though, even before we get into this conversation that you had those thoughts, like, is this really gonna work? Am I gonna be successful in this? I love that you shared that about that journey. Let's just dive into it. What would you say is one of the biggest obstacles or experiences you've had to get through and overcome?

Di: I had a few, if I were to go back into obstacles, I would always, think about as when I was a child. So I am actually from Brazil. You can hear a little bit of the accent right now. so let me give you just a little bit about my background, I have a little note because I want to read it to you. So I don't forget anything because many times, like this is how we connect with people. This is how we understand that we got to be unique. Then we have our own gifts, go through our own struggles. And that comes from where you come from, because who are you going to become, is going to be all about your experiences. The people you're going to be around, like coaches or mentors for what your interests are, but when you're born, you don't have a choice, right?

You're going to be born in a different country, speak a different language. You're going to have your parents. You didn't choose any of that. It's just who you are. And once you embrace that it's going to be so much easier for your entrepreneurial journey. So let me read it this, so I don't miss anything. And you might resonate with some of those too. So I was born in poverty. I did not have any money. My family didn't have any money. We didn't have a name, that's what I knew. And I was very happy with that. Because that's all I knew. I didn't know anything different, but I was born in a third world, country, Brazil, and the name of the city is Recife. I was raised by a single mom that could not write for read.

So right then if you don't have a strong mindset, you are ready to be thinking, okay, if she can't write or read, like who am I, who I'm going to be as a grownup. Right. but that's not what this is about. I made a lot of my own toys with plastic bottles because we couldn't afford it to buy our own toys. I was touched by adults when I was younger, my mom didn't have any idea, but I've been touched when I was younger. So I know that we all women here. So let's be real and talk about the truth. Right? I wasn't raped, but I was touched inappropriately, the ways I'm not supposed to be as being so young, and English is my second language.

So, if you are from a different country and you try to build a business in United States, anywhere you want to go, just believe in yourself and it's completely fine. You can do it by being a foreigner. It's completely fine. Trust me. I had many periods in my childhood that I felt insecure. When you don't have that much money, for some reason, it breaks your soul a little bit. When you see all the people have more than you, but that's all, you know. So it's fine, after my teenager years, I had a period where I didn't have any money. Do you know when I was 18 years old and I graduated from high school, I ended up actually going into England because my aunt lives there, and I was cleaning toilets because my dream was to go to anniversary.

So as I told you guys, my mom did not have any money, so by 18 years old, I knew that I had to do it on my own. So how many of you feel that way? That for anything to move, you're going to have to move, right? You're going to have to get the second job, to put yourself through school. Well, I did that. I ended up cleaning toilets in a different country. And I remember many people looking at me and just like, you're so pretty. Why are you cleaning toilets? That was my opportunity. You know, that was my opportunity to be able to save money. I was lost in a world without God. And my first encounter with God was when I was 16 years old. But I think I was too young to really grasp and understand what is the walk in faith and with him and trusted him.

I basically knew about him and I went through my life without him for a while. And then I was, addicted to cigarettes, badly, like a pack a day. So if you're on that journey too, it's going to be the fine. You're going to figure some things out. And, the nightlife was my life. I love going out every weekend. I wasn't very responsible. And I believe because I did not have those examples either growing up, I just remember seeing my cousins, my uncles, all going out in parties, even though they were older, they're still doing the same things. I had to learn really quickly, if I want it to be successful in life, I had to change my habits. I was someone that, many times I didn't have credibility.

I didn't have any money. when I was younger and I got married when I was 19 years old, got divorced at 22. So I don't know where do you find yourself in my story, but you're going to find yourself somewhere because I want you to find yourself , because you got to believe that is your past. That's the things that happens before you were about to become, just as stepping into your God. God is exactly what came as one to talk about. Is this the part of it that you go to find who you are? But I, because I was living here in United States when I was 19 years old, I was 3000 miles away from my family. So I did not have any family support. I was on my own. I had credit card debt of at least $15,000, that's no longer in there. Thank Jesus. I have been remarried. I have been in a foreclosure. I have always been between 155 to 225. So I have a big problem when it comes to self-love and self-image. and you probably look at me, I don't know what she's talking about. She's gorgeous. Right? I hear that all the time guys, but guess what? You can be pretty, but right here in your mind, you can be a completely different person. So trust me, I had that many times, a self-image that I don't feel good about myself. And it's hard because when people tell you, your pretty and you just can't see it that way. You just can't see it. that's just a little bit of the beginning of my story. And, it's all about overcoming and you are an over-comer. You definitely are. So I'll leave it at that for the beginning of my story.

Kimberly: I love it. Wow. You know, you shared so many interesting aspects and what I really loved about what you were saying is you kept going in and out of your journey, your story clear until you're in your twenties, all these different pieces. And we always have so many obstacles and limiting beliefs that come up for us all the time. And when we're walking about that, and we do heal on some level from what we've gone through, I always say you could be walking through the grocery store in the soup aisle, all of a sudden have a meltdown, because you never know when it's time to heal some more. I want to touch on a couple of things that you were saying, one of which is, as a child growing up, knowing your mom couldn't read or write, and then also being in poverty. I know you mentioned that you didn't know any different, so it didn't affect you on some level, but as you were growing up and realizing that there is so much more outside of your family and other people's parents can read and write and stuff, did that affect you in your decision-making as you were growing up?

Di: Absolutely. Absolutely. I didn't know any difference what it means to be poor or rich. I didn't know the difference between what kind of toys is supposed to be playing with. I just knew that I was a happy child growing up, until I started to figure it out, you know? And that was probably around age six or seven years old. You know, that's when you started to figure it out that your mom actually cannot write, or read and that your babysitter's the one teaching you. And I wanted that so bad. I want her to sit down with me at the table and tell me like, this is your homework. This is what you need to do. And even I was so young, I remember clearly like, it's happening, that I hurt on the inside that she could not do this for me.

And my babysitter at the time just told me she was like, your mom cannot write or read, but this is what I'm here for. So she made sure that she provided someone else that knew what they were doing to help me. And from that, point on, I felt that my mom wants the best for me, that she didn't want me to be just like her, that she wanted me to be better than her. And to be able to give more for my own kids. And I could feel it, because my mom was never a person that actually talked negative, even though she couldn't write, she couldn't read. She had a really positive mindset. And I hear many times from people say oh, my parents were so negative and talk down to me and said, all those things. I did not have that, but I have many others struggles in my life.

Kimberly: You always hear in conversations about how we grow up and our parents, and even us now, as parents, you're doing the best you can with what you know, and how, and you can't feel guilty about that, but your mom, there was something that you needed that she couldn't provide. And so she got you this babysitter, so bless her heart for that. I love how you talk about your mom, and you felt very loved, and you felt like you weren't in poverty, you didn't know anything. And you were a happy child, that says a lot about your mom and how she was really trying to help you.

Di: Yes. So for me, that the reason, I guess I never really felt like, or, understood what that was. It really was like her hugs, her making sure that even though, I couldn't buy lots of clothes or I didn't have my own bedroom, for example. whatever I had, she made sure that it was clean. That it was nice, that I took care of it. So in a way, I think the way she, was showing the love for the thing she gave to me. I could understand it. I believe that to me, it's probably like, I felt rich without being rich.

Kimberly: Exactly. Yeah.

Di: You know she transferred that through, that one toy, through that one piece of clothing. That one pair of tennis shoes, because all the things that I have was just one, and I had to take care of it. You know, I couldn't break it. If I break it, I didn't have another one as my kids right now have, they have so many toys. Like I literally have to, pile like boxes and boxes to take to Goodwill. And when I was growing up, I didn't have that. I made my own. So I, appreciated if the way she, brought me up. I really am.

Kimberly: I want to go a little deeper on that really quick. And then, we can talk about something else, but I think for us right now, as women understanding that even if we only have that one thing, or that one experience or whatever it is in the positive, that we can really embrace that and love that, and really understanding, just being happy with that. We don't have to have all this other stuff, we don't have to have multiples, obviously there are goals to get to certain points in life that we want, and desire and deserve, but really embracing and just being present with what you have, I think is really something, there's a lot of power in that.

There's a lot to be said about really appreciating what you do have and how it helps you in life. And so I really liked that you brought that up. I want to go back to; you were talking about growing up and having those moments where you were inappropriately touched. I love that you differentiated that for one. because even as women, we tend to sometimes wind up in relationships where that can happen and we need to really own that power and say, no, learn our no, and make it very firm, I have a lot of conversations with domestic violence victims and really embracing that is very important.

At what point during your life, did you really recognize how you wanted to change, given what you'd gone through throughout your life? Be it poverty, be it, those inappropriate moments. What was it for you that switched in your mind that you were going to have better?

Di: I had many points in my life that I have an encounter with Jesus, so I would say it's a few of them. It's not just one. And I just snap my finger and it's like, woo, it's all gone. I would say I had many encounters with God and that's what my points of it. So the first one that I ever had, it was when I was 16 years old. When I went to that one church from one visit at one time, I raised my hand, the pastor give an alter call and I came forward and I just dropped on my knees. And I remember just crying like a baby. And that my boyfriend, at that point, that was my first boyfriend. He could not understand that, like, what was going on, and it was all that burden at that point.

It was all the burden of like where I came from, being touched in appropriately, not being assertive, who I was, because I was only 16 years old and what I was going to be. And basically, I fell to my knees, I just asked God to take me through this journey with him, and even though like at 16 years old, when I got out of the church, I didn't stay in church every week. I had him with me and we went through this beautiful journey together on my teenager years and my twenties and my thirties. And throughout those years, I have many other encounters. I had my second one, I would say when I was 18 years old, and I had to leave my country again, and go to a different country and, clean toilets.

And I remember as I was in Home Depot, it was a Home Depot that I worked, and I was just like cleaning the toilets. And there were 26 of them. And I was just like, God, look where you took me, you took me away from my country to clean toilets in a different country to save money, to be able to go to school. And, I was crying. I said, thank you for preparing me. Thank you for putting me on the bottom of the bottom that I never thought I would do. So I could be a little bit more appreciative whenever I went back home, I appreciate my mom or I appreciate my friends more. I appreciated everything. So from that point on, I always, always woke up in the morning, feeling grateful and that feeling of gratitude.

That's really what, changed my life from being more of a complainer and negative and feeling sorry for myself then to just, I gotta be grateful because from now on, I get to make the decision for my own life from now on. And whatever happens, it will be because of my own efforts. And I have to clean toilets to understand that it was my own effort to scrub the toilets, to be able to get paid. And with that money, instead of just spending the money and complaining about my life, I saved it and put myself through school. So that was, one of them in my twenties. Another encounter was basically driving back home, really drunk at five o'clock in the morning, smoking a pack of cigarettes.

I said, God, you've got to help me. I said, you've got to help me because I'm about to kill myself or kill somebody. If I don't change my life. And at this point I had a job. I made good money. I was married, but I was still like drinking. And, they had this beautiful church and I was living in St. Louis, Missouri, at this point, this beautiful church, St. Louis, faith church, it was huge, it fits like 5,000 people. And that church keep drawing me in. Every time I drive on the highway, it kept drawing me in. And one day I just said, this is it. I went home. It was a Sunday. I came home and overnight like party and all the kind of stuff. I came home, I took a shower and I went to church and, that's when God, called me back.

Like truly he called me back and said, this is it. I've been pursuing you this whole time. I was with you, but I've been pursuing you to be able to give you everything that I always wanted to give it to you. So, to me, it was from 16 to 28 years old,

I was living on my small box and God had this huge box for me, full of blessing. But I couldn't get to that box because I was over here. I was thinking small. I was just thinking small. I was just thinking about partying and hanging out and doing all the things that would not grow me to be the woman that I'm supposed to be, the mom that I supposed to be. And when I say yes, Kimberly, Everything really changed because I became a mom.

I graduated from school. I then started my journey, that was to open a nonprofit organization, which is Christ fest PC and doing events and Christian concerts. And then after that, when I could not believe it, I said, God, you blessed me with so much, like what else? And he's just like, just wait. And, two years later now he prepared me to have a nonprofit organization, to be able to give me a real business, which means a traditional business. Two years later I was talking to a few people. And, I started up a company which is a distribution center for cleaning products, for a small business. And I opened that business in 2016 from ground up, I invested, I would say probably over a hundred thousand, in two years and no profit, no nothing.

And I was just kind of a little upset with God that you helped me do this Christian concert. Now you are helping me here to open this business. I have put so much money into, I have invested so much and I'm not, I don't see anything. And, then I kept working full-time I was working full time in a hospital with kids and the business. I was fulltime, 60 to 70 hours a week. I think what really kept me going, I'll tell you, I'm going to go back into the beginning. Right? I was born in poverty. I had been touched before. I have so much struggles with credit card. Being addicted, being so many things that has happened to my life. Like being in a foreclosure, that whenever you are in a tough place, that two years later you have a traditional business.

I Invested a hundred thousand dollars. You think you're about to lose everything. It's something inside of you. Like the fire that comes back and said, who are you as I am not a quitter. I'm going to keep going. I'm going to make this happen because I've been through so much that now your able to grasp it too. And you know who you are, you still the same little girl, that strong girl that came out of all of that, to be able to impact thousands of people. If you don't keep going, you're going to have 14 families that's not going to have a job that you already gave them the opportunity. So I kept going into two years later, the company now ended up, they became a seven figure company. We're going into a fifth year right now. And then the third one, since I build a business, a home.

So now I don't work in a hospital anymore. I live in the United States. I'm now married. I have two business running, and then comes the third one, which is network marketing. I said, I'm already at home. So why not do something to impact more people. And that's basically what I did. So I impacted people spiritually with a Christian concert. I impacted people when it comes to have financially with more income and with a traditional business, giving people an opportunity. And now I'm just able to impact people with products, and also with an opportunity to make an income as well. And then, because I went through all those things, when I was younger, I'm able to relate with so many different women because some woman, they are a single mom and I'm like, you know, I was raised by a single mom, some women's that come and talk to me say but I don't have any money. I was like, I know what that means. I didn't have any money. So it's so much easier to connect with people. When today I have a clear, a clear understanding that I had to go through all the things that I needed to go through to be able to be here today and be able to connect with so many amazing woman and a woman like you, right, I was able to connect with, some amazing women like you. So yeah, I'll leave it at that.

Kimberly: Amazing. And you're right. I always tell people, your journey is what gets you to this point, this is who you are. You're meant to go through all of that in order to be able to connect on a much deeper level. That's how I feel about my story. And that's what I share about every woman. I want to just say that for me, when you're talking about all of your story, there's like this thread and this theme about being worthy in all of it, and you, you keep coming face to face with that and working through it, you go through it, and you're worthy. You're deserving. You're enough. You're perfect and amazing just as you are. And I love all of it. Even the moment when you touched on the weight, like we all talk about that. We all have a situation like our closets have what? 10 different sizes?

Di: Yes. Yes. Mine does, and forget about the bras.

Kimberly: That's definitely lifting up the girls. This conversation could go on and on and on. I can't wait for you to come onto the TV show too. Cause we'll dive in a little bit more that way as well. And with your business. I want to end though, with, if you could go back and tell your younger self one thing, what would it be?

Di: If I go back to my younger self, I would tell her you're playing small, everything that you want, it's already done. I want to tell her that she is so smart. Oh my God, I'm going to cry. I've got chills. I want to tell her you so smart. You have no idea how creative you are. You have no idea how many people are so grateful to have you as a friend and that you are truly beautiful, even though you don't think you are at times and believe in yourself and do what you're meant to do, stepping to it. Don't be afraid and it's okay. It's going to be okay because it's always okay. He is with you. God is with you. He has bigger plans. And, you're going to be in shock what he's going to do in your life. Because now going back, I think about at 18 years old, if somebody would tell me that I would have a seven-figure company, somebody would tell me that I'll be doing interviewing podcast or, become an author, a number one bestselling author. If somebody would tell me that, I will have amazing, beautiful twin kids. I would not believe it, Kimberly. I wouldn't, because I tell you the truth and everybody that's here. Often we look into our family and we think that we're going to be somewhere kind of like them. And that's not the reality. It's your choice to change it. You got a choice to change it and step into your Godness. Right? You've got to step into it because if that was, if that was it, then I would have been alcoholic. I would have been a prostitute. I wouldn't be so many insane things. I wouldn't be someone that can write and read. I would still be in poverty. I would never dream. because that was my past and my family. So you just go do what you need to do because the gifts it's inside of you. And you just have to take the first step and just keep going.

Kimberly: Amen to that, and with that. You are amazing and brilliant. Thank you so much for sharing your story.

Di: Thank you.

CHAPTER 8

My Mess into My Message

Kara Maldonado

WHAT IF I TOLD YOU THAT YOU COULD LOSE INCHES THROUGH A MASSAGE? *At Real Bodies Period, we believe all bodies are beautiful! I am Kara Lynne, a Certified Cryotherapy Technician and the Founder Real Bodies Period. After suffering from my chronic illnesses, my mission is to change one person at a time by providing an overall holistic approach to weight loss and pain management. Some of the specific treatments are: Lymphatic Drainage, Permanente Fat Removal, Skin Tightening, Supplements, Detoxing, Nutrition, Fitness and Mindset Coaching.*

https://www.facebook.com/kara.maldonado1

https://www.instagram.com/myreyoflite

https://www.twitter.com/Cali_Kara

https://www.realbodiesperiod.com

https://www.facebook.com/susancmadden/ videos/10219245418393886/?d=n

http://bit.ly/3hTrt43

She had a secret, and she almost died, but she survived, now she is thriving. ~KA

Kimberly: Today, I am talking with Kara Maldonado. I am excited to talk to you. We are talking about overcoming limiting beliefs, trauma, obstacles, and I am looking forward to your story. Thank you for being here with me today.

Kara: Thank you for having me, Kimberly. I'm super excited.

Kimberly: Me too. I want to know about what you do. This is amazing. You're the founder-owner of Real Bodies.

Kara: Yes, yes. I help women and men achieve their ideal body goal, in weight and in physique, and how I do that is through localized cryotherapy. We administered it in a massage technique through Cryoskin machine. Many people refer to me as the lady with the magic wand. Cryotherapy is a technique for permanent fat removal. If you have that last 5 to 15 pounds, and you've done everything right; you're hydrated, you're trying to eat right, you're exercising, but we've got some things that we're fighting against right now. You know, look what's happened, COVID hit! And then gyms closed. We couldn't get out, depression, hormones, age, all these things are not on our side, we're struggling. If you're struggling to get that last bit of weight off, I come in and I help you with that. Remove those last five inches in five sessions, it's a 30-minute treatment. I'm giving you a massage, and whatever the target area is that you're concerned with, it can be anywhere, double chin to your ankles, whatever it is, your abs, arms. I will massage you, with a warm to hot, to freezing technique. Sub-Zero cold to do the fat removal. Then I do, the skin tightening and body contouring. But to add to what attracted me to the machine is the detoxifying of toxins in your body. This happens through lymphatic drainage. If you are suffering from chronic pain, chronic illness, like auto-immune, post-cancer, rheumatoid arthritis.

It does wonders for you, good gut health, because it's cleaning out your system, taking all the inflammation out, all of those yucky toxins that are hiding in those fat cells to keep you unhealthy. I took this cosmetic machine and repurposed it to help you holistically. The treatments are non-invasive, there's no downtime, there's no pain involved. And the side effect, if you will call it that is you, loses inches and you lose fat cells. It's a win, win for everyone, and if you want to get healthy, and you don't care about losing the inches, I mean, it's the well-rounded situation for everyone. I'm super excited about what I do and the lives that I've changed, and it's for all ages.

Kimberly: It's wonderful. That's awesome, and so important, especially for those looking for the detox side of it, or weight loss with the benefit of the detox. But I wanted to be clear. It's only for those who need to help with the last 15 pounds. I mean, you can't come in there at the start of your journey. So, I have clarity.

Kara: Oh, no, absolutely not. There is a way that I can do it for people that have up to a hundred pounds, it's a longer process. There are layers to it, like with anything. I have developed a 360 degrees Weight Loss Maintenance program that is more involved. Through my program, I have resources I provide customized nutrition, there's a personal trainer, supplement subscription of 92 minerals out of the 102 that your body requires daily, and a mindset coaching. I help no matter what your goal is, I'm there to help you from start to finish. I do a maintenance program as well. Once you've achieved the goal, I set up support in maintaining it, there's a quarterly treatment that goes along with that. When I say the five to 15 lbs., it's those who want to do something quick and a couple of months, without doing some invasive type of procedure, I'm your girl. If you have a long-time term goal, we have another package that we can also help you with.

Kimberly: That is fantastic. I love it. How did you get into that?

Kara: Yeah, that's part of my story. When I got sick, it introduced me to the cryotherapy. I was trying to find different modalities to help me get better. This was one treatment that it introduced me to. The lymphatic drainage was helping me to get rid of the cellulite, excess water and unwanted fat that I was carrying. When I realized it was taking toxins out of me, I said, "you know, I want that machine. I want to tell everybody about it." That's what brought me into leaving my 27 years of multi-management, corporate real estate career and stepping out on faith and saying: "I don't know what I'm going to do with this machine. I don't know how I'm going to reach people, but I I'm going to do something with it". And three years later here I am.

Kimberly: Love that. You're a walking testimony, let alone the founder and owner of Real Bodies, period.

Kara: Yes.

Kimberly: Awesome. Let's dive into your story. You touched on; you got sick. Is that where you want to start? What is the biggest obstacle you'd say you've walked through?

Kara: Well, you know, I used to jokingly say that I should be a 99 cents crackwhore. I know that sounds abrasive. I used to say that in my home and not say that to everyone, but I need to say it now. I need to really, turn my Mess into my Message! That's why when you came across me and invited me here, I felt, this is the platform that needs to hear this. I thank you for that. There's always been secrets, every family has secrets, mine started at six. My father was killed, and it left me alone to care for my three younger brothers. My mom she remarried quickly, and I was confused. But you know, when you're six, you don't understand; you go with the flow.

There were a lot of things that weren't talked about in my home, a lot of physical abuse. A lot of things that were not explained. I remember being five prior to my father dying, being in a car parked somewhere on the side of the road. I remember seeing the sun come up and I'm in the car with two babies, my brothers. This is how it starts. I'm wondering what's that all about, but that's kind of my life. When my mother remarried, I became responsible for my siblings because her life moved on. She had two other children by my stepfather, they became her interest.

After my mother remarried and had two more kids, she finished her doctrine. The priorities shifted and my priorities at a very young age became taking care of the household and taking care of the children on top of maintaining Honor Roll at School. All the other things that come in a household that had alcohol, drug and psychological abuse and thing unexplained! I don't think it became very clear to me until I was in my teens what was going on because at the time you think is normal. I'm a real Empath. I'm easily manipulated and told that you're supposed to do these things and it's a part of what your life is planned out to do. You can be quilted into a lot of things; in which I was. And that within itself was abuse. A lot of that started there, again, me thinking that was normal; I went into my first marriage, and I married the same type of person. That's my children's father. I allowed that same behavior to keep happening to me. That relationship, it lasted for 20 years and out of the drug abuse continued that same thing. I finished college, doing the things I needed to do while he was doing what he was doing.

He ended up fathering a child with another woman during our marriage. I am still accepting some of this behavior. I'm supposed to understand and do my part and be there for my kids. At that point I had a nine-year-old daughter, and I said, she can't think this is okay. I checked out! I tried to get away. By then you're damaged. You're like what is wrong with me. I keep allowing this, because I hadn't done the work and I'm making excuses and I'm hiding, and I'm covering up and not saying anything. I wait 10 years, because I'm waiting for my daughter to get older; before I get into another relationship.

I get in a second relationship that is twice as bad, now the physical abuse comes in. In the last 10 years, I have gotten out of that relationship. It was very physical. I believe that was the onset of the autoimmune that I now suffer from. I have fibromyalgia and lupus, again with me not telling anyone in the family, no one knew. Maybe they knew. No one talked about it because I didn't talk about it. I walked around being very successful in business and a wreck at home. Hiding and covering what was happening, I thought I was protecting the kids and protecting the person who I was with. Thinking, oh you're going through a hard time and whatever you're emotionally dealing with or whatever, because I didn't understand addiction. I didn't understand what it was doing, or so I thought. It's a sickness and they're sick, that's what it is. I had to be a better person and take it until they got better, but they weren't getting better, and I was getting worse.

It wasn't until I guess I had been sick six years ago when it hit me. I was passing out at work, and I had to get blood transfusions almost every two months. I could not maintain red blood cells. And through all of this, I'm dealing with this person who found every reason to barrage me. Put me down and not show up if I had an emergency or if I had a special doctor's appointment.

I'm saying, "can you get me to this appointment? I needed to go to, and I am terrified." Cause I don't know what's happening to me. I'm thinking I'm dying, and I didn't want to tell my kids. They wouldn't give me a test because I needed to be dropped off and picked up if I had to be put under and he wouldn't show up. I was going through those types of things. It got terrible. I ended up having to run for my life out of that relationship when it got to the point of me getting my jaw fractured and a threat to my kids. And I'm like, I don't know what's happening to me. I'm going through every CT scan, MRI, blood tests, everything. This is what you're doing to me. When I decided, I had an exit plan; it took a couple of years to get that all together. I had to make sure my kids were safe.

I had kids that were staying in the Bay area and my daughter, and my two granddaughters were coming with me back to South California. Everybody had to be accounted for and had to be safe because I would get threatened. If you leave me, we're going to come after your family members. All those types of things were being told to me. It got so bad where I had to make a police report and it had to be that kind of intervention; it had to happen. For me to get out, I did that, and I got down here and I felt so great. Oh my God, I can start my life over. And you know, I'm with my daughter. I have my two granddaughters down here. Everything is going to be different. We had a big, beautiful home in Irvine, and we had decorated. Everything was great. I'm so happy. Oh my God, three weeks into that, I pass out, fall down the stairs and my secret was out. I couldn't hide my secret anymore. I woke up, and my granddaughters were at the foot of the bed as if I was going to die. And so, that was when the ER doctor said, we're going to send her to an oncologist. She came in here and my hemoglobin was 4.6. Women are supposed to be 12 to 15. By the time it hits 11, they're scared. Right. I was walking dead. Like he called me, and so long story short, they still took another year.

I had five different specialists and they still couldn't find out what was wrong with me. My eldest son was the one who ended up finding out what it was. He narrowed down by asking me to send my journal to him, to journal every day for 30 days what I was eating, what I was drinking. All my activities, what the effects were. From that, he took it to some of his colleagues because he's a professor. He told me to have them separate your Ferritin, test your Ferritin, do all these batteries of tests and separate this, isolate it. And, have them do that, your oncologist and tell me what the results are. And once they did that, I came in on a Tuesday. They read me my results. They said, yeah, that Thursday I started, chemo. And I had, my cancer was attacking my Ferritin, and I was not reproducing red blood cells, so that six blood transfusions in a year.

When I did that, going through all of that and then having the fibromyalgia and the lupus developed all from being in such a toxic relationship that started at birth. For me not knowing any better and being groomed to accept the narcissistic behaviors of other people and not knowing. Having the strength and the love and self-belief in myself to care about myself, do the right things to get out of it. I accepted it, and I hit it, and I dealt with it, and I put up with it. It broke my body down until my body said no more, no more, but by then I was on 39 pills a day and, and taking treatments, twice a week.

I was... I was dying. I was dying; it wasn't until my now three-year-old grandson was being born, first boy in over 10 years. I said, I can't do this anymore, he gave me that purpose to say; I need to get up. I was stuck in my bed for a year. gained 130 pounds, I said, "I want to live." Three, almost four years of my life, gone. I don't have much memory of it. That was when I got introduced to the cryroskin. Me getting out and saying, okay, now that I'm trying to get up and walk, and do things and get out, I have cellulite.

It's pretty incredible what happened. What we allow to happen to ourselves. Last year when the entire world shut down,

I did the work. I took a lot of courses, life coaching and spiritual coaching. Had to clean that up, to clean my closet out, and I realize it was not good baggage and stuff to be carrying around. It was not okay to do that. That was why it was so easy for me to decide, not go back to doing what I was doing, selling real estate, building and managing all the people that I was. This gives me, this helps me, so much, if I help one person get off of the meds, they're on, helps them with their diabetes or help them lose 10, 50, 20 pounds, get that pressure off their legs, their hips, whatever it is. It's so much better to let them feel that way. When you're feeling better about yourself, you're able to have choices, you get stronger, able to say no and not feel bad about it. To do things for yourself that you wouldn't do before, not allow people to take advantage of you. Unfortunately, you know, that's what I've learned.

Kimberly: Wow! What an incredible journey you've been on. I'm happy you're sharing it with us. I kept hearing in my head, as you were talking, that from six years old on you, I would imagine, you've always felt stuck. Like there's something stuck, even though you kept doing well. You were successful on the outside of the world, viewing in on the inside. There was this feeling because you were watching your baby brothers. Stuck to have to deal with all that was going on in your life. It's incredible how you can keep moving through those things. Here you are today and you're recognizing it now. You said, you know what, now I'm able to get out, and it took your body to go, you're done, that's a moment of looking in the mirror going, okay, it's time for me. Right?

Kara: I don't regret it, sometimes people say, God, that's so terrible what you went through that. I'm sorry, you went through that. I say, you know, don't say, sorry, God does everything for a reason. I believe in that, like this whole COVID thing; it gives you the opportunity to look deep at your journey and what's going on and the surrounding people. I could see those who stood by me. I took care of many people, my brothers, their kids, everybody. When I got sick, it was just me and my daughter and my granddaughters. No one showed up. And not that I need anyone to do anything for me. I didn't ask for anything in return, but it allowed me to see that I didn't have to feel guilty when I say I can't do something for others.

I will not do that anymore, I realized no one appreciated me spreading myself so thin to where I almost died or taking time from myself, my kids, or my grandkids that needed me. No one appreciated that. Why am I losing sleep? hurting in this painful situation, worried about all this other stuff? It gave me that ability to look in myself and say, I got to refocus and take care of me. If I can't take care of me, I can't take care of those that count, you know? It shows you who is worthy. You know, it, does. It's unfortunate, but it gives you a very clear picture.

Kimberly: Time is our most precious, valuable commodity. We're spreading ourselves so thin. We forget about ourselves in all of that. You can't be present in what you're doing. Incredible. I wanted to go back and ask you, what was it in your first domestic violence relationship that helped you get out of that?

Those are the conversations that I think help women know; it's, not this big, magical thing that happens. There's something that clicks inside you. I know it was for me, but I'm curious, what was it for you on the first one? I know what you said on the second one. It was that physical moment, but what was it on the first?

Kara: He wasn't physical with his abuse. He was very psychological and emotionally abusive. That could be worse because I keep hearing, "look at you, nobody wants you", "you are worthless" and "I'm the best thing you're going to get" those kinds of horrible things. I think what got me was when he referred to my daughter. Her first language is Spanish. he went for her and said that "she was going to be stupid because she couldn't speak English." That was it for me; you can do a lot to me, but don't hurt my kids

Kimberly: Oh yeah.

Kara: I was like, no, I've got to protect her. I have to get out of that situation. He was not only a cheater, but a misogynistic! I couldn't let her see that as a girl growing up that this is okay, this is how women are to be treated. I did everything to get out of that and situation. I said, go, this is not acceptable. Left that relationship, did not ask for alimony and let him take whatever he wanted. Walked away with nothing, so that I can have my child respect me. And it was worth it. Money, all that stuff, is not worth my daughter thinking the behavior is okay. That a man should cheat, and he should have to do all this, and it's okay. No! That's why I refuse to have any other outside relationships. All my kids knew was their dad until they were 18 and out of the house. I still didn't do the work for myself. Now I've done the work, it would be hard for anyone to come in and try to replay that again.

Kimberly: That's awesome. I love that. You're stepping into your power. You've stepped into it. What would you tell your younger self? If you could go back in time?

Kara: Oh, my goodness. Baby girl, baby girl. Oh, my God. You are special. You know, it was not your fault, and you did nothing wrong. God loves you. And you are strong. You have a purpose!

Kimberly: So true, that gave me chills. You've gone through many things. I love that you're able to sit here and share that from an empowered space, because many times, a hundred percent in agreement that psychological and emotional abuse, all of that, it's worse than the physical. It hurts, then you're bruised, and you have proof of it. All that other stuff you don't, and it can still come up. I know, for me, even when it comes up every couple of moments, you're like, Oh, okay, okay. Okay. But you have tools in your toolbox to say "that's not true" it comes up (and it's going to come up) but it's okay.

Kara: Yeah. Took me 40 something years later. Or 50 to now get that. But you know, it's never too late ladies. It's never too late. You don't want to leave this earth and not know, even if it's your last breath you take. You want to combat that, it's the devil, it's evil. It's nothing, not you, it's their projection. It's theirs of themselves that's coming at you. Took me a long time to realize that and to accept that it's not me, it's them. Now I have the tools and I feel good. I want to give that back to all women. Also, men that are there, many go through this, they're not exempt and it's unfortunate.

Kimberly: Incredible story, incredible journey you've been on. Thank you much for sharing it with me today.

Kara: Thank you. Thank you for the opportunity. It was, okay, it was tough.

Kimberly: You did amazing. And I'm proud of you, you're so brave and strong and you're radiating. I would never have known that you were walking dead, as your doctor said. You look incredible.

Kara: Thank you. Thank you.

CHAPTER 9

Overcoming Fear & Finding my Joy

Kelly Smith

Kelly D Smith learned that fear has the power to control her life if she let it. She could be a victim or a victor. Her choice. Fear is a word that is powerless unless she gives it power. The word of God freed her, healed her, and set her life on an amazing path. She holds a master's degree in Special Education. In 2017, Senator Morrell awarded her The Woman of Distinction, City of Menifee. President Obama recognizes her with The President Lifetime Achievement Award 2016. Kelly is an author and dynamic speaker. She co-authored 4 books. She is a #1 Best-selling author in the states and internationally. Her book Your Amazing Itty, Bitty Book on Faith, 15 Chapters to Overcome Fear and Live a Life of Victory, is available in digital and paperback from Amazon.

Contact info

Warrior Princess 4 God

Website: www.warriorprincess4god.com

Email kellywarriorprincess4god@gmail.com

Phone: (909) 471-1894

She had to breakthrough fear, finding her joy. ~KA

Kimberly: I am with Kelly Smith. She is an author and a speaker. Kelly, I'm so happy you're here with me today.

Kelly: Thank you, Kimberly. I'm so happy to be here. It's so exciting.

Kimberly: Tell us a bit more about your business. You're an author and you're a speaker. What have you authored?

Kelly: I have authored "Your Amazing Itty-Bitty Book of Faith, 15 Chapters to Overcome Fear and Live a Life of Victory." And it's available on Amazon. I've co-authored several books. I Recently did the one, it's all about showing up.

Kimberly: We're both in that one you're talking about "It's All About Showing Up," from the one and only, Robbie Motter.

Kelly: The power is in the asking, which is true. I've been a co-author of an anthology for a writer's group. I have a children's story written in there, which is coming out in a picture book with illustration. Really excited about that coming out soon. I Co-authored a book with The Information Diva, Deborah Thorne, and its "Entrepreneurial Women Sharing Their Anchor Scriptures." I've co-authored several books. A lot of pictures books coming out soon, which I'm really excited about. I love to write children's books. I've been in special education for over 21 years, and I love to read kids' books and write for children.

Kimberly: Definitely felt your passion coming through on that one. Awesome. Let's dive into our conversation. One of the first questions I always ask my goddesses: What would you say is one of the biggest obstacles that you've overcome? We're still working through them. We know.

Kelly: It would be fear. When I was 22, I was robbed and raped at gunpoint. While the guy held the gun to my head, he said he's going to blow my brains out. I used to be an extrovert. I used to smile and laugh all the time. I was the life of the party. You knew when I walked in the door, right, loud talking all the time, chit chatting. That day, the smile left my face, and the fear entered my heart. It didn't just enter my heart; it took root in there and grew and grew. Once you get fear in there, it's hard to get it out. I found myself depressed. Other things started setting in, this roller coaster effect, the snowball effect. And I lived in fear off and on, I would say for a good 20 years.

Kimberly: I can imagine, you said it took that smile away. I can imagine it ripped a part of you away as well.

Kelly: It did. I used to smile and laugh all the time. It's like the smile left, the laughter left, the joy of life left. Then I went through a divorce and a lot of other things started happening. As you think, you're getting over the fear than something else happens. It felt like this rape followed me throughout my life. They released him from prison and then of course all the fear sets in again. You think, oh, he's going to hunt me down and find me, because I prosecuted, he's going to kill me. You know how your mind just goes wild; the fear sets in again.

Then I'm remarried, and I'm in a terrible marriage, he's mentally and verbally abusive. It seemed like things got worse and worse. When I was growing up, I always had hope. I always thought, things will get better, or today's a bad day, but tomorrow will be better. This was an awful week, but tomorrow is going to get better, always had hope. There came a point in my life where the pain in my heart, I had so much pain. I couldn't deal with it anymore. I remember leaving the grocery store, loading the groceries up in my car and asking God to kill me. I didn't want to be alive anymore; it's really sad because I had two little girls that I adore, loved. I needed to raise them and be around for them. The pain in my heart hurt so much, I didn't want to live anymore. Thankfully, God had other plans. He didn't answer that prayer. Sometimes ladies, when God says no to a prayer, be thankful. He said, no, life has become exceptionally good and full of blessings. When you're in so much grief, pain you don't feel you can ever get out of it. You can't see past that light that there is joy ahead. There is hope, something better ahead. You got to get through this dark time.

Kimberly: Having a prayer like that, there's much finality to it. One conversation that comes up often is when we become a victim of something, there's more than us as that one victim. That the thing happened too... It's the surrounding people, our family, it affects everybody. Like you said, you were married during that time.

Kelly: I was engaged. Then, we went ahead; we got married. I always feel, divorce It takes two people. It's two parts, it goes wrong on both sides, both people have to work on it. I can't say it's all my fault, I can't say it's all his fault. But I believe that the rape, the robbery, that influenced the divorce. When you're with someone, that's happy and friendly, and then suddenly you have this depressed person who doesn't want to get out of bed anymore. I always think it's a good thing I never liked the taste of alcohol. I would have become an alcoholic to drown myself in the pain. It's sad to think about that. I used to think that because

I only found one drink that I ever like, Peppermint Schnapps, because I love mint. I wouldn't go out and buy a bottle, but if I had been a drinker, I could see myself going that route.

You kind of look at people in a different light when you've gone through things, see where they're at. You can look at someone and you can't judge them because you don't know what they've been through. Maybe that person's drinking a lot, to drown in the pain that they're in. They need somebody to come, encourage them. Let them know that there is hope and you can get through it.

Kimberly: What were some steps that you started taking to get that back, to change from getting out of that depression?

Kelly: I had gone to church off and on as a child. My parents didn't really take me to church. I would go with friends. My husband and I, we started going to church; we had taken our girls with us. It really involved us in the church. I would cry. Some messages would just really get to me. I would sit there and cry. The lady sitting next to me one day she asked if I wanted to accept Jesus. And that's really when my life changed. I started going to Bible study. She invited me to her house to a Bible study, and I started getting in the word and I really started reading the word. And it really started changing my life.

For some people it's a quick change, for me, it was a slow change. It's like, God said, "okay, we're going to work on this. We're dealing with this one thing. Then it's okay, now we dealt with this. Now we got to deal with this. And okay, now we dealt with that." It was the slow, full recovery, the slow healing. But I can say I have my smile back, my laugh. I have my joy back. I'm not fearful like I was.

Yes, we still deal with things. When Satan knows where your weaknesses are, he comes after you. Just like the bridge story I told you. I'm fearful of driving over bridges that are over water.

I'm driving down to Southern California. I have to drive over the Richmond Bridge near Oakland. Somehow, I end up on the wrong freeway and have to turn around. The map app on my phone takes back to San Francisco, over the Golden Gate Bridge in the dark, to loop me around and take me over the Richmond Bridge again. I'm just crossing over bridges with water. It's like, okay, Lord, you're going to take me over that bridge again? On my way home, I decide to go a different route. This route takes me inland and I end up crossing over three bridges, all that are over water. Two are draw bridges. Then I drive by a large body of water. I'm thinking, God is working on my fear of driving on bridges that are over water.

Kimberly: Lessons, lessons, lessons. You know, I want to touch on something that you said; I think is really, really important. And that was, I'm going to focus on this one thing, work on that one thing. Then I can move to the next thing. I think that's really important because we think we have to just wake up one morning and have all that joy and be all that happy. Act like everything's great. It's not, and it's also okay to have either thing happen. Whether you felt great, something makes you feel good all over and fantastic. But to also recognize that there're those moments where you have to go, okay, one thing at a time, one more thing at a.

Kelly: Yeah. When you go through abuse, whether it's in a relationship or an assault, it really affects your self-esteem, how you feel about yourself. You have to learn to love yourself again, to accept yourself for who you are. It's really hard to love others when you don't even love yourself. Start by liking yourself, right? Learn to have confidence in that voice that says "hey, I can do this and hey, I'm okay, the way I am." And it's okay. It's okay if you have scars. It's like some people have visual scars, which you can see, which I have a few. Many people have scars on the inside. It's okay if you have scars. The way I look at it... it's time that you've been through something, but you healed. Only when it's bloody and pussy and messy, you know that you're not healed, when it's scarred over it's healed. I look at my scars. It is something that I've been through, lived through, I survived this. I'm better because of it, a different person now because of what I had to go through. Then I would have been If I had never gone through it.

Kimberly: YES. It's your warrior goddess marks, right?

Kelly: Yes. You know, the name Kelly means warrior princess.

Kimberly: I love it. That's awesome. We're always trying to hide our scars and we think we have to have this perfect image about ourselves from head to toe and the scars are there for a reason. It's to remind you how strong, brave, and amazing you really are. You went through that; survived it. Now you can be a survivor. You can be a thriver.

Kelly: Yes. And you know, there's a quote that I love. I don't know who said it or the first time whoever said it, but it's pretty popular, I love it. It's fitting for this interview. The quote is that "courage, isn't the absence of fear. It's being afraid but doing it, anyway."

Kimberly: Yeah. I've heard that one. I can't think of who said that, but I absolutely love it.

Kelly: I do too. I would love to know who said it, to give credit to it. It's so true. My daughter, she went on vacation to Switzerland. (I have two daughters, but one went on vacation to Switzerland), and she went on the highest suspended bridge in Europe. It's 10,000 feet, it's not over water, it's over mountains, but her words are exact. She says, "mom, I'm scared, but I'm doing it, anyway." Sometimes we have to push ourselves outside our limits, out of that comfort zone, out of being scared, doing it, and pushing past it. Because it's only by going through there, can we grow and move on to the next level?

Kimberly: Yeah. That's where greatness is. It's not your comfort zone. So good. One thing at a time, I'm curious, what were your first couple of things that you were really focused on moving through to help you find your joy again?

Kelly: You know; I was to where I wanted to hide knives everywhere in the house in case someone broke in the house. Seriously, under the couch cushion, hide one under the bed cushion, hiding it in the medicine cabinet. I've got to have a weapon, every place in the house. Afraid to go out alone, to go to the grocery store or whatever. Simple things that most people would think are pretty simple to do can be scary sometimes. And just pushing myself to do it. I have to do it. No, I don't need to hide a knife under the couch or in my medicine cabinet.

Kimberly: So not having to do that anymore was your first step.

Kelly: Just feeling comfortable enough, safe enough, being where I am, whether it's in the home or driving in my car or, getting out and walking to the parking lot, to go to the grocery store. You know, I still, to this day, I still drive with my windows up and my doors locked. I figure it's safe. I'm not being reckless. Lock my doors in the house, when I go to bed, the doors are all locked. It's not like I'm saying, be reckless. Of course, always remain safe. I've learned to relax in it. I can have nobody else in the house. It can be dark, and I can be home by myself. I'm comfortable. I'm not afraid to be home by myself.

I'm not afraid to drive somewhere, I've learned to drive all over the place by myself. With my daughter, we went all the way across the United States, all the way to South Carolina. It's to the point of just telling myself I will not let fear hold me back. I'm going to learn to do something. I'm going to be smart about it. I'm going to be safe about it, but I'm going to learn to do things I wanted to do and that I want to experience. I will not let fear keep me from getting on an airplane and traveling out of the country or just even going for a walk, taking my dog for a walk, simple things. I put the leash on the dog. We're going for a walk in the neighborhood.

Kimberly: That's a huge first step too, after what happened to you, how long did that take you? If you don't mind me asking, how long did that take you to actually get to this point?

Kelly: It's been a long road because I've dealt with a lot of things in between that, it's been a long road. That's all I can say. Some people may get through things fast. It was a long road with me, since I started feeling pretty comfortable, but even like getting my self-esteem, my confidence back and believing in myself. That's a big thing, believing that I can do something, that I'm capable of doing something.

Kimberly: That's huge, that sometimes takes the longest. In these conversations, often, we talk about how, I always say Shrek and donkey put it so well, it's like an onion and peeling layers back and you keep healing through it. Do you find that you still have moments where either you get anxiety or do you kind of stop a bit because of your past? I know for a lot of us that have had a happening, we'll call it that, there're moments where you're able to move through it a little quicker. You're able to recognize what's going on. It doesn't worry you in life.

Kelly: It doesn't cripple me anymore. I always say, you're healed, but you don't forget the memories. The memories are still there, but you're healed you don't let those memories stop you. Don't let the memories hurt you anymore. You will not sit there and cry over it anymore. Move on, you move past it. But the memories are still there. They just don't affect you the same way.

Kimberly: Yes. That's what helps you in the healing process, too. I don't want to say dissociate, but there's a little of that too, it's more of a, I know this happened, but that's not me right now. It's not happening right now. I'm able to move forward. I'm able to be at home alone, go somewhere alone and it will not affect me like that. But I will always know my surroundings.

Kelly: Yes. I am always very aware of my surroundings. I'll see women walking down the street all the time. They're not looking around on their cell phones, walking around and I'm like, it's not being safe. I'm not saying you got to be panicked, but you need to be aware of your surroundings. You really do and know who's around you and what's happening around you. You shouldn't be so on your phone that you don't know that somebody is walking up to you. Right.

Kimberly: I've seen people even with two earphones, that's not necessarily the safest thing to have both in your ears. At least pull one out so you can hear too. If you could go back and tell your younger self one thing, what would it be?

Kelly: I think it would be to not let fear stop you. Fear can be very debilitating. Fear can stop you from achieving your dreams. Just an example. I always had a fear of going to college because I always felt I was stupid. I wasn't smart enough for it. The reason being is that I struggled my whole life with math, math just never comes easy for me. And I almost didn't graduate from high school because I couldn't pass the math proficiency test. I had to take a math proficiency class to prep me, to take the test again. I always felt I wasn't smart enough for college. Math just wasn't my thing. You can be smart in so many other things, but it doesn't mean you're smart in everything.

And as I went on, as I got the courage to go to college, I ended up; I got masters and a credential in special ed. I had a 4.0 grade point average when I graduated, from someone who thought they were too stupid to go to college. Don't let fear stop you from pursuing your dream. Get help, ask for help. Don't be afraid to ask for help, seek help. My brother helped me every weekend with my math homework. I would stay after math class, stay, and go into the math lab. I would get help with my math until the math lab closed. It was taking me all weekend to do my math homework. I would show up to math class half an hour early, and some kid would come in, say I didn't do my homework yet. He'd sit down on the floor, and he whipped out his homework really quick. I'm like, I just spent two days at my brother's house, like 10 hours each day doing my homework. And you sat and did it in 20 minutes? And that's okay. Math is his gift. It's not mine. That doesn't mean I'm not smart. It doesn't mean that I can't excel in other areas. My thing is, don't let fear stop you from living your dream or put limitations on you.

Be safe. Of course, always be wise, but don't let it stop you. Pursue the things that you want to pursue. Even if you don't have someone that wants to do it with you. Because there were times, I was afraid to do things by myself. I didn't want to do it by myself. If I couldn't find a friend or a family member to do it with me, I wouldn't do it. I always had the dream to write. I couldn't find anyone that would go to a writing group with me. You know what? This is my dream. I want to do it. I'm going to have to do it by myself if nobody will go with me. Nobody I know has the same interest I have. I finally went by myself. I made a friend and we've been friends for I think it's like eight, nine years now. It's like I went in there without a friend. I ended up making a friend along the way and my daughter was the same. Well, my other daughter is the same way. She couldn't find anyone to run with her. She joined a runner's group, and she met friends in the runners group. Sometimes we have to do things, even if we don't have someone to do it with us. We make friends along the way, don't let the fear stop you from pursuing your dreams and the fun activities in life that you want to do.

Kimberly: I love that. Just get out there and do it right. You never know what's going to happen. You made me think of one of my favorite quotes by Albert Einstein. He says, "if you judge a fish by how well he climbs a tree, he will spend his entire life thinking he's an idiot". That is to the point of what you were saying. Here you are, this brilliant woman, smart. And in many things, just not the math side. There's lots of people that have that. You can't think that you're anything less than brilliant, just because you're not good at this one thing. I love that. Don't let fear hold you back. Especially if you think you're not smart enough to do something.

Kelly: You don't have to be the top in your field if you're loving it. Even if you love to paint, but your painting is never good enough to sell, but you love to do it, do it anyway. You love it, hang it up in your house, display it for yourself. It's something you love, your dream, your passion. Pursue your passions.

Kimberly: Oh, I love that. Yes. You never know who might actually love your painting,

Kelly: Right? Exactly. For everyone right, there totally is. I've seen some paintings. I'm like that's considered art. There are many styles of art and yes, some things I wouldn't consider art is actually considered an art. You could be the most creative, unique styling and come up with a new trend. I heard a story too, of this lady that her whole life doesn't think she had any talent or anything. In her eighties, when she started painting, turned out, she could paint the most beautiful paintings, but she never took painting classes. She never messed with paint on her own. She never knew she could paint. A lot of us we have these hidden talents, they haven't been drawn out yet. Don't be afraid to try new things. You know? Like I tell my daughters, you don't know what you're good at until you try it. If you're interested in it, try it, try it, painting class. If you didn't like watercolors, try acrylics, or you like to cook, take a cooking class or a baking class. Try things. You don't know what you're good at because you haven't tried things, who knows. You could be fantastic at something you don't know because you've never tried it. Although I know I can't sing. So don't ask me to sing. I tried it. I actually went to take music lessons and the music teacher gave me back my money and told me she couldn't teach me to sing because I was tone deaf. Yeah. Don't ask me to sing our little secret, right?

Kimberly: Oh, that's such brilliant advice though. I love that. Go out and try something. Especially if you're feeling stuck and in the mundane and you don't know what to do, go try something new. You never know. If you don't like that, that's okay. You gave it a whirl. Try something else. You're not bound to take up whatever it might hike, and you hate it. Try something else. It's so simple. The choice is yours. The decision is yours and don't let fear hold you back.

Kelly: Or gender, there's some wonderful women mechanics out there, you don't have to be a man to repair cars.

Kimberly: I absolutely love your bravery and your strength. I appreciate you sharing your story because something like that absolutely can rattle you to your core. It rattles you to your core, it can paralyze lifelong, you moved through it, move past it. You're doing amazing things in the world. Thank you for that.

Kelly: Thank you for having me. I've enjoyed being here with you. Thank you.

CHAPTER 10

Save Yourself First, Everyone Else Can Wait

Kristin Arilus

Kristin Arilus is the founder of The Foreplay Factory, a creative marketing agency designed to help you build sales funnels that SEDUCE your leads, SELL your offers, and SECURE sales on autopilot. Using the power of email marketing, as a result of working with her agency, clients have: hit their first 10K month in their first 90 days of business, closed $24K sales in two months with a $57 product, and booked $55K sales in 30 days – ALL DURING the pandemic!

When Kristin is not chasing after her dreams, you can find her chasing her two toddlers, enjoying a crime series on Netflix, or practicing her calligraphy skills.

contact@theforeplayfactory.com
https://theforeplayfactory.com
https://www.facebook.com/kristinarilus/
https://www.instagram.com/kristinarilus/
https://theforeplayfactory.com/application

She was born with it, wanting bigger, better, and more. Now, she is creating it, creating her legacy. ~KA

Kimberly: I am so excited to introduce Kristin Arilus. Thank you so much for being here with me today, you're the founder of The Foreplay Factory. Very cool, let's start there.

Kristin: Thank you for inviting me. Sure. The Foreplay Factory is my marketing agency where we're basically helping people make money. I built this business because I wanted to make business fun, sexy, and profitable. That's actually the slogan I started using. We basically use the power of email marketing to help our clients make sales, but not just make them like one-off, we want them to make them consistently and we want them to, what we call them, have Moneygasms™. I help my clients automate their ability to make money, so that they can step away from the business, spend more time doing other things.

Kimberly: That's definitely needed in business for sure, but I love the name. I think it's awesome. It's brilliant. Let's dive right into the meat of this conversation and talk about what it is you've overcome in your life. I know as women; we do a lot. We overcome a lot, but what would you say is probably the number one?

Kristin: The number one I will have to say is my fight to keep moving regardless of my background. I was raised in a household with seven other siblings, actually I have nine siblings' total. I am the oldest of my parents' children. I was the one that really created the; I don't want to call it a blueprint, but I was the one that went to college first. I didn't graduate because I joined the military, but I really started paving the way for me to live life differently than what I've seen. There's definitely a cycle of brokenness in my family as far as living in poverty, needing government help, and sexual trauma in my family. A combination of all of that kept my family where they are now, but I decided I don't want that to be my story. I've pushed myself to make sure that my kids have a different story. I built that foundation so that I break the cycle, that their lives could differ completely from what mine was growing up. I know that was a little vague, but I'm not sure how deep you want me to go. I'll leave it there for now.

Kimberly: That was good. The deeper, the better, because it's where we heal in these conversations and sharing what you can make it for others to heal as well. When did you have that thought process of, I want to do better? When did that start?

Kristin: I feel like I was born with it. Like my mom talks about it a lot. I was her kid that didn't want to do things how everyone else did. I questioned everything. I questioned why we have to live how we live. It wasn't like a horrible upbringing; it was more so we wouldn't have money for something sometimes. I'm definitely that family that understands what it's like going to school and then coming home and everyone's huddled in front of the fireplace because the electricity is off or going to my older sister's house to go shower because our water is turned off, things like that. I realized this cannot be life, like I'm watching. We didn't even have cable. I'm watching sitcoms; I'm like these people living these fancy lives. If they could dream it, I know that's because some people are actually living their lives like that. I want a piece of that.

I went to a predominantly white college in Franklin, Indiana; I was one of like 32 mixed colored folk on the campus. I looked at how these other kids were living their life. I'm working three jobs to keep the bills paid in my mom's household. In class with people who literally would have frat parties all night or hanging out in the cafeteria all day. I was like, what did their parents do differently that their only job right now is to finish college compared to I'm finishing college, working three jobs, I even was walking a neighborhood dog for money, all kinds of things, my family could survive for me to be in college. I think that's when it really started honing in for me that there's something off here and I need to figure out or discover what that looks like.

Kimberly: Wow. That's interesting. I've talked to a lot of women, they often have stories like that of being poor, my mom being one of them. I can understand that story. You want to flip that script basically and get out of that mindset. Even the victim mindset on some level, right? Because you're living in this way, but you're seeing others live the other way. My mom started working at nine years old to help support the family. Nowadays we'd be like, what? that was a different time. I completely understand where you're coming from, when you're living one way and watching other people live in a different light. Would you say that when you talk about always no matter what your background was, where I would imagine you've seen that come up for you a few times as you keep moving throughout your business, graduating college and all of that stuff.

Kristin: Yes. I haven't graduated yet, and I haven't decided if I want to go back. I haven't decided that, but it definitely shows up, meaning I know I struggle with shame. It presents itself at every new level I achieve in my business with my family. I have two toddlers at home. I'm a military spouse. I've noticed that as we up-level our lives on what it looks like for us, I struggle with shame, but it represents itself in different ways in my life. Especially in my business, as I am growing my agency, bringing on new clients, I'm currently celebrating that I'm literally $3,200 away from my first six figures in business. To know that stuff is happening for me, but to also know that I have a family that is still on government help. I used to feel like I needed to be the superhero or the person who saved them.

I'm actually going to use a reference that unless you watch the show, you probably won't get it. But I am in love with the show "This is Us". I watched the latest episode last night, in the season or in the show, there's three siblings that all grew up fairly poor, but they didn't know that they were growing up poor. One sibling got rich and famous, he has a lot of money. The latest episode had a conversation between him and the spouse of one of his siblings, about the lifestyle of him and his girlfriend. They all had babies, not trying to go too deep, but it's like his family doesn't have to care about money. They could book a flight, they could do the things, they could go out there and basically live life.

Finances are not a conversation about if they can do it, compared to his sibling and her spouse. It's like they're getting hand-me-downs for their kids. They don't have the latest tech, the latest thing and something that the superstar in the show or the guy that has the money said made me realize that's how I live my life. He saw that he and his family could live in a compound; he wanted to buy a compound, where all of his family, their kids and all the kids that are raised together, grow up together. I realized that was a dream that I had for my family. But I also realized that it's my dream, it's not necessarily their dream. They don't want to come out of where they are for me to make the money. I wanted to buy an apartment complex, have all of us living, like not me, but, you know, having bought an apartment complex and having all of my siblings, their spouses and kids living in this apartment complex I own. They don't have a worry as far as, is the roof going to stay over their head? But I realize as long as I keep fighting to push them into wanting more, the more I keep myself stuck. It's like this repetitive cycle of shame, because my kids won't know the lifestyle that I grew up in. My kids are definitely a little privileged. They know Starbucks, Chick-fil-A, Target, and they are only five. Those are not things I even knew existed until I was a teenager.

Kimberly: Wow. You touched on a lot of things. I want to go back to something that you said about you feeling the guilt because you're being so successful. I think a lot of women can resonate with this because we have changed our mindset. We are stepping into that new chapter in our lives, we're able to do things, seek the things that we need for ourselves to grow and heal. We want to bring everybody with us. Feel guilty when they're not coming. That adage of you can lead a horse to water, but you can't make them drink. I mean, that fits perfectly right here, a lot of women feel that way. They feel that guilt and shame, even feel shame because you're doing well and it's hard to celebrate that. Would you agree?

Kristin: Yes, I absolutely agree. I am reading a book called a happy pocket full of money. In that book, I'm literally at the beginning of the book. It's an amazing book, but he says something that I cannot get out of my head. We all have the same time in a day, but you cannot go into debt with time. There's no way for you to. Like you have to live in a moment. Live in now. There's no way for you to go into debt with time. There's no way for you to jump into the future and move things into what you want. Like, I know I want a multimillion-dollar company, but I can't make that happen tomorrow. I can collapse the time over a period to make it happen.

But it made me realize in that book that I had shame, I had shame. Let's say I'm a recovering shame on myself. I don't know what you would call that. I was ashamed, but I also realize my family, my siblings, my mom, they have the same amount of hours in a day as I do. They have access to the knowledge that I have. Before I started making money in my business, I was giving out all this stuff for free. Like, come on, let's do the thing. Here's the information. But I realized, no matter what I do, they're not ready. I need to allow them to go through the journey that they need to go through because I've been going through mine to get me to where I am now. If I try to push them to come with me now, I'm actually robbing them of a life experience that they need to have, for them to actually enjoy, sustain wherever they're supposed to be in life.

That made me realize I can't rob them. I know where I am now. I had to go through a learning process for me to actually cope with everything that I'm going through now. I don't mean to cope with them in a sad or mean way. It's scarier when you make money. It's scary to put yourself out there, open yourself up and share vulnerable sides of yourself. But I had to go through that, those smaller things, those smaller failures for me to have the confidence that I have today to show up how I show up. If I try to collapse that for them, I'm literally robbing them of the foundation that they need.

Kimberly: Absolutely. So powerful. I love that book. It's a great book. Everybody should read that book, what a poignant, thing that you said about robbing them, because we all have our journeys, we all have our life lessons and you can't bring them along with you in that moment, because like you said, I think it was so well put that you're robbing them from what they need to go through, to have that success. Maybe that's not their plan, their dream or their want or desire. They have to still go through what they're going to go through.

Kristin: Yes.

Kimberly: I think being one of nine siblings, you said, that I would imagine it magnifies those feelings too, right?

Kristin: Right. Absolutely. Yeah. I have siblings that range between; I think it's like 32 and eight. Like a lot of us, I'm like right in the middle at 27, But I know that each one of us has to go through our own journeys. Once we lay in our bed, we have to figure out how to get ourselves out of it. Because if someone else helps us, like I've noticed every time I help someone or want to bring them with me, they didn't learn a lesson and they ended up in the same situation. It might not look exactly the same, but it's at least similar and they're expecting me to come bail them out again. Whereas if I would have left them alone, initially they would have learned the lesson too. Like, I'm not doing that again, because that was stupid or whatever the situation is.

Kimberly: Would you say that it's the victim mindset too, that people fall back into, it's kind of a comfortable space if you will, even though we don't like to talk about it like that.

Kristin: Yeah. I would call it a comfortable space. I wouldn't call it a victim mindset. I think it's a comfortable space where, actually; I don't think it's a comfortable space because it's very uncomfortable, but it's what they know. They'd rather be uncomfortable with what they know than to be uncomfortable with the unknown. Yeah. I feel like I'm dropping some gems. I'm going to have to re-watch this.

I feel like it's more the fear, about if I change what I'm doing, I'm not sure what that will look like. I'm not sure if I will fail or rise. I feel like it's a combination of fear and a combination of they're in a box. I don't know any other way to explain it other than I'm the only one that left the state to attend college, and to do anything. All of my family is still in Indiana. They never left the state for anything. When I left the state and realized people don't live like that, there's a much bigger world out there. I realized when I went back home, they're in this box. Because they don't know that there's a world or existence outside of this box, they don't even think to think bigger because it's not even seeing anyone in there, like the surrounding people, aren't doing it. It's not something that they see, even though they see it with me, they think I'm the exception too, because they don't see more than me doing it in their lives, it's kind of like, oh, she's blinking, but I don't think I can do it. I'm noticing that. I think it's definitely a combination of fear and the fact that they're living in a box that they don't even know that they're in.

Kimberly: What I hear you saying to them is take the chance.

Kristin: Definitely, it's actually deciding that you want it, taking the chance and working through whatever happens.

Kimberly: Yeah. That forward movement, like you were saying initially.

Kristin: Yeah. Like deciding what you want and figuring out, you don't have to figure out all the steps. I know I want a multimillion-dollar business, but I also know I don't have the mindset there to map out a multimillion-dollar business right now. My next step is to close $3,200 to get the six figures. Then I'm like, well, I hit the six figures. Let me collapse the time. Instead of doing it in nine months, let me do it in six months. Let me do it in three months. Let me do it in a month. I focus on what that next step is for me to get closer to where I want to go and focusing on that next step. I feel like I'm positioning myself, to have the connections, the experiences, the whatever I need for me to figure out the next step.

Kimberly: I love this, your mindset. As you grow, your expansion, you're able to receive on a larger level, you're expanding on a larger level, where you're able to create it. I think it even talks about that in that book too. Really understanding your capacity to even have that million-dollar business, because I would love that as well. But I know right now I couldn't do that tomorrow. And understanding that and having that grace with yourself to do what's next, that next step, that next step, because that next step is going to get you there. Love what you're saying here. Going back to when you thought you had that shift in mindset, but you're saying you always kind of had that in you, which I would absolutely believe, then how do you think you were able to really own that, and do what you've done? Because a lot of women we feel like we want to; we want the bigger, the better, the more, but we stay stuck. So how did you get from that point?

Kristin: I kind of already said it. I feel like it was me making a decision that this is not what I want. I don't know what I want yet, but this is not what I know that this is not what I want. It started with me joining the military. I mean, it started with me going to.

College and then I finished like a year, like a semester or two before I met my husband online. We got married; I moved out of state, and we started growing our family. Then I got into entrepreneurship, but I feel like I was open to the fact that I didn't know what this looked like, but I will take at least one step to figure out like, maybe if I'm standing here, I can't figure it out. But if I take one step to the right, maybe I could figure it out then. I was trying to take one step at a time, not try to overwhelm myself and it's been happening. As far as I also recently found out that I am in human design, if you take a human design test, you can Google it, you can find out what type of creator you are and I'm a manifesting generator. By the time I was 22, I was already married. We had already bought our first home, and had our two kids. And the house we had was the dream house. I even tell people when I married my husband, I had a list of 40 things I wanted. He had 38 of the 40. The two he didn't have, he can't sing or dance, but I'm okay with that, I realized maybe that's the answer.

It's being clear about what you want, not knowing how to get there, but clear. This is what I want. I knew I wanted to go to college. I literally decided a week before I was supposed to move on campus, I made it happen. We decided we want to buy the house. Well, I married my husband in three months. After we met in person, we got married in three months. We've been married for six and a half years now. When we bought our house, we decided we wanted to buy. I think in April, by October we had closed the house and was moving in. It was like these things. Once you decide what you want, I feel like our brain fires help us see all the information we need. It's like the puzzle pieces are showing up for how we need to lay that next brick or whatever for us to take that next step, to get where we need to go. Maybe that's the long way to go. It's being clear about if this is not what you want, what do you want? Then start positioning yourself to attract that or bring that into your life.

Kimberly: That's good. It's like you're saying, making the choice, then doing it, acting on that decision and having absolute clarity because you can't fail. Even if you do, you fail forward. You keep going. There's no such thing as failing. Really. There's finding ways not to do it in that moment.

Kristin: I call it graciously failing forward, taking massive imperfect action. It will not be perfect, but you acted.

Kimberly: Absolutely. There is no such thing as perfection. I always say progress is perfection. Keep going.

Kristin: Absolutely. Yes.

Kimberly: Keep going. I'm going to ask you one of my favorite questions to ask. If you could go back and tell your younger self a piece of advice, what would it be?

Kristin: Stop trying to save everyone. Save yourself first. I spent my life far. I mean, I know I don't have a lot of it yet, but the life I have, I spent it trying to save everyone else. I

Started working at 15, through high school, sophomore, junior, senior year, I worked three jobs. I did three different childcare facilities, worked weekends, early morning, afternoons, I was sustaining my mom's household at that point. I went to college and did the same thing. When I got married, I purchased our first; we had an apartment, but I purchased a car that was way too big for our family, because I was envisioning being able to adopt my siblings so that they could live with us. I'm paying for this big car we don't even need. They never came to move with us down to the house we bought.

I bought a house that was way too big because I wanted my siblings to come. I know for some people it's, oh; you know it was going to happen. You're preparing yourself, but I realized I would've saved so much money. So much time, so much headache. If I would've purchased what I needed. Once it was completed that they were going to come live with us, then expanding it, going to the next step and doing the thing. Even throughout this process, I've been married six and a half years. We've had four different couples, or families or people live with us because I have a big heart. It's like, oh, if you're struggling, I'm going to let you move in. But I decided I'm done with that. It was like, if I could tell myself something, it would definitely save myself first, let them figure it out on their own. I feel like I wouldn't be in debt right now because I would have been taking care of my lonesome, my family, and get what we needed to get done. It wasn't until I made that decision that I stopped being people's default when they needed help. I'm their last option. Because they know Kristin will not help unless it's serious. Like absolutely not. I feel like if I would've done that way sooner, Oh my gosh. I couldn't even imagine where I would be right now.

Kimberly: That is definitely a powerful gem. You dropped right there. I think a lot of us do that. As you're talking, I'm sitting here going through my mind, like, wow. Yeah, I've done that. I do that. Those big hearts we have, we want to grab, gather the flock, bring them with us on this amazing journey we see for ourselves, think about all that wasted time, energy, money, buying stuff, getting the big car, the big house when you didn't need it in that moment. Powerful. I think a lot of women can definitely resonate with that. I was sitting here, like I said, I was going through my mind. Yup. Yup, yup. Checking off the boxes.

Kristin: I think it's because what I'm realizing is this, this is how I'm living my life now, I don't apologize about it. Because they're not a problem. Like when I was at my lowest, I'm incredibly open about what's happening. My husband and I sold our house early

2020, because we financially could not afford it anymore because I got so much in debt trying to save everyone else, that they couldn't even help me out of my situation because they weren't willing to help themselves out of their situations. We ended up selling our home. During that period, our credit was shot. We had to come up with the deposit to get this apartment I'm in now. No one helped. I was always the first person there trying to help them. I'm not saying to completely back off. I'm saying I'm no longer their default. I made the decision that I have to take care of my family first, because one else is going to take care of my family, the way I take care of everybody else. Once I realized that for myself, even now, I regret nothing. I'm living my life proudly, meaning my family is still living on government assistance and don't really have money for stuff. However, they have more gifts under their Christmas tree than I had for my kids. My kids had three gifts each because we decided we wanted money in savings so that we can eventually take a paid in cash vacation in the future. I'm not judging anyone that does that, but I'm saying, it made me see, that's how they're spending their money. Why save them? Because you're making money and trying to help pay their bills.

If they're not being smart about it themselves and they won't even listen to the information, help them do what you did to get yourself out of it. I feel like I was totally about to go on a tangent, but it made me realize like we started putting it ourselves first. Meaning in the last 12 months we have house cleaners now that come by weekly to help me, like my husbands in Japan, me and the kids are here in California. We have housekeepers that come by weekly. I had a meal delivery service weekly, but my kids stopped eating the meals. We're going to figure that out. But I did that for at least six months. I literally started a monthly membership for massages now that they're back open and I'll be honest, I'm living my life.

If you can't pay whatever it is you're trying to pay and I'm only relating it to money, because I feel like that's what a lot of us try to put our help, even if we don't have it ourselves. I will not feel bad about the fact that those are now necessities or essentials for my household, for me to keep continuing to build my empire, because no one else is going to come and clean this house for me. No one else is going to come help me make these meals to make sure my kids are eating. No one else is going to help. I was like, okay, if I had all the help that I wanted, what does that look like? Financially, that money is already taken care of. I feel like I'm definitely going into the money side of things because it's gotten to a point where if a family member wants a loan from me financially, they have to apply.

I am not an ATM. I'm not a money tree. I am like a bank and you need to apply to get the loan. When you apply, I need to know how much you need. I need to know what is for. I need to know when you're going to pay me back. Then if, if all of that makes sense and I'm like, okay, I don't mind loaning you this, now I need you to go through a budgeting course that I created. I created a budgeting course for my family. I will not keep repeating the same thing over and over. You want money? Okay? Here's my course. I need you to send me your budget. Once I see it, here's the video, it's like a quick 30-minute video about how to create a budget and I want them to create a budget and send it over to me. I'll help them manage their money better so that I don't have to bail them out again. When I started doing that process, suddenly they didn't need my money any more. A few people have gone through it, but many of them, like I had to do all that. I might as well go to the bank. OK! Go to the bank.

Kimberly: I love it.

Kristin: I'm like how do I need to show up? I realized every time I saved someone else I'm taking away from my kids' legacy. The money or I want properties in our names. The more I help other people, the less I have to give to my kids when I pass away. I want not j my kids to know my name; I want seven generations of my kids and my grandchildren, great, great, great - grandchildren to know my name. Because great-grandma Kristin made sure that we had property in our name, she made sure we had this, this, this, these assets. Every time I help someone else with my time, my money, my energy, any resources, I'm having to really put it in my head. I'm taking that away from what I want my kids to have. Because that's the leverage I saw in college. Those kids didn't have to work because their parents had assets in place that made sure that I paid the bills, that they didn't have to take out student loans, and stuff was in cash. All he had to do was get a good grade. If they want to play a sport, they are playing for fun.

Kimberly: I love it. Instead of trying to get scholarships, I love it. This is such a powerful conversation. Let go, make choices. It's taking the oxygen mask first. They always say on the airplane. You put it on first and then you can help others. Absolutely a brilliant conversation. I am thrilled that you were here with me today. You're amazing. Thank you so much.

Kristin: Thank you so much for having me.

CHAPTER 11

When Tragedy Becomes Light

Lupita Garcia

Lupita is a woman on a mission. Her goal is to open a nonprofit organization that will help and empowered kids and families in need. Using their own stories as a source of empowerment and other resources to get them through life's challenges. She has been working out of her home, helping her community whenever there is a need. Her biggest project is a school considered being below low income with #657 kids. Using her FB page, she gathers up her supporters, starts donation drives for almost every holiday. She does it for #657 kids, has been for the last 5 years. All this more while fighting cancer. She's the definition of boss but too many she's a warrior.

Contact Info:

https://www.facebook.com/mrsgarcia6801

mrsgarcia68@yahoo.com

(213) 925-2368

She had to hit rock bottom before she finally was ready to say, enough is enough, now she is leading the way. ~KA

Kimberly: I'm excited to be here today with Lupita Garcia. Lupita, thank you so much for being with me today.

Lupita: Thank you for having me. I appreciate being here with you.

Kimberly: Thank you. I'm excited. Let's talk about what you do because you really help in the community a lot.

Lupita: Well, I try to help as much as I can. My goal is always to teach people we can help each other. Basically, when there's a need for help, whether it be a family, kids, or someone in the community, I'll put it out on my Facebook, or I talk to my people to say, this is what the need is. Let's put it out there, see who wants to fill the need. Amazingly enough, every time that I ask, the need always gets filled. It's amazing how many people want to help. They don't have the guidance. I guess I provide that guidance for them. Since I've been doing it for long now, they trust me, which is good.

Kimberly: Absolutely. That's incredible. You also want to start your own nonprofit, is that correct?

Lupita: Yeah. That's the goal to have my non-profit where I can actually help, do more, because I'm limited now. I don't always have funds, sometimes I use my husband's funds, that doesn't go over very well. The community can't always help. Everybody's struggling right now because of COVID. As you know, many people didn't have jobs, but still we came together as a community. I tell them, every penny count, everything that you give always makes a difference, it all adds up in the end. The goal is to start a foundation. I want it to be geared to helping families, kids, anybody who is in need basically, geared more towards families and kids. Because that's what my target is always, especially because I target a school of 657 kids every year for the past four years, every single kid leaves with a present for Christmas, for Mother's Day, we make flower pens for them, and they get to take it mom. Halloween, they get Halloween costumes, it's about making kids happy, making families happy. We don't have enough happiness that we can see. We can actually say see that smile and know we were part of that. It's an amazing feeling. I always get told, it feels good when you see kids, thank you. Happiness, that's what it's all about in the end.

Kimberly: Ooh, that was good. You gave me chills. I love it. You have an incredible story. I'd love to talk about that. What would you say is one of your biggest obstacles that you've gone through?

Lupita: The easiest way to sum that one up is life. Life for anybody I think is a challenge, especially nowadays, but for me, I think it was every moment that I put myself at risk because in the end it was me who put myself in situations that landed me where I was. Involved in gangs. I did a lot of awful stuff in my younger days. I was a product of the environment that I grew up in and because of the people that I grew up with. My biggest obstacles were getting out of gangs, getting out of drugs, staying away from all that awful stuff. I was brutally gang raped; I survived being shot, stabbed, incarceration. Life wasn't perfect.

It wasn't perfect once I got sober either, or away from all the bad people. It takes time, it's not a simple thing to walk away from, especially that life that you're so used to, that you can easily run to when everything else is failing. I did that a lot. It wasn't an easy road; it's never been an easy road. I still struggle to this day with a lot of things that go on in life. When I get angry, I go back to that old Lupe. I call her the old chola Lupe. Don't bring her out. We don't want her out, but you know, I've learned so much. It took me a while to understand why things were happening to me, or why I go back to the saying.

I put myself in a situation, not that I deserved it, because of stuff that I went through, but I don't regret any of it because I am who I am today because of all those moments. They've been horrible moments. I don't want to wish on anybody, but it's made me a better person, a better mom, a better friend, a better wife. I've been able to take my story, teach others, help them, and show them, hey, you see where I was at? Well, I came out of it, look at my life. It's not perfect because nobody's life is perfect, but we can come out of it. We can change. This is it; I'm going to show you, I'm going to give you the steps, you take whatever you need; you go with it.

I think that's one of the important things that I tell people. You always have to share your story. Your life is your story. You don't know what difference you can make in somebody's life. You may think that your life is irrelevant or that you haven't had tragedy or something. You don't need tragedy. Some of you could go through something that somebody else can relate to and be like, oh, and they don't know how to deal with that. When you share your story, no matter what it is or how it is, you make a difference in somebody's life; you help somebody you might not know right away, but you'll know. That's what's important to you. We're like, we have to, because we have to help each other. That's why I also have my love thy neighbor page where we help each other. It's about loving your neighbor. If you can offer your neighbor help, why wouldn't you, you want somebody to struggle as much as you did? I don't, I wouldn't. If you have questions, ask me. I have so much to say; I don't want to like bombard you with so much, because it also gets a little, people are like, Ooh, they get taken back. If you have questions, please ask me. I'm an open book, but I also realized that when I talk to people, they feel bad. I see that pity look; I don't like that, I'm here, survived a lot. I'm still surviving cancer. I'm still surviving life being off the streets. Because that's an everyday thing, you know? If you have questions or you want to ask me anything, please feel free.

Kimberly: I will, this platform is perfectly situated to where you're able to share. Whatever comes up for you, share. I will not interrupt you if you talk about something. Please share whatever, as much as you want to, be as vulnerable as you want to. It's like you said, it's sharing our stories that we can help impact and inspire somebody else. They're powerful.

Lupita: Yeah. I think I wrote it in the little bio that I put when I was reading everybody's bio. Not that I have nothing to bring to the table, but it was a little intimidating for me because they're bosses on a whole different level than me. I know that I have people's powers (my husband calls it people's power) because I can take people, convert them, bring them together and create a movement in which I have. I created a moment too, to help people. That's what I want to do. I look at it this way. I take my life, all the awful stuff that I did, I want to pay back for all the awful stuff that I did. All the junk that I put into this world, all the bad, all the bad vibes, everything that I did. I want to turn that around, give back to the world. I think that's how I started my journey to why I help people. When people tell me, why do you help people, it's because I can. I want to give back because it took so much when I was young; I did a lot of damage; I want to show people also like, hey, look, you can do all that. When you're done, this is what you can do, stuff like this, you feel good about yourself; it changes you; it transforms you. Not only that, but you're also touching other people's lives. I call it the trickle effect, especially with the kids. The kids are like, oh, you know, I helped this lady that was walking. She needed help with the groceries, or like I helped the students. They needed a pencil. It's little things that make the difference because they remember. I learned it from her. That's what I love to hear. You know? Those are the moments that make me happy. I'm doing the right thing, or I'm making a difference. That was important to me because sometimes I'm like, am I doing, am I doing the right thing? Am I, where I'm supposed to be? It always comes up, brief moments come up at the right time that remind me, yes, I am. You know, it's hard. It's not an easy thing to do, like to motivate people to want to help or get them to donate or whatever, because sometimes they want to hear a tragic story or they want to hear this, like, my God, tell me what, why, why do they need this?

I'm like, well, sometimes I don't want to tell you that, what sometimes it is, if they need help, it doesn't have to be something big and ugly. Sometimes we need to help each other get through the day. It could be like a smile. It could be anything. We have to make a difference in each other's lives. We teach that to our kids, for a long time I thought bringing my kids into it. I was like, no, I'm not going to, they will not be a part of this, but I made them a part of it because I want them to know what it's like, I said, my kids will not go through what I went through. I can give them what they want. They will get it because I remember what it was like not having what I wanted, or not being able to do what I wanted, the way I wanted. I did little things because I was in gangs. I lived a whole different lifestyle. I did not want that for my children. I said, I will keep that away from them. In doing so, I protected them much that I shielded them from all the awful stuff. It worried me and thought, do I need to go expose them to the bad stuff? No, but you know, I shared so much of myself with everybody that I didn't realize that I didn't share with my kids. Eventually I had to, and it strengthened us. Especially with my fight with cancer. It brought us all closer together. I think of all the things that I've been through in life, I've been through a lot, I've survived a lot of stuff, you know? I've survived.

The worst thing ever for me, that I think I've survived besides this cancer, is a being left in the field when I was gang raped. The cops set us up. In Rampart district, they used to hog tie us. When we didn't have money or didn't have the drugs on us, they would take us to our enemies' neighborhood. They would leave us there in zip ties. Hey, we got somebody here from whatever neighborhood was their mortal enemies. They would drop us off. The one time I didn't have my homeboy with me, I was by myself; I was there. They caught me. They took me, a bunch of them rapped me and they left me for dead, with a broken bottle inside me and everything. And in the field that I was in, I was found by a little old man, like he was picking up cans, and if he wouldn't have found me. I would have died. I lost a lot of blood. And that was like the most, the most heart wrenching for me, because I realized who was there and who wasn't there, where I was at and why I was there. And look at me, look at me now, like I'm so broken and I' still am the one that has to pick up all the pieces, you know? For me, that was one moment where I started realizing like, do I want to keep doing this? Because this is where this is what's going to keep happening. And guess what? I still kept doing it. It was that wasn't enough for a change. It wasn't enough, like, boom woman, come on. Like, isn't that enough to wake you up, but I wasn't ready? Then I realized that you have to be ready to want to change it, to be in a position where you're able to change, because of change, but are you able to change? Are the circumstances there for you to change. I didn't have any of those circumstances. I was still living on the streets. I was still homeless. I was still doing drugs. So all that stuff, but for me now, where I'm at now, looking back, that was walking in the park compared to what I'm going through with cancer. I've been fighting it for 16 years on and off. It's been the biggest struggle of my life. That's because it's affects me, but my children, my husband and everybody that cares about me, it affects them.

I have fantastic people that I'm surrounded by they help me and we do stuff together. It's changed us in ways that I never thought, it has brought us closer together. And it's also driven people away from me. People I thought were like my actual family. It's an eye opener. Even now, to this day, I'm still struggling with a lot of stuff. And trying to navigate myself what are the right choices for the medication. You know, I have a bad heart because my mom was a bad person, whatever. So much that it's overwhelming, I have to be careful. I still want to help people. I run myself down. My husband looks at me like I told you, but that's what drives me. I love to help people because it's their smile, or when they say thank you. That's what fuels me. That's what makes them happy. Because then I know I did something good, out of all the bad crap that I did. Now, I'm doing something good by me. I'm making a change. I'm making a difference in somebody's life. That's my goal is to make a difference to show that, even if you're a bad person, yes, we all have it in ourselves to be bad people. But it's what comes after, that's important. What do you do with that awful stuff? You make it better. You teach somebody; take that bad stuff; we make it better, recoup their life. That's what I'm always doing. I hope that everybody that meets me takes that with them, that I'm not trying to help you. I want to change you. I want to impact your life. I want you to impact somebody else's life and get them to that point as well, it's a lot, but I know where I belonged. I usually know people would say, Hey Lupita, I know somebody that was going through this. I know when I can help. Then I know what my limits are. And I also know that sometimes you need to reach out for more help. I did that too. I took my life, and I also shared it, I went through a homeless program, and they actually paid for my school.

I was a social service provider for many years. I became one of the youngest program directors in Hollywood. It was amazing. I spoke in front of the Senate regarding HIV and AIDS awareness, in the middle of all that when the HIV/aids Pandemic was going on. I learned a lot. I was actually passing out bleach kits and condoms on sunset and Santa Monica, to the transgender community. Because I learned that's a whole different world than what I grew up. When I say that we all have our own tragedy or we all go through something different and our story will help somebody else, it will because I learned from them, they learned from me. It's an amazing world we're living in, how we treat each other. It's sad now, but we can be better. We have to be better because if we want a world for our kids; we have to love thy neighbor then.

Kimberly: Absolutely. So many things.

Lupita: I told you, I can overwhelm you a little. That's why I said I have too much to say.

Kimberly: Oh no, I will not stop you. Because when we share like this, like you said, we have impact, we can help somebody else. You never know who's going to resonate with our stories and how we can inspire them. You never know. I will never stop you from speaking.

Lupita: Sometimes people won't even tell you because they're scared because they don't know how to, and that's why you have to., If it's a serious story, or even write it down, people read stuff all the time, people in silence, do you help people like that too? You never know where that helping hand is going to reach out from and know that it will, know that somebody somewhere out there is going through something that you went through, and your voice will reach them, eventually.

Kimberly: Yeah. You went through many things. I wanted to ask you. One thing that you mentioned after that tragedy, that happened to you, you were still not ready to change your life. I want to touch on that because I think it's really important for people to understand that we take to be ready. Doesn't matter how bad or what we're going through. If we're not ready to change, we will not change. I wanted you to talk a little more about that, because that was a horrific thing that you went through. You still stayed in what you were doing.

Lupita: Yeah, it was because I was angry. That moment made me even more angry. Made me want to get revenge. Beat this. I got deeper into drugs; I didn't. It was because then I also had a recovery process that took close to eight months to a year. It was a long process because there was a lot of damage. I was all by myself. I had my one homeboy that took care of me. If it weren't for him, I think I probably would've killed myself. I was in so much pain on so many drugs. He was the one that would always snap me out of it. I did a lot of that by myself or with him. I wasn't ready to change because I had felt so much anger; I wasn't letting it go.

I could've let it go. I walked away, but I didn't want to. I wasn't ready for it. People don't realize that we may want to, the need and everything, the right circumstances have to be there because until everything falls, everything has to fall into place before you make that choice. It pushes you when everything falls into place, that really pushes you. Because now you're like, okay, everything's telling me it's time, it's time. You know, when it is time, your heart will tell you, now if you're being stubborn, that's a whole different story. There is a difference between being stubborn, then wanting and needing to. Eventually you realize you need to change? Why? why else, because I want to live and be better. You make a choice as to for what you want to change whatever choice it is that you make you go with. I wanted to see my daughter; I wanted to see my daughter; I wanted to see my kids. I wanted to have a life with the man that I married to now. He lived a similar life like mine, he's from a rival gang. It wasn't easy.

It was really hard because I lived in the same neighborhood. So, to walk away from it, where was I going to go? Still everybody's around me. You can't change until you leave and that's why it was really hard to do. And it took so much for me, to be so angry and to hate so much, that it wasn't until I started being a part of that homeless program I wanted to be better, because I had seen other people be better. I wanted to be a part of that. I'm tired of being a part of all the destruction. It's not until something clicks in your mind that, you resonate with or that you can relate to them and be like, hmm, well maybe, maybe I can do that, because you're told for so long that you can't, or that you're not good enough. You can't because of the type of person you are, or because you got all these tattoos, or you look like a chola, or whatever, all the negative, it stays with you. And when you're trying to change, or you're trying to make that step, it's right there echoing in your mind. And you let that go, if it's still in your head, then you won't be ready for it.

Eventually, that time comes for everybody when we decide. And I'm sure that, you know when you say it enough is enough, that's it because where else am I going I'm already at rock bottom. Is there anywhere else, sideways? No, that's it. Do I want to keep being here? Do I want to see what's out there? What else is up there? If I've tried all this horrible stuff, now let's try something a little better. Why not? Right. We already experienced the worst why not experience the best, or at least try to get to the best. I look at it back I'm like, why did I continue on that path? But it was because I wasn't ready. There was still too much anger, plus I was still living in it. I was amid it. It's not a simple thing to walk away from.

Kimberly: Right. But you did.

Lupita: Yeah, I did it. I'm glad I did.

Kimberly: That's awesome, something that keeps coming up, in all conversations that I'm having and going through all of that stuff. We wouldn't be who we are today. We wouldn't know what we know. We can't help at the level that we can help now, had we not gone through all those things that we've gone through, and you went to that homeless shelter, and you started seeking help. And it gave you an idea that you can get better. You can get out of it. And then you were in that child welfare to help you graduate.

Lupita: Social service provider for kids that were homeless, HIV positive and stuff like that. Yeah, because that was that's where I graduated from. I knew I wanted to be a part of something. I knew I could help. So why not use my life to help them it's different from when you learned it from books when you live it, because you can actually speak to it. You have the backup; you have the proof, the paperwork basically, because they knew I was being sincere and then it was easier to help them that way.

Kimberly: Yes. That's why these stories are important too because we've got all that experience, we'll call it, we can share that with others. You took that used it to help all those kids. I think that's remarkable.

Lupita: Yeah. In the beginning, it was really hard. Like I said, it's a lot. I knew when to say what, because I have much experience speaking to others. I also knew when I couldn't help someone. I Knew that there were things you can't talk to kids about someone else had to... If I needed to talk to a rape victim or something like that; I knew what to say, because I was there at one point. I knew how to handle them, as opposed to somebody who did not know, who had never dealt with it. They would want to speak with me because it was the way you approach people. That's why I tell people it's important for you to, to share stories, to help people, because it'll make a big difference. It'll impact somebody in a way that you won't even know, because if somebody helped help you there was that person for me, it wasn't somebody that actually went through it, but she connected me, impacted my life. And that's how I knew I had to share my story too, because it would make a difference.

Kimberly: It makes a difference, and it helps.

Lupita: It helps you heal too. I think for me; it was a big healing. A big part of my healing process of sharing it, realizing that it was all bad. It was bad, but you know what, I'm making good of it now, I'm turning it around and it's going to work for me. It was always against me. Everything was always against me, but now it's for me. I'm going to use it to help to make a difference in somebody's life, not to ruin it. No more crying and all that stuff. No, enough is enough. I already did that for too many years. Now that my story is going to be proof of something good coming from it, you know? That in the end, that's what I want people to take from it. Like, yes, I went through all this crap, but you know what, as much as I hated those moments, as painful as it was, I don't regret them.

People sometimes look at me like what you don't even regret it. It took me a long time to get to where I'm at. It does because it's a process. Things come up where it hits home. I realized that I've impacted the lives that have impacted, I've learned and helped many people. I don't know what else, I read that my story has done. I know that it happened for a reason, for so many reasons. I'm grateful for it because I, became a better person because of it. Now I appreciate life, when I didn't appreciate life, I didn't care about it. If I was living on the streets, being a part of the recklessness, I didn't care about life, now I love life now. That's why when cancer came up and I was like, My God, this is something I cannot control. That's why I said, it's the hardest fight for me because you have no control over it. I see my husband break down, my kids, I'm like, I can't do this. There were times that cancer has made me want to give up, like, I don't want to do this anymore. But then my husband always brings me back, he's, my rock. He always reminds me you survived so much to let this thing take you down. I'm I say, okay, okay, I get it. We have to have those moments of like, hey, wake up, did you forget who you are? Remember, I told you I was reading everyone's bios. He said, hey, remember who you are, remember what you survived. You're a survivor. I always have to remind myself of those moments because, sometimes I say, I'm basic. Everybody looks at me. No, you're not. You do all this stuff for the community, it's not that I need to be reminded, because I don't look at it in a way as if I'm doing this for that, I do it because it's from my heart. And that is there's a need. And when, if the need happens, if I know I can do it, I'm there. If I can't, then I'll try to have them get to get the help or somebody who can help. I know it's hard to do because I'm always going to be the one to help because; I have the people behind me. I'm glad that my story has become something, or my life has become something that I can help others with, you know? It wasn't all wasted on bullshit, I'm grateful that I'm still alive to share it with people and you're helping me share it too.

Kimberly: Absolutely. Because as we share our stories, we heal ourselves on deeper levels, it lets other people know that they're not alone, they can get through it. Hopefully our stories, by telling them, can collapse time for them and help them get out of their situations faster or heal from their past situations faster.

Lupita: Knowing that you're going to help heal people or help someone survive it gives you hope. It gives you that little life. That is the life that you've been waiting for. It's like, okay, maybe I can't do this. You know? Then sometimes that's all you need is that reassurance. Speaking to it, forget what you did, you did it. That's sometimes all. We need to realize that because we were stuck in the ugliness and the bad of it, that we were in the bad for long, it feels like black clouds are always over us. That's what I used to call it, my own black cloud and let it stay. You do not need to stay here... I had to stop dwelling on it eventually it's going to leave and there's going to be a way out, People need to know that there is a way. That's why, again, share your story because people need to realize like, there's bad times, but we eventually all come out of it. We all come out, there's always a way.

Kimberly: I always say there's light at the end of that tunnel.

Lupita: You've got to look for it in a corner, open your eyes.

Kimberly: Yes. What would you tell your younger self if you could go back?

Lupita: Oh, wow. I would tell my younger self. Well, that's a good one. The first thing that came to mind when you said that was to be patient. I had no patience when I was younger. I didn't. I wanted to go, go, go. I was always the one that was going through the stuff and then no planning, no patience. To slow down, life isn't going anywhere. It's still going to be there, slow down and appreciate life as a young person. We don't appreciate life. There was so much that I missed out on. I mean, I missed out on a whole different way of life. I lived a whole different life, but I missed out on the good stuff. The normal stuff, like playing with Barbie's, doing, stuff like that, for all this other fun stuff. So patience and slowing down. I think for me anyway, for the lifestyle that I was in, this was to have the patience to slow down. I was always crazy.

Kimberly: You have an incredible story. Thank you so much for sharing it. It's powerful. I hear from other people you're such a warrior goddess because you've gone through all that you have, you're helping so many, you're standing in this light and being powerful. Thank you for all that you do.

Lupita: Thank you. I appreciate it. Thank you for helping me share my story. And I hope I know it will impact somebody. I always tell people, if anybody wants to know my story or know more about it, I'm always an open book, I don't mind sharing or helping people with it, because that's, what's important. That's, what's important to me, that's what I always preach. I always practice what I preach. Thank you so much, really appreciate you for this interview. I hope we get to see more and more of everybody's interviews as well. Thank you.

CHAPTER 12

Recognizing My Reflection

Natalie Renn

Natalie Renn is a Motivational Speaker and the Founder/CEO of The Pink Bags 501 © 3 nonprofit organization in Phoenix, AZ. The bags are freely given to women survivors of domestic abuse who are currently in a transitional housing program.

Natalie is a proud partner of Inspiring Women and UnSilenced voices. Natalie created, organized, and hosted the 1st Annual Conference of Hope in April 2021 and has planned The Conference of Hope2 coming Spring of 2022.

Natalie is a subject expert on domestic abuse, as she herself is a survivor and tells her story of how she nearly lost her life.

She received The Congressional Recognition Award in October 2020. She has also been chosen and honored as a Service Hero by The Service Hero Show, for her work with vulnerable communities.

Natalie is a mother to 4 beautiful daughters' ages 9, 13, 21, & 25.

Contact info:

natalie@thepinkbags.org

Her passion and compassion fuels her to help others. Facing fear and walking through it. ~KA

Kimberly: I am talking with Natalie Ren. I am so excited you're here today. Thank you for being here.

Natalie: Thank you. Thank you for having me. This is so wonderful. I feel honored to be a part of this amazing project.

Kimberly: Thank you. You're the founder and CEO of the pink bags. Why don't you talk about that for a sec?

Natalie: THE PINK BAGS is an Arizona based 501 C3 nonprofit organization, and we serve women survivors of domestic violence that are currently living in transitional housing. Getting the resources that they need, having the support that they need. I create beautiful hot pink purses that are actual purses that they can use. I fill it to the brim with over 30 items that are bath items, beauty items, some stationary items to help them. There is a journal, along with a fancy bling pen, there's a photo album, there're postcards to send to their friends and family. I include stamps and I deliver these bags to help these women on their healing journey.

Kimberly: I love it. That's incredible. I'm grateful to you for all that you do in the world. Thank you for that.

Natalie: Oh, it's beyond a pleasure for me. This is a blessing, a huge blessing that I have in my life.

Kimberly: Absolutely. Well, let's go right into it. What would you say is one of your biggest obstacles that you've overcome, gone through?

Natalie: I'm not sure obstacle is the correct word in my life. It's more like a barrier. It's been a huge barrier, the tallest, thickest, hardest wall to break through, now at the age that I'm at, I have the awareness of what exactly has stopped me, what has held me back from experiencing wonderful things in my life. That is my lack of self-belief, believing in myself. I have struggled since I was a tiny little girl because of the abuse I endured by my stepfather. I never believed in myself. I wanted to. There was no one that ever believed in me, either.

Kimberly: How has that shaped your life growing up and what have you done to help yourself move past it, move through it.

Natalie: I haven't conquered it yet. I haven't been able to move completely through it yet to where it no longer affects me and my life. It can debilitate. The fear of rejection is horrible. The fear of failure has prevented me from participating in opportunities in my life. I have been asked to be a part of things that I could have helped define who I was, and shaped me into someone, a better version of myself. I missed out on many things my whole life, even as an adult. There was a time where my self-confidence, self-esteem and my self-belief was intact, I was very strong, when I was a surgical assistant at a trauma center, because there was a manager that saw something in me I've never seen in myself. He believed in me and because of him; he was the first person ever in my life at 26 years old. He allowed me to do my clinical rotation there in the operating room. I became a talented assistant. I thrived, I flourished, I blossomed into this amazing person. I felt what it was like to be sure of yourself to know that you can do things that nobody else could do. It allowed me to specialize in several specialties, in surgery, and I thrived even more. Then I got lost after a horrific rollover car accident, and I suffered a brain injury and everything that I had worked incredibly hard on completely disappeared. I have struggled since 2014, that's what really devastated me, my abusive marriage that I was in for almost five years. The abuse robbed me and stole away what bit of self-confidence, self-belief and self-worth, self-esteem that I had inside of me vanished! I second guessed who I was as a person.

I second guessed my decisions as a mother raising my daughters. I couldn't trust myself. I wasn't able to know I could do it again. I wanted to. The abuse robs you of every good thing that there was, you're left empty hollow, now I've been rebuilding it slowly. The pink bags literally have been life support for me. They pump life into me. They allow me to breathe, to be productive, to have a purpose in my life, once again helping others. My entire purpose is, I don't want another woman, that's been in an abusive relationship to experience what I experienced. I completely stopped performing self-care, I stopped wearing makeup, stopped dying my hair. I wore the same clothes for several days. I had bags under my eyes from insomnia because of the horrific Complex PTSD. Until one day, after I had kicked him out, I looked at myself in the mirror. I couldn't believe what was looking back.

I didn't know who she was. I thought she was ugly. But then I said to myself, my two precious baby girls, I need to at least put some kind of makeup on to hide how I feel, what I'm dealing with. I need to heal. I want to heal; I'm learning how to heal; I'm trying to do what I can. That was a very monumental moment in my life. From that day forward, I never go without a full face of makeup. It was the first step of taking my power back. I knew an incredibly traumatic incident had occurred that was a defining moment in my life. I knew at the end of the incident, I would never, ever be who I once was. Something happened to me. I felt myself die as I was on my hands and knees in my closet. I was different. I would never be the same, and I'm not. I never will be. It is. I made sure that my little girls didn't need to see my pain.

They didn't need to look at their mommy's face and see abuse all over it. Then I dyed my hair for the first time in five months. When I did that, and I looked back in the mirror, who looked back at, looked familiar, I recognized her, and it was me. That's how I slowly performed Self-care, because it is incredibly detrimental, not only to keep our bodies healthy, but what it does for our mental health is astronomical.

It allows us to have the ability for our healing journey to begin. Finally, we begin to can heal, that's critical to us being able to move forward.

I didn't want another woman to have to ever experience what I did. I created the pink bags. Everything in them pertains to self-care and all kinds of stuff. They go crazy when they get their pink bag. Every time I've sent them, I love it. It's the most joyful experience you'll ever have in your entire life. The gratitude that pours out of them, that thankfulness, the joy, that smile on their face, makes it all worth it. It's like my life's important. I'm on my healing journey. It will be three years, December 23rd. Yes, more healing has taken place I am in a much better place than I've ever been, but it's not over yet. I still have quite a road to walk, to get to a place where I can say I'm no longer just a survivor. I'm now finally a warrior. I'm a warrior. I will get there, I will.

Kimberly: Wow. you are a warrior. We're always on a journey of healing. It's never something that is one day we wake up and we're completely healed, and completely better. Those kinds of things go with us throughout life. We now know, and are aware of, what we're feeling, what we're going through, we're able to move through it faster as the healing journey process.

Natalie: Yes. That's what I mean. When I say the pink bags, are like my life support to me. They have allowed me to heal faster than what is the normal pace. My therapist in my medical team are amazed at my progress, where I'm at considering I deal daily with a severe form of Complex PTSD, as well as extremely severe anxiety. They can't believe that I'm running a nonprofit, that I'm creating what I'm doing. That I will host my first ever Conference of HOPE on April 24th. They don't know what to say. They're proud of me. I'm proud of myself for facing fear for the first time in my life. I am slaying it, facing it right up front, walking through it, and I am not letting it hold me back. It has robbed me of much goodness in my life. It will not rob me of anything ever again. Enough is enough. It's time to fight the fight for it once and for all. That's what I'm doing.

Kimberly: That's why you're a warrior and a goddess.

Natalie: No, sometimes I feel like I'm always on a battleground. It's exhausting to fight through this. It's a lot of work.

Kimberly: But we're paving the way to help others in their journey.

Natalie: Absolutely. I don't have hundreds and thousands of dollars, that I can leave my four beautiful daughters when my time comes. I'm not sure I ever will. I don't even know if I'll ever be able to get life insurance because of my brain injury, but there is one thing I can leave, that's my legacy. I can leave them my legacy.

Kimberly: Absolutely.

Natalie: That's what I'm trying to do. Well, I'm trying to help other women heal faster, even if it's one day of healing, to help them. If there's self-confidence, they can look in the mirror, after they use the bath products, they smell themselves; it provokes positive emotions in them, then that heals us, those positive emotions, they replaced the negative self-talk and the more positive emotions that are provoked in our lives, the less negativity we hear, the less negative self-talk we do. Good always outweighs bad, good always wins. Always.

Kimberly: Absolutely. Oh, I love it. I want you to really know, though; you are a warrior. You are brave. To say those words that you were not letting fear hold you back. That's powerful.

Natalie: Fear is not from God. He does not instill fear in us; it comes from a really horrifically awful place. Has nothing positive to offer us. It still kills, it destroys our lives, robs us of good things that we deserve to have, it's exceedingly difficult to work through it. It's very difficult to not give into it, when it's pulsating through every vein in your body, you're terrified, you don't know what to do to make it go away. You can't shake the feeling. You're scared, you're all alone, you don't know what to do? No one there to help you. My faith has pulled me through, my faith, the blessings that were given upon me when I was wounded at the end of my abusive marriage, it was, is indescribable what God did in my life. The miracles that he performed, the healing he did, immediately took place so that I could fulfill whatever purpose. I do not know what that is, to just to clear that up, what has in mind for me. I don't know. The only thing I know is I feel deep down inside of me is I'm meant to help somehow, some way. That's all, that's the only thing I can put my finger on. I've been like that my whole life; I've always been one to offer help. I always gave myself freely, receiving nothing in return. I was always okay with that because it came from my heart. I didn't have any expectations.

Kimberly: It was unconditional. What I love about these stories is that even in those moments, like you were describing where we feel alone, we are completely broken. We really aren't alone.

Natalie: No, I wasn't. That became known to me because he came sat beside me. I felt his love flow through my body. I realized my father was there. I felt him. That is when I could say to myself to realize I was important to God. I was valuable to God; I was loved immensely by him. I am his greatest creation. All humanity is his greatest creation. As soon as I realized those three powerful words, my negative self-talk was absolutely horrific. What I did to myself disappeared because I walked around and I told myself nonstop. I'm important. I'm valuable and I am loved. Even if it's only by the Lord, I'm okay with that because that's all I need. I had lost all of my friends that I'd had my entire lifetime. They all turned their back and walked away from me. It was the grief that I endured. The loss from the depths of my soul was insurmountable. I can't even describe the pain, the loss that I felt in every facet of my life, every facet of my life. There was nothing but destruction.

Everything had been destroyed. The abuse had affected me in every way, multiple times, in multiple ways. I prayed for different things. For restoration to occur, for God to please bless me with new friends that were believers, that would be good people. That I could have the wisdom to recognize that you sent them to me for me, not to be blinded again by the enemy, for me to see that it was you that brought them and placing them in my life. He has answered that prayer. I have a tribe that is unbelievably remarkable. I'm blessed. I'm so blessed.

Kimberly: So good. I want to touch on something that you spoke about earlier, that was when you went back inside yourself in the mirror, after you started taking care of yourself again, what was that moment for you when you, went from not recognizing that person in the mirror. I thought what you were saying was so powerful to recognizing your reflection again.

Natalie: Right. When I first put a bit of makeup on, all I did was put foundation on and I think mascara, that was about all I could muster, but I wanted to hide the bags under my eyes that were so bad. My little girls didn't have to see those if I could help it. The very first time I did that, I still didn't completely fully recognize me, but I looked familiar. I knew that person, that person I was aware of. I knew her, as each day went by, me continuing to and consistently apply my makeup for the sake of my children, and with my hair, a ball on top of my head and hit a button. I hadn't got that far yet. My hair wasn't in part of the problem or a part of the story yet. But each day that passed by, I became more and more familiar with the reflection in the mirror. I want to say, it probably took about a month before I could look in the mirror and say, that's me. There's Natalie.

Kimberly: You are sharing many wonderful steps that you took without even me asking you to share them. I love how you helped yourself move through all the hurt, the pain, and the fear. One step at a time, one day at a time putting on the makeup, self-care, knowing you're not alone. I don't know if you knew it. I know I didn't, going through what I went through, but there're many resources out there for women to tap into. That's one thing why I even created this platform was to help get the message out that there are so many resources. You're not alone, shape, or form. Many women that have gone through things, there're resources out there, and now, for people who even receive your pink bag, I think that is so incredible.

Natalie: it created The pink bags from a very humble, selfless heart.

Kimberly: Absolutely,

Natalie: Expecting absolutely nothing in return. If I could make a difference in one woman's life, I have succeeded.

Kimberly: Absolutely! If you could go back and tell your younger self one thing, what would it be?

Natalie: I guess it would depend on what age I would refer to; you know what I mean. What I'd tell myself when I was six is a lot different from what I'd say when I was 13. You know what I mean? Well, I don't think I can answer the six-year-old one. And the only thing the 13-year-old, in eighth grade, getting ready to go in, into high school as a freshman, I was incredibly insecure. I had felt ugly my entire life. I had never looked in the mirror and saw anything pretty about myself ever at all. I had been a tomboy; my mother wouldn't let my hair grow out. My hair was short, it was ugly. She never showed me how to style my hair or how to make it pretty.

I was never taught how to apply makeup or when I could have makeup, my mother did not teach me any kind of self-care, or any way help me feel pretty, ever. She just didn't. She was a tortured soul, lost in her addiction. They left me to my own devices. That 13-year-old girl was very wounded and tried to do everything she could to have friends, to be happy, to be included. I would tell her, you know what, friends aren't the answer, because at 13, no 13-year-old has the ability or the wisdom or knowledge to know how to really be a good friend, how to nurture that relationship so that it blossoms, shines, and grows. I never had the ability, never experienced having wonderful friendships or relationships. I had never been taught how to do that. I now teach my daughters the importance of it, because of my experience. But when I think of myself and how I lived at 13, in my private school uniform, that was hideous. I would let her know she is good enough, worthy of every beautiful thing that the Lord has placed on this earth, and that she is going to have the most beautiful life. Don't lose your faith. Don't stop believing. Hold on tight, I would let her know. When it's all said and done, it's going to be okay. I promise it will be, so that she can hear some comforting words for once in her life. I'm sorry.

Kimberly: You are sharing such a heartfelt piece of you, being vulnerable. That's what makes these stories are so powerful. Don't apologize. I could feel that in my soul. Thank you for sharing all that you shared, and being an incredible warrior goddess that you are.

Natalie: I can accept the goddess before I can accept warrior, it's crazy how we've used things, but I'm a champion. I don't go down with the first blow. I'll hold on with everything that I have inside of me until he takes my life away. I will never quit. I will never stop fighting the good fight. I will never stop fighting the good fight, because I know what's at the end of this. I want to spread the word and the awareness that these women that are in hiding, that have not been helped yet, they're not able to use their voices yet. I will speak up for them we are here. They're not as alone as they think.

Kimberly: Thank you so much for sharing your story.

Natalie: You are welcome. I know it's not a really cheerful story.

Kimberly: It's powerful and it will help someone. That's why we do this.

Natalie's: Then we've succeeded. That's all that matters. That's all God asks us to do is to help one another. I appreciate so much that you chose me to be a part of this amazing, beautiful experience in my life. What it's doing for me, words cannot explain. Thank you so much.

CHAPTER 13

Learning to Love Me More

Nephetina Serrano

Dr. Nephetina L. Serrano Relationship Expert, Certified Marriage Counselor, National Empowerment Speaker, TV Host 3x Best Selling Author, Publisher, Certified Life-Coach and Mentor Co-founder of Covenant Marriages, Covenant Rescue 911 501c3, and Covenant Marriages Institute. She supports couples in transitional phases within their marriage to achieve balance and stability in life and in business through Biblical principles to build a more effective communication in marriage and in relationships. Dr. Nephetina Serrano along with her husband Co-host their show, "Your Marriage Matters"; on Dominion TV in over 35 countries around the globe. Dr. Serrano co-authored the book, The Marriage Corporation, which Highlights the organizational needs of a covenant marriage. She is the Publisher of Marriage CEO Magazine, "For The Entrepreneur Who Leads, Building Legacy" a publication tailored to meet the relationship needs of couples and individuals. It also provides a learning platform for singles preparing to embark on their marital journey.

Contact info:

www.marriageCEOs360.com

DrSerranoministries@gmail.com

She had to believe in herself and love herself enough to know she could do anything. ~KA

Kimberly: I am here with Nephetina Serrano. You are a relationship expert. I love this. Thank you for being here with me.

Nephetina: Thank you for having me. I'm super excited. I'm glad to be a part of this amazing project. Kimberly you're awesome. What you're doing to bring about awareness and support as we support one another. This is great. I love it.

Kimberly: Thank you. Thank you. Let's first talk about what it is you do. You're a relationship expert.

Nephetina: Yes. My husband and I work both in ministry and in life together. We actually also work for the government as well, but we basically support you to achieve both balance and stability in life and in marriage, through biblical principles, to give you a more effective communication in both life and in relationships.

Kimberly: I love it, so important. They don't teach that stuff in school. We need this conversation.

Nephetina: Absolutely. We love working with couples, marriages, and families. And as counselors and relationship experts, it really brings us joy to know that we can help another family grow together and work things out.

Kimberly: Absolutely. Let's talk about your story. What would you say is one of your biggest obstacles that you've gone through?

Nephetina: I mean, one of my biggest obstacles was believing who I am, understanding who I am, realizing that what God made in me was beautiful, that I didn't have to live up to everyone else's expectations learning to create my own expectations for myself. I'm being myself, never apologizing for that, be who I am, and I can appreciate being that way now today. But you know, one hurdle was learning to love me, because until you really love yourself, it's impossible to love anyone else. I think learning to appreciate who I was in all my differences and uniqueness, because growing up, I was incredibly unique. I was very different. I got teased a lot and things of that nature. Learning to be completely settled and free. The skin that I'm in was really one of the biggest obstacles for me.

Kimberly: It's a mindset shift too. It's a perspective shift in being okay with you and loving yourself. What made you so unique as a child?

Nephetina: Actually, it was, of all things, Nephetina, starting with my name, right? The kids teased me over it. I got a little teased and bullied growing up. In the beginning, I hated my name. I cried when my name was spoken or mispronounced when they had to call my name. I cringed. Not understanding how amazing that it is, my name means love and everything that surrounds love. And it's like, wow. You know, until I really came into an understanding of what Nephetina meant, deriving from Queen Nefertiti, the goddess of love, understanding what that really represented just in my name, that I was fearfully and wonderfully made too, to be this queen and goddess that I am and understand that God, what he made was beautiful.

It's okay to accept that about yourself, to not make apologies or excuses for who I am. Being teased, not having my name called right. I was told I spoke too proper, as an African American young lady growing up, I got teased about that. It's how I speak. And even today, people still question me, it's like, that's really how you talk. Yeah, that's how I talk. Like what's wrong. I mean, really adults, not even children, now we're talking about grown folks. I dressed uniquely. I was a dance major, and artists, no matter what part of artistry we're in, whether it's writing to drawing or speaking or dancing they call us unique people. But I received that now. Yes, I am unique. I received the fact that I was not made to fit in. It made me to stand out, and it's okay with me.

Kimberly: I love that. What do you think that really shifted that thought process for you regarding your name and embracing who you are?

Nephetina: My family, my mom, my family always encouraged me to be myself and be who I am. I had a sense of confidence about that. Although I was teased, maybe bullied a bit, I didn't lose my confidence. I was always confident in who I was. And I felt like I loved me, but I realized, you love yourself, but you're still living in the shadow of the expectations of others. You don't have to do that. Love who you are, be who you are, grow through that process. It was a realization of one day to be perfectly honest. I remember this young lady, a little girl, I was a little girl; I remember this little girl that used to live up the street from us, and she was a friend that I had. She would like to pick on me, then she would want to fight me. My grandmother, I remember one-day running home, my grandma was like, you're going to stand and you're going to defend yourself or I'm going to get to your butt. Well, I was like, oh, well; I guess I'm going to have to work this thing out. You know, I stood up to this little girl. After that day I never ever took crap from anybody anymore. That day I Rose up for myself and I stood up for myself, I said, I'm not running from anyone ever again. I will not allow people to bully me or to talk to me in any kind of way. If that means I travel alone or I have to take this journey on my own. So be it. I kind of settled that in my mind as a little girl, but I would not run away from people anymore. I was going to stand up for myself and be who I was.

Kimberly: I love that. It's interesting hearing that you decided that as a child, that's a very adult mature thought process to go through.

Nephetina: Well, I had a little help though from my grandma. Listen, that fear from grandma, you will not play with that. I will stand up. I will not run home again. No. I remember that my confidence level changed because I stood up to this little girl and she was. Oh, she's not running. No, I'm not, I'm not running. I'm going to be who I am. If you don't like me, then you won't be my friend. I don't really remember playing with her anymore after that. I think, for me that was kind of like I was that girl that sometimes had to. I was kind of loner. I found myself not in large groups in crowds, but often doing things on my own, alone.

I don't really know why that was. I know people teased me about how I dressed. I was kind of punky Brewster. I had the leggings and the different colors; I was something else I'm telling you. So yeah. I was unique. People would often tease me and to be honest, they would call me, I'm a white girl. They said that I always acted and things of that nature. And I wrote that. I wrote part of that story before, because I don't believe people, I mentor young women. I think we need to make sure that girls understand loving themselves for who they are, to appreciate who they are and what they offer, not worry about what other people say they are.

Kimberly: Yeah, absolutely. When you started hitting the older grades of high school and so forth, did you still have moments where you had to deal with that or were you just like, this is it I'm done, moving on?

Nephetina: No, in high school. I had friends; I had a diverse group of friends. I was very blessed to go to a very diversified middle school and high school. I went to a school that was a college preparatory school, but it was also a performing arts school where I was a dance major. I found people in my space and place that accepted me for who I was. That was awesome. I found myself exposed to many nationalities and races of people, because we had people from the Naval yard that were students at our school. We had students from anywhere from Cambodia to Italy; we had students from all over and that was a joy, a pleasure. I think for me; it was one of the most beautiful parts of my upbringing was being able to meet people from different parts of the world. I think that helped to cultivate a part of my life today because even now I found my ministry is global. My work is global, I find I get along with many variations of cultures and ethnicities. I think it's a wonderful thing to be that way.

Kimberly: Yes, definitely. I totally agree with you. I grew up in Hawaii. It's a hodgepodge of everybody. I love that. How does that help you in your business? I'm curious, what you've gone through, all your experiences. How do you think that helps you as a relationship expert?

Nephetina: As a relationship expert? It helps me because I have people from all over. I'm a Christian, I'm very much faithful to that, we've counseled Muslims. Jehovah witnesses. We've counseled all different ethnic groups and religions; they understand from which principle I'm coming from. It's okay. Why, because we're able to have that commonality of understanding God, knowing that we didn't create ourselves, realizing and recognizing that there is certainly that God, who is greater, more powerful than us, who had a purpose for creating us in this world. Having that diverse background has really brought light into my world, because I have found that I've been accepted into so many cultures, as well as I embrace them. I embrace them as well; it brings beauty and in the relationship expert area, because I also had teaching in schooling in this multicultural as well. It all kind of boils down to allowing, seeing through the eyes of others sometimes, right? Everything cannot be from your own cultural experience and you; I allow myself to go there with my clients so that I can have some insight into what it's like behind their view. When you do that, it helps you to bridge that gap of differences find those areas of commonality. You realize we're more different than we are not. Those differences are beautiful, beautiful points. You know, the polka dot dress with all the different sides, sizes, circles, but every circle is unique in its own shape though different yet the same. I love it. I love what I'm able to do to impact lives, families, husbands, and wives and children. It has been a joy in my life since I was little. I was always counseling people. I was a child that had the old spirit that adults always will allow me to be in the room when all the other kids had to go to bed.

I believe that was part of my rearing up in this area of counseling and coaching. It's definitely helped me to be better at what I do, but life wasn't always easy, I was cared for. I had a nice upbringing, a wonderful family that loved me. But then I had issues within the home like other children have, then some of my issues weren't the same. Right. I think going through living in a home where my parents worked hard, but there was abuse in my home, physical abuse and that brought a whole different dynamic to things. That wasn't easy. That was very challenging.

Kimberly: How are you able to take those lessons, growing up, going through, like you said, you were bullied and so forth, standing up because grandma gave you that nice little push for yourself. Do you find that even with the abusive situation, when you were growing up, that you've learned how to really step into that confidence, but having moments where you're like, Ooh, that it brings stuff for you?

Nephetina: You're making me reflect right now. With that reflection, it reminds me I'm very; I believe I'm humble. I believe

I'm a pleasant person genuinely, right? I love people and I love to see people happy. I like to see people say I'm not a confrontational person, but I still find that even in this adult life, that there are bullies, adult bullies and they will try to push you to that limit. I find sometimes still a struggle in standing my ground, for myself. Because I find I will defend, be there to support someone else a lot quicker sometimes than I will for myself. I very much, I won't say that I struggle with it, but I will say that there are times even in this life as an adult that I find sometimes a challenge to stand my ground.

Kimberly: Isn't that an interesting concept to think about, how quick we will help somebody else, but we don't help ourselves or stand up for ourselves. It's so much easier to do that for somebody else.

Nephetina: You know; it really shouldn't be. That's part of that self-care journey I'm kind of on right now, loving me more, it's not that I'm not loving others, but I'm learning to love me more. That gives me more of a perspective to say, when enough is enough to know when to walk away, or when Kenny says, you got to know when to hold them, walk away and know when to run. I have mitigated through those times. Should I stand in this relationship, is it time to shut the door? Do I need to walk away, or do I need to run? I found myself in every one of those positions where it was like, this is definitely not the road you want to go down, no, it's not for you. I Quickly bounced back out of it, but then you find yourself in a position sometimes where it's not as easy to back out, to walk, to run out or to, to leave. You literally have to back out of it slowly.

Kimberly: Oh, so true. I like the philosophy though, know when to hold them, know when to run. That's a great, great philosophy. Now I'm going to sing that song in my head.

Nephetina: I was a Kenny fan growing up? I loved him.

Kimberly: He's amazing. But I love how you are saying that you can literally, when you step in that space of being in self-care, if you look at that in each relationship or in anything that you're doing, that's a very clear picture of how you can decide what's going to be the best thing for you. Makes it so simple.

Nephetina: Yes. It can be a simple process. You don't have to kill yourself or beat yourself up about it. Recognize, be willing to love you more and willing to love you more.

Kimberly: That's so important. We forget that. It's interesting too, when you're talking earlier, when we were saying, we're quicker to jump into helping somebody else than we are ourselves. I know coming from the side of domestic violence and having many conversations with that, one of the key things that helps us get out of those situations is we don't want our kids to go through that. It's all about the kids. I am a huge proponent of, if that's what gets you out of that situation, then dive head deep into it. But it's an interesting thing to look at, to know it takes thinking of the kids, instead of ourselves and say, I don't deserve to be in this situation.

Nephetina: That's right. That is so true. I was as a young person growing up in a home where domestic violence existed between my parents. We were never physically abused as children, which is really strange. Like we were never struck in or any of that, but to live with watching our parents go through that, watching my mom go through that, that was horrible. It had great, devastating consequences for my brother and I as the older siblings, because my younger siblings were so much younger than me, like one a decade, another one, almost an additional five, six years. They were much younger. They didn't really experience what we did.

My brother and I realize the support that's necessary for children that lived in domestic violent homes, how they come out of that situation, traumatized with such devastation and for the male and the female. It's two different traumas because for the male, it's the, I wish I could have done more. As the male, I should have stood up for my mom. As the female, your kind of in a position where the hurt goes deep for that parent, you internalize it all and you have to get up every day, go to school, leave home, knowing that there's a possibility that your parent is going to be harmed and to have to function every day. Children don't know what other kids are going through. Teenagers don't care what you're going through at home, you know? It becomes a very lonely alone road for that child because you don't want everybody to know what's going on in the home, but you're hurting for your parent. Going through that, it was rough. It was really rough dealing with that. I have to say, when I think about one of those moments, that was one of those moments in life that was really hard.

Kimberly: Definitely. It's something that we keep secret, can't let that secret out. And even if you're in it as the parent, it's still a secret. We hide it; we hide it; we're protecting somebody else.

Nephetina: Yeah. Unbelievable. Right. It takes a lot to rise out of that, but I'm glad that I could live, to see my mother rise out of that situation. And hearing the story, as you stated, she did it for her children. I had already left home at that point. I wound up running away from home and leaving home in my last year of high school, which presented an enormous challenge because I was an excellent student. I was an A student, to not finish high school, that year was very devastating for me because my goal was to finish high school and go away to college, not have to deal with this life and that didn't quite happen for me. I wound up going back the very next year and finishing, but it was very hurtful that I felt like I had to give up something in order to seek sanity.

Kimberly: Survival. I mean, you kick into survival mode, whatever that first thought is, that's what you head towards. If you could go back, tell your younger self one thing, what would it be?

Nephetina: I really believe just love you more, love you more than enough because God does. I believe that if I could tell my younger self; it doesn't matter what people think about you, what matters is what you think about you. I'm glad that I never gave up on myself. Sometimes I wanted to give up. I think there was one time I gave up a bit, but mostly throughout my years, I was determined I was going to make it. I was determined I was going to make it. If I can look back at her, I would say, girl, rise and love you more.

Kimberly: That's so good. Such an important thing to hear, you don't hear that either. I love that. Powerful. I felt that when you were saying it, I could feel that right into my soul.

Nephetina: Yeah. Yeah. Once I learned to love myself more, the desires, the hopes became a true reality of achievement. Like I could do it, I can do this. I can get through it. I can pass that test. I became my biggest competition. I'm in my biggest competition. Like defeat was not an option in my mind. Not in school, not on that test, not on that job interview. The one thing I was going to do was make it. The one that I was going to do is make something of my life, be somebody special, do something great. That's what I wanted. I wanted to be better in the world and to do better. I wanted to make it. I wanted to prove to me you can make it, no matter what you can make it. I learned I could make it no matter what I had to go through, no matter what I had to endure. I was going to make it. I believed in myself, no matter what. On every job interview I ever went in, I felt like it's mine. I got it. There weren't many jobs that I didn't get on a first interview. I started working at an early age too at 14, and actually at 13 I went to the Mayor Summer Youth program. They took me in because I was right on the brink of that birthday. They took me in. My first job was with the counseling, the university of Pennsylvania here in Philadelphia, one of the biggest, most prestigious schools here in Pennsylvania. I worked in the Wharton school of business.

My first job was as an assistant secretary in the counseling and psychology department. Hence, here I am.

Kimberly: You're showing up on your path, didn't even know it. I love it. What an incredible story. You are truly a goddess and I love your name. Nephetina, It's beautiful. Thank you for being here and sharing your story.

Nephetina: You're welcome. Thank you for having me to be a part of this amazing project and to be in your presence. Even hearing your voice is very calming. You have a presence that I don't even; I know that you probably get it time and time again, but you have an amazing presence. It really does. I can feel it when I hear your voice, now seeing you and having this face to face, it feels good. It feels right. I know I was purposed to be a part of this.

Kimberly: Absolutely. Amen. So great. Thank you.

CHAPTER 14

From Self Doubt to Super Dope

Nikki Bradley

Nikki Bradley is a brand strategist who specializes in helping women entrepreneurs build their personal brand alongside their business brand so that they can bring out their biggest, baddest, dopest version of themselves so that they can show up as more of themselves to serve with more impact and sell with more confidence. She also works with organizations to empower their business leaders to become powerful brand ambassadors, position themselves as thought leaders, and build their own personal brand.

Contact info:

NikkiBradley.net

info@nikkibradley.net

Even when she was winning, she still questioned herself. Now, she embraces her dopest self. ~KA

Kimberly: I am excited to talk with Nikki Bradley today. You are a brand strategist and business coach. Tell us about that. How do you help your clients?

Nikki: I help women entrepreneurs, service-based businesses primarily, build their personal brand alongside their business brand. Because many women focus so much on, here's my business, here's what I do. Here's my thing that I offer, but then when it comes to their face, being a part of their business, they're like, oh no, don't look at me. I'll stay back here behind the curtain. I'm all about helping you to be the biggest, baddest, dopest version of yourself, that you can serve more, sell more to the people that you're meant to serve in this world, do that in all assets of your business, all aspects of your business from, putting yourself out there more, being more confident about who you are, your power, your expertise, to showing up in the best, biggest version of yourself. That's what I do.

Kimberly: I love it. Before we go into our deep conversation, I want to go back to how Important is it for us to have our personal image become a part of our brand image, that seems to be a big deal.

Nikki: I think that many of us — this was the case for me too — especially because I came out of the corporate world. Everything was about the business. You kind of had to hide who you are. You had to wear a mask a lot of times. Like you had your corporate self. You had 'this is who I am at work, then this is my personal life.' I had to keep everything separate. When I became an entrepreneur — I hear this so much from the women that I work with — we keep it all... we like to keep it all separate. But now everything merges, you can't really do that anymore. People want to know who it is that they're working with. They want to have a connection with you and people don't buy your product, don't buy your thing. Don't buy your service, they are really buying you. They're buying, getting access to you. I know we hear this all the time — trust factor, it's real. They will not hand you their credit card unless they feel like they have a connection with you. They're like, Oh my gosh, 'she's my people. Like she gets me, I get her. I want to be around her.' We worry about, 'Am I smart enough? Do I have enough experience?' A lot of times that doesn't matter much to people as if they feel like they know you, they have a connection with you. If we hide ourselves, if we don't create a personal brand around ourselves, where people feel like they know, like, trust us, the rest of that stuff doesn't even matter so much.

Kimberly: It adds that human element too. I think that's what's been missing in the branding for so long. It's business, we don't see the faces behind it. That makes sense. I was one of them. I don't want to be out there, but here I am. We struggle with being out there, that has to go together. We want to know, like, trust people. We want to feel like we know them. That's good. Let's talk about your story. What is it you would say is one of your biggest obstacles that you've overcome or experiences that you've had to go through?

Nikki: Oh man.

Well, there are lots. I think one of the biggest ones for me, especially when I shifted from going full time in my business, was a couple of things. One trusting I was enough. The other was when I left my corporate job. The company that I was working for (how ended) it wasn't the best situation for the company. They had like a big lay off of people. I had a lot of shame in that. The business went out of business. But I had these great relationships with all of my customers that I had been serving for years. I had a lot of corporate relationships. For a long time, I was very hesitant to put myself out there in my business, because I was like, 'gosh, these people that I knew in the corporate world knew me as this, are they going to accept me in this new thing?'

Even though I had been building it on the side for years, I was nervous about putting myself out there more fully, because I had been doing it kind of on the side. Now that I was full time doing it, I wasn't going after any corporate business with the clients that I had been working with for years that I had these relationships with. I was afraid to approach them to do business, because I was like, what if they see me under this veil of how things ended with the company that I wasn't with anymore? Will they think that I'm enough on my own? Even though we talk about success amnesia, we forget about the things or the successes that we've had, the wins that we've had, that I had sold multimillion dollar contracts with these people, these big companies for years... for more than a decade. Those were things I did. I still, I didn't lose that experience. I didn't lose that because now I was doing this on my own. But it took me a while to embrace that, to bring it into this new stage of my evolution.

Kimberly: Isn't that fascinating how here you were successful in this corporate space, having massive success, creating relationships, and then you questioned yourself if you were enough still to handle it on a different level, it's amazing to me how we think that way. We go right to that. Am I good enough?

Am I worthy, am I deserving, can I do this, forgetting the success. I thought that was a significant point that you brought up too, because we forget that we've had those successes, we accomplished all that amazing stuff. Then we're sitting here going. I'm not worthy. Are they going to judge me? How do you help yourself get through those moments? Because I would imagine every once in a while, that's still brews up for you.

Nikki: Oh, absolutely. I stayed off of LinkedIn for a year and a half for that reason. Thinking I don't want them to see me in this new, this new thing. I was like, I'm going to learn Instagram. I'm going to focus on Facebook, cause they're not over there. Yes, they are.

Everybody's on those platforms. Yes, they are. But it'll be different over here. Cause it's not like business connections. Yes, it is. It's connected. The thing that got me over that was I actually had one of those clients reach out to me, to check on me and it's like, 'Hey, I haven't seen you. And oh I had this opportunity that I think you'd be great for.'

Sometimes we need somebody to see something in us we don't yet see in ourselves. When that happened for me, — I didn't realize it at the time — but that's something that I had always done for other people. I realized that it's one of my strengths. We talk about our gifts, whether some people say it's your spiritual gift or whatever it is, but that's one of mine that I always have been able to do for people. Somebody had to do that for me at that moment. I'm not the type of person... I think many of us women put on like our capes and we're like, you know, 'I'm independent. I can do it all.' But sometimes we need people around us to ask for help or sometimes to accept, receive the help even when we don't ask for it.

Kimberly: Oh yeah, we're super women, we think we should do it all. I think there's a huge lack. I love you brought this up. We definitely lack in that department of asking for help. We run ourselves ragged, to exhaustion, overwhelm, then we get resentful, then you're going down this whole other spiral and all it could have been this one simple, hey, can I have this help?

Nikki: Yeah. Actually, I had to create a one page about my business, my offering, a bio for that opportunity. In creating that, it forced me to take inventory and write out what made me so dope, because I love using that word. I'm such a nineties chick and a Hip hop head. All of those things. I mean, clearly, I'm wearing Beyoncé today.

It forced me to write out why I was dope. It had me think about why she, or anybody else, should hire me. I encourage anyone to do that. I literally just had a call with some of my clients today. I have a client who had her first $20,000 month. She was having trouble really receiving that, accepting, wrapping her mind around that. She'd done nothing like that before in her business. She was like, I'm trying to get the confidence to own it, really. I was like, 'okay, I want you to journal, make a list of why I am the dopest at fill in the blank, what you do in the world.' I had her do that, I had actually had everybody in the group do that as homework.

Cause that was what I had to do for myself. I recommend everybody do that, even revisit that list, update it from time to time. It has become something that I use; I go back to and pull from. It becomes fodder for my content. It becomes things I update my bio with, that I use for different things to build my personal brand. Because if we don't talk about how dope we are, who else is? Our clients end up doing it at some point, but especially when you're getting started, sometimes you have to be your biggest PR person.

Kimberly: I love that activity. I actually do a similar version of that with women's groups. I think it's an important piece that we can incorporate into our lives by recognizing what we've done, who we are, what makes us uniquely ourselves. Right? Do you still find that you have moments where you think, Am I enough? Can I take on this next client? Are they going to judge me? We're businesswomen, but oh my gosh, that stuff comes up all the time.

Nikki: I had one of those recently, when I hit my first six figures. I would not celebrate it on my own, but I'm always talking to my clients about celebrating their wins big and small. I talk about it in my communities too. I was reminded that I needed to celebrate my win more publicly, because I'm always talking about it. I realized a long time ago that my purpose is to show people what's possible in all aspects of my life, not my business, in my family, in my relationships, in everything. That's what I want to do with my life. I realized I wasn't being in integrity if I didn't show people, especially women and even women of color, what's possible. When I see the statistics that only 6% of business owners hit six figures and many people are trying to get there to see that somebody who looks like me can do it. You can, too. I needed to share that, but I had all the thoughts about what that could mean, what people would think about me sharing it, talking about it. What that could mean from even people who currently worked with me and people who might work with me, what they might think about it. As a business coach, would they think, 'how much of my money was in that? Did I help her get there? Or is that even enough? Is she making enough to be my business coach?' All the things, all of that. It still was. Am I enough? Yeah, that came up. I've had that thought come up at different points in my business, I've had to learn how to deal with those thoughts. When it comes up, I know how to deal with it. I get a little better at dealing with it each time. This time when it came up, I knew I had to not just talk about it one time. I needed to do it again so that it wasn't just me talking about it and being like, 'Ooh, okay, did that now I can leave it and run?'

I had to do it. I had to talk about it again so that I could shut my brain down for good about it. The good thing about it was sometimes I think we worry so much about what other people will think. We always go to the negative of what people will think. We surprise ourselves, because when I talked about it, I was so ready for backlash because that's what my fight-or-flight brain was thinking would happen. It was the exact opposite. It was, 'I don't even know how many comments are on that video and views and things now.' But it was people with an outpouring of support and leads. All kinds of positive things that came out of it, and people sending you messages, calling me saying that it inspired them either to do something in their business, or even inspire them to be more vulnerable about something else totally non-business related in their own life. You never know whatever you're afraid of doing, or that your brain is telling you that you're not good enough for. If you push through that, if you allow yourself to be vulnerable, if you allow yourself to show more, show up as the biggest, baddest, dopest version of yourself, whatever that looks like for you, you never know what's on the other side... how you might impact somebody else.

Kimberly: Yeah, for sure. Especially being vulnerable. It's hard to be vulnerable. We're used to shutting that door and hiding behind it, then not celebrating our big wins, let alone our little wins. We do them privately and behind closed doors. Instead of, that's scary. Why is that scary? Isn't that an interesting conversation? Why would that be scary to celebrate you?

Nikki: Yes, we celebrate. We celebrate everybody else. We celebrate everybody else but ourselves.

Kimberly: It's an interesting concept. It's an interesting conversation to analyze that. We overanalyze everything. Like you said, even to receive that, make those posts or videos. You went through all of those different thought processes over-analyzing everything about it because we're in fear of who might say something. It's amazing. Why do you think people don't want to celebrate their wins? Then I want to go back to the receiving part of it.

Nikki: I think some of it... Sometimes it's not even recognizing the wins, not even giving ourselves credit for the wins. I know in my case I didn't even realize I had hit six figures. I was deep in the doing, in the just keep going, keep going, I didn't even take a second to stop, look; I had hit it and blown past it and was onto the next. Then someone brought it to my intention that I should look at it, check. I looked, and I was like, oh man, wait, when did that happen? When did I do that?

Kimberly: So, slowing down then.

Nikki: Yeah. Similarly, and interestingly enough, the same client that I was talking about that just hit $20K in a month, we're doing a case study about her tomorrow. Because I was like, we need to talk about this. Cause it's a thing. She did 15$K of that this month; she wasn't counting it. How do you do $15K in a month, and you're not counting it? Because she had been focused on selling one program, that she had been selling $15K of something else that she wasn't counting. That revenue counts. Everything counts.

Kimberly: Yes, it does, I wanted to ask you; you mentioned your client. It was hard for her to receive that. That seems to be an issue with women in general. We have a hard time receiving everything. Getting help, that's a big one. We don't ask for help. So, it's this whole thing about us receiving. We were built to receive. Hello. That's one of our biggest, biggest obstacles as women is to receive all the goodness.

Nikki: Yes. Not only to receive, but when we receive, to cultivate and grow something to even be more than what came to us.

Kimberly: It's fascinating to me, if you could go back and tell your younger self one thing, what would it be?

Nikki: Oh gosh, you are enough. You're enough always and forever, always.

Kimberly: Did you ever feel you weren't enough in your childhood? I'm always trying to dive into the deepest moments. Like where does that stem from?

Nikki: I have thought about that. I can't really pinpoint to one thing because I grew up in a family of high achievers. Everybody in my family has a college degree or multiple degrees. It was not... getting anything less than A's and Bs was unacceptable. Totally unacceptable. Like excuse me, what is it? We don't know what these other letters of the alphabet are. It does not compute. I have one of the most supportive families I could ask for. Like, my parents got divorced when I was six years old, and I grew up with my mom. But my father's side of the family, we are probably even closer to. My cousins on that side of the family, we grew up more than siblings. My aunts and uncles... My aunt, my father's brothers stepped in and because my dad has had some issues and things. His brother stepped in and we're like, okay, we're here. What do you need? I've tried to figure that out. I don't know that I can pinpoint when I've ever felt like you're not enough. I think it was something that I put on myself over time, because maybe growing up in that environment of everybody does this level. I think inherently I want to be the best. I love personality assessments, so I'm always in that achievement type. That's me. I think that it's something I've put on myself.

Kimberly: I think we do that a lot, but when you said that it made me think of if the standard is up here. You're seeing that the standard is always here. Like you said, there are no other letters of the alphabet. There might be this sense of, am I enough? Or am I good enough to maintain that. Do you know what I mean? I guess subconsciously am I going to hit it or maintain it?

Nikki: I could see that. Definitely. I always will move the bar even for myself. Like, that's good, but can we go a bit more? We do better than that!

Kimberly: Yeah. Overachievers, here we come.

Nikki: I'm working on it. I really am working on settling in. I don't have to make it hard. It doesn't have to be hard. I've gotten a lot better at that than I used to be. I will definitely say that. I chill a lot more than I used to.

Kimberly: Well, you're definitely enough. You're more than enough. You're amazing. I really appreciate your insight, your wisdom, thank you so much for being a part of this.

Nikki: Thank you for having me. This is fun. I'm glad you're doing this. This is definitely something that is needed for women. For us to see in other women what we need to see in ourselves reflected back.

Kimberly: Amen to that. Absolutely.

CHAPTER 15

It's Only Temporary

Nora D. Richardson

Brand Positioning Strategist, Nora D. Richardson of Spot-On Branding, saw that Entrepreneurs were pouring their profits into a million marketing efforts before they had a brand plan in place to secure success. Bringing her 20+ years of knowledge to a wide range of businesses, she connects those dots with a 6-step.

Process which zeros in on The Relatability Factor that will speak to an audience's heart and unlock their wallets. Nora enjoys working with entrepreneurs that have plateaued in their sales and want to break through to reach their revenue goals. Leading her clients to prosperous results, Nora has worked with a vast array of clients, brands, and categories. She believes you are never too small to look big. Most notably, Nora D. Richardson has worked with Kahlúa, the Olympics, and Northwest Airlines but favors working with entrepreneurs. Recognized by The New York Times as an industry leader, Nora is an adventurous spirit who enjoys traveling the world with her husband.

Contact info:

Spot-On Branding LLC,

843.814.0114

nora@spot-onbranding.com

www.spot-onbranding.com

Her superpowers are trusting herself, and her
unwavering belief that her situation was
only temporary. ~KA

Kimberly: I am excited. I have with me today, Nora D. Richardson. You are a brand strategist, start by talking about what it is you do.

Nora: I have the best job in the entire world. I get to hear people's stories and help them dream… what they want to do, how they want to show up in order to change the world for the better. It's about taking who they really are at their essence plus something they love, doing at their core and positioning them and their origin stories in front of an audience that will relate and buy from them. It is extremely rewarding, and I love it.

Kimberly: I love it, too. That was such an awesome example of what you do. Let's talk about your story. What would you say is one of your biggest obstacles that you've had to go through or overcome?

Nora: Today, I am a successful business owner that has been in business for 21 years. I am in a loving marriage of 24 years. I own a home with two acres of land and traveled all over the globe. I even put myself through college, being the first person in my family to earn a four-year degree. These things could be seen as remarkable achievements knowing about my childhood.

Prior to adolescence, I was mentally and physically abused by my mother. Luckily, I lived a good portion of my early childhood with my grandmother. When grandma died, I was 13 and my mom decided she would rather live her life without a dependent. Essentially homeless, it forced me to navigate the world by myself. I understood there was only one scenario that would get me out of this ordeal, so I wouldn't become a statistic. It took hard work, determination, resiliency, and grit to swap the narrative of where I was to where I wanted to be, but I knew—even at 13 years old— that I needed to finish high school and go to college in order to become the person I am today who has achieved many wins.

Kimberly: Wow. That's one reason I love these conversations, is because we walk into a room and we compare, "Oh, she's successful. And she's pretty. She's this and that," but we don't know her journey that got her to that point. I love these because it takes that comparison with. We get to meet that little girl, that woman, and hear what brought her to that success. It creates compassion. We have empathy and we can cheer you on. So, 13. That is such a young age. You're officially a teenager. Your grandma passed, and that's when your mom decided she was going to go live with her life?

Nora: Yes. From 13 to 18, five years, I had 20 different homes— not foster care homes. The first two places my mom found and dumped me off. The other homes I found. I always knew that my childhood life was a temporary situation and that when I could decide for myself, I would actually make better decisions. My first decision was to treat my education as something that was going to get me out of my current circumstance, that I would have a better second stage of life. Although it was hard to juggle, I knew I needed to focus on my education, no matter the personal life distractions.

That unwavering thought process helped me through those hard times. The Foster Care System was an option, but I knew it was not the right solution for me. I believed it would not get me where I needed to go. I felt it could actually derail me from my objectives. I lead a dual life, making sure that they did not find it out—I was essentially homeless and had to find my own roofs, food, and clothes. Ages 13 and 14 was precarious because I wasn't old enough to apply for a job. As soon as I turned 15, I got a job and started thinking of myself as an adult—more in control and self-reliant—able to see my progress and achievements.

Kimberly: Wow. It's amazing to me to hear you talk about this, because one at that age to have such self-awareness and determination is huge, and I'm thinking, you kicked into survivor mode at a really young age. I'm curious. Do you find that has become like a knee-jerk reaction, as you kept going through life to get to where you are today? Or is that something that you're like, okay, I know that feeling I'm never going there again. I'm going to keep pursuing and pursuing and doing better, getting better.

Nora: I really have never thought about it that way. I knew my first goal was to graduate high school, and from there get into college, then graduate. These were the milestones. There were no other options. For someone in my circumstance, those were lofty goals. Anything else would have been distractions. My known strengths were artistic; I could draw, and I was creative. That narrowed my options, so I focused on going to college for art. Before my grandmother died, she said, "when you graduate high school, you need to go into the Air Force." And I toyed with the idea... for 2.3 seconds. Just like the foster care system, I knew I was too independently minded to be a good fit for the military. I was extremely creative and a strong, self-reliant individual. I was a thinker, a planner, and a goal-setter. I was resilient, driven, and determined to achieve those goals. Military training is all about following the rules without question. Following somebody else's rules was not in my world... I figured I was not exactly what the military was looking for.

In knowing that the military was not the right place for me to thrive, I already knew who I was and who I wasn't. I imagine when you 're forced to make adult decisions early, you learn who you are a lot sooner.

Kimberly: Yes. I'm curious your primary focus at that point was to get through school. You knew it was the first step, get to high school, graduate high school, then get to college and all these things. Was there something, or maybe from your grandma, that instilled that in you, or how did you come to think that school was your way out?

Nora: You're right. Although I was the first one to graduate from college with a four-year degree, education was absolutely the cornerstone of childhood. My mother and my grandmother were highly intelligent, well read, and well-traveled. Speaking proper English, using proper grammar, sounding educated was drilled into me at a young age. I knew the only thing that I could do at as a kid was an excellent student, and trust that, and graduating would miraculously change my life. I had no clue how that was going to unfold, but I knew an education was my golden ticket. That's the only thing I had to hold on to, and that's what I did. It armed me with hope.

Kimberly: That's amazing. I love that. Were you an only child?

Nora: Yes. Luckily, I was an only child. I say that, because I don't know if I would have been able to do what I could do if I had someone tagging along. I had to make quick decisions, and I only had to think about myself. If I had to think about others, I don't know if I would have made the same risks.

Kimberly: Yeah, because then you're thinking about more than only you, it's not as easy to make the mistakes. If you have loved ones, you are tagging along with such as siblings; you don't take those risks.

Nora: Exactly. Either you're tied down by them or they're tied down by you—depending on who is the strongest or eldest.

Kimberly: Definitely. Do you have a relationship with your mom now?

Nora: Yes, I did until she passed. We stayed in touch the whole time. Even when I was not living under strangers' roofs, we communicate briefly. She didn't want to be a mother. My grandmother forced her into it. My mom wanted her mother's love. When grandma said, I am dying of cancer; I need a granddaughter. Mom saw this as THE chance to gain the love she had always craved. She jumped at the chance of getting this love from her mother by having a granddaughter. I was born because my grandmother wanted to be a grandmother, rather than because my mom wanted to be a mother. There is a difference. Once grandma died, mom's role was, in her eyes, kind of done. She had done what she was supposed to do, now it's time for her to live her young adulthood that she missed out on. She thought I was old enough.

Kimberly: Well, back in the day, 13 was old enough.

Nora: True, but not in the eighties, though.

Kimberly: What an incredible story. Again, the self-awareness that you had at 13 years old to know that you needed to do these certain things. Was there anyone thought that really kept pushing you? I would imagine, as women we have meltdowns going, oh my God, what am I doing? Am I good enough, worthy enough? Am I going to make it? These questions to have that on your shoulders at 13?

Nora: I knew that this whole situation was temporary. I kept telling myself that. I knew that my circumstance would not define my life or my achievements. These were the things that were going to strengthen me in life. I'm incredibly grateful for all the things that I've gone through because I'm the person who I am today. I really like myself. I've liked myself all along. All these things that I have done and gone through throughout my life, makes me a stronger person, especially when you compare other people to yourself. It can be humbling. I wonder if they would have had my background, would they be going through this issue in the same way? A piece of me wishes they had some of this knowledge I was graciously given. Even though I went through some grueling times, I got through it and am a grounded person on the other side of it. Anything that comes my way, I can handle it because I've handled similar stuff or worse. It's, easier for me to trust myself. I know I'll make the right decisions—no matter what.

Kimberly: Ooh, I like what you said there, to trust yourself. I think we have those conversations all the time as women too. We don't trust ourselves, but you were gifted in experience that allowed you to see a bigger picture, from a different perspective. That's what I try to help others understand is that our stories, our traumas, our experiences aren't. It happened to me, all this awfulness, it opens your eyes. It allows you to have this completely different perspective of everything. You can see life through a whole different lens, really have that compassion, empathy and help others on a different level. Even as a brand strategist, you can hear these stories and go, okay. You can make it benefit them, in the sense of their business. Then I would imagine that's completely helped you in your business too.

Nora: Yes. That, as well as me being an Empath, has really helped me strengthen my knowledge of the world. Since I've graduated, I've traveled to five continents experiencing and understanding people from all walks of life: different cultures, classes, and ages. This gives me a good foundation to meet people where they are then pull out what we need to extract, that they can actually do what they really want to do.

Kimberly: Absolutely. Oh, I love that. That's good. Everybody needs you. Ok at 13 years old, I'm going to keep going back to this, because this is such a profound age to shoulder all that you went through. What was the number one struggle I'm curious that you kept running into, was it finding food? Was it finding shelter? Was it your own belief or mindset?

Nora: It was finding quality people to help me on my journey... whatever I needed at the moment. Sometimes it was a roof or a couch or it was food. Sometimes it was a shoulder for me to cry on. I found good people, and I found, okay people, I found not so good people. But I was pretty wise. I could assess people pretty quickly. One of the cooler skills sets I developed was directly from my mother's poor choices in men. She had several boyfriends who would treat her poorly. I got introduced to what men look like on first dates, versus who they are six months later. It was a fantastic lesson in psychology, and how to assess people. Being able to assess people is useful in my branding work. Branding is very personal, revealing and one can feel vulnerable. Most people want to hide themselves and not want to be totally exposed. Assessing people can come in handy as to tell if they are telling me the whole truth or not? They may not realize they are eliminating the truth until I do a deep dive. At 13 I was assessing people. I was saying, okay, this is a truthful person. I can stay here. This is a person I can rely on that's how my world worked.

Kimberly: Incredible, too bad we can't bottle that kind of knowledge up and hand it out, right? Like, okay, you're 13, here you go. You wouldn't have any heartache.

Nora: We all have to go through something. We don't know what's well until we have experienced what's bad. We all have to go through something that shapes us into whom we're supposed to be the growth you must gain in order to appreciate it. I feel I was lucky that I got my really enormous struggles out before 18. There are many l people that had a wonderful childhood then get slapped in their twenties, thirties, forties, fifties, and they don't have the equipment, the knowledge, the grit to properly get them through. (Or at least they don't think they do. They do. They always do.) But it can be much harder for an older person to navigate tragedy or suffering or struggles. I think being a child, when your normal changes, you are more accepting of your new normal. The goal hasn't changed. How do I pivot? How do I adjust myself to get to the goal I need, and who do I lean on to help me get there?

Kimberly: I love what you said about how, as, we're kids, we're able to go, okay, this is it. This is my normal, this is my new normal, we're really in the flow of whatever's coming at us. We're dodging, jumping on that horse, and riding through it as we get older. Cause I was one of those, I'm one of those people that it hit me at 18. It slapped me in the face at 18, and thought, wait a minute. I had a great childhood. What the heck am I dealing with now? You don't have any concept of what the heck's going on.

What do you tell people when you're trying to get out their stories, how to help them through that as they're getting older and really understanding that do you ever share any insight? I would love to hear what you have to say, telling somebody who might go through something.

Nora: Wow. well, I dislike giving advice without knowing somebody's details. Normally I would know the struggles a client is going through now, before I would ever give them any advice. But I believe that between the age of eight and 15, everybody sees the world differently. From one til eight years old, you're following what your parents have told you. Their beliefs become your beliefs and even your core beliefs. Sometime between eight and 15, your beliefs kind of change, in the sense that you can think and see things for yourself, not trust an adult and trust your parents. I would tap into that energy, whatever that strength was, whatever that minor or major issue you saw that was wrong with the world from that time period... tap into that now as an adult.

What does that look like for you? What did you think about at that period in time? What was the problem that you saw? How did you see how you could change it—make the world better? Tap into that feeling of empowerment before maybe you've told somebody your dreams. It's this passion for something specific that I find is our north star. That's where we get and find comfort when we die. We dive into that little, whatever that was, we get strength from that young person who we were becoming. That nugget of information of yesteryear can actually help us find where we need to go today.

Kimberly: Mmm that's so good. What would you tell your younger self? If you could go back in time.

Nora: Trust yourself, keep trusting yourself, keep doing it. You're on the right path, you are on the path of success and all that you are dreaming of and more.

Kimberly: You learned at an incredibly young age to trust yourself, trust your instincts, trust your intuition. Do you find you do that supernaturally now as an adult? Or do you have moments where you're like, oh, I don't know.

Nora: Yes, I totally 100% trust my instincts at all costs. I can say that if I hesitate, I always come back to my initial heart and gut reaction. Every once in a while, my brain will interfere and ask, "are you sure?" And I'm like, yes, yes, brain. My brain needs to check off some logical boxes until it's satisfied, but on the whole, I usually circle back to the heart and gut.

Kimberly: That is awesome. I always say this, your initial reaction feeling, gut instinct, whatever you want to label. It is the right one to go with.

Nora: You have to satisfy the gremlins in your head. If you're able to justify what your heart and gut are feeling, over time, your gut and your heart being always right becomes one of the check marks. Trusting yourself, but it's logical to question to make sure. I would always say, satisfy that brain, and prove to the brain that your heart and your gut are right. Then you go head on, you have no questions. You don't deviate, keep going and follow the path. Because you know that you've got everybody on board, all three parts.

Kimberly: Yes, I love that, teaching other people to go, okay... The brain is always questioning. If you can check off, okay. First heart and then gut are a hundred percent. All the time, you are maybe averaging 25 to 50%, depending on the thing. Then check mark, whatever those boxes are that you need to check for your brain to go, okay. Yes, heart is right. Gut is right. Let's do this. Let's move on. It's a good thing. Great advice!

Nora: If you don't get the brain on-board, then you find that the brain will divert you onto other paths. To get anywhere quickly, you have to be totally in alignment. If you're not in alignment, then you veer off the road to follow every squirrel that is on the side paths. Now, I believe all paths lead to the same direction, but there is a direct path and there are curvy paths, too. It is up to you which one to take. Do you want the lollygag on the scenic route, or do you want to efficiently get to the destination? It's always up to you.

Whichever path you pick, you will learn things that will shape you and your knowledge and help make you the person you're.

Kimberly: Absolutely. We could keep talking about that. I Thank you so much for sharing your story and your wisdom. It's been amazing.

Nora: Thank you for doing this. Thank you so much.

CHAPTER 16

Designing Your Life

Samantha Buckley Hugessen

Samantha is an American Certified Coach originally from Seattle Washington, now as an expat, she lives in Cabo San Lucas Mexico; she had a 7-year layover in Whistler, BC, Canada. With 2 amazing sons' a wonderful 20+ year marriage, plus 3 fur babies. Sam is a force at 6'2" tall, she is foul-mouthed (CENSORED), but she is super effective and passionate about helping people design and live lives they love. She has been managing and leading people her entire adult life and started her "Personal Life Coaching, Sales and Leadership Training and Mentoring" company full time in 2011. In October 2019, Sam released her first Book UNS*UCK YOURSELF – The Guide to Designing a life you love, gaining AMAZON Bestseller status in 4 categories. Her company is perfectly named "A Designed Life, LLC"

Contact info:

www.adesignedlifellc.com

https://www.facebook.com/adesignedlife/

@a_designed_life_llc/

https://www.linkedin.com/in/samanthabh/

She's living her life by design, so powerful! ~KA

Kimberly: I am excited to talk with Samantha Buckley Hugessen today. You are a leadership and mentorship coach. I love this. Let's talk about that.

Samantha: Okay. Hi. Happy to be here with you and other goddesses. I'm a life, sales, leadership coach. Mentor and Trainer because coaching, mentoring, training are actually three different hats. I thought I'd better tell people that because many people say, Oh, I'm a coach. And really, they're telling people what to do. It's like, no, you're mentoring or training when you do that. You're not really coaching. my history, my corporate world history was a lot of training and sales management. I'm good at that. I became a coach back in 2010 professionally because I was trying to solve everybody's problems for free. My husband said, charge people for that!

Kimberly: Definitely... what is your company? What is your business?

Samantha: My companies called, A Designed life LLC. Ideally helping people discover their purpose, discovering what they would love to do in life, then doing that, being a partner in believing with them, and introducing them or reinforcing their faith versus fear.

I've got thousands of stories, probably like many people do. I have evidence of how it works. Right. Then I wrote a book. I wrote a book a couple of years ago. This is it, "UNS*UCK Yourself - The guide to designing a life you love," it's really about life design. We either live by default or by design. If you get to wake up and breathe today, you have a choice. Life's either going to happen to you or through you. It always happens through you, but in our minds, many people want to say, this is happening to me. You don't know what happened to me. It happened to you. We may not know why, but the sooner you figure out it happened for you, the sooner you can get clear on where you're going.

Kimberly: I love that. That is a great segue into my big question. What would you say is your biggest obstacle, or what have you gone through in your life?

Samantha: Well, my greatest obstacle was also my greatest gift. God, that sounds hokey. Doesn't it?

Kimberly: It's true though.

Samantha: I grew up in a less than ideal childhood, which many did. I'm not special in that way. My mom was married seven times. That has nothing to do with even the boyfriends or all those types of things. They weren't healthy relationships. You can imagine what comes along with unhealthy relationships, abuse, those types of things. Then I started going down the same road. I married my very own abusive alcoholic when I was 22. That's kind of. When I hit the brakes, what's going on here? I even remember going to therapy and the therapist calling me out, I'm 20 years old, the therapist calling me out and says, if men are the problem here, because I was convinced, that men were evil, bad and dah, dah, dah. Why are you seeing a male therapist? I'm like, I have issues. I got mommy issues. That's what I got. I realized then; she was supposed to protect me; she didn't. I for sure had mommy issues. I drew a line in the sand, and I did a ton of work. Through these experiences in life, it helps me to mentor. It helps me to say, hey, come on, I'll put my arm around you. I have been there, done that or something like that. I have empathy, but I also don't allow people to stay stuck in their old story. I'm not down with it. I know you can design your life. I know greatness waits for you, if it is possible for one, it possible for everyone. Like I said, at the top of our conversation, I've got probably thousands of examples over the lifetime of it working out. By the way, anybody listening, or reading this, it's always worked out. If you're listening to this, you're still breathing. It always worked out. Maybe not how you want it, but could you imagine if you were in design mode rather than default mode?

Kimberly: I love that. What were some of the first things that you did, taking those steps to help yourself? Because you obviously, like you mentioned the first part of your life, you saw a lot of stuff. What were some things that you did when you were 20 years old?

Samantha: Well, I think I started before that. I literally got my first job when I was 12. Independence was really important to me to not be the prey of, or not be relying on, anyone. Then I had to unlearn that... it's okay to receive. I love the saying, "you do you", like Sam, you do you. I became independent, sought help, went to therapy. Went to a lot of therapy, think therapy is great. If you have the right therapist, I'm not a therapist unpacking your past. Your kind of going to unpack things you've been cramming, shoving in there and didn't know existed in the basement. But as a coach, a leader, I'm all about looking through the windshield. Okay. You don't need the review right now. We're going to go forward, going to drive ahead. I think it was getting help, acting, knowing that was true in the past, or that might've been true. Yes, those are all facts, but now I choose... XYZ for my life. We were all given freewill, thank goodness. Aren't we lucky?

If you don't like the decision you made, make another one. Universe has perfect hearing. You've heard that. Right? Perfect hearing. Perfect GPS, whatever. How many times have we heard? Oh, my gosh. I was thinking about this; it showed up; it showed up. I think once we realize this was me, once I realized that wherever I was putting my thoughts, or my energy toward, I was getting more of it. I was really. Putting my thoughts on, "I don't want to marry a loser" that was a lesson that I had to learn. I'm not married to him now. By the way, here's the funny thing about that one. That guy that I was married to back in 1989, he ended up being married five times. By the time he was 30. Talk about what a correlation that was between my mom being married so many times and him, it's like that there, I was totally manifesting going down the same rabbit hole, different piece, different end of it. Same rabbit hole. We create our realities.

Kimberly: I love that you're acknowledging that, it's about taking full responsibility.

Samantha: But there's a caveat to that too. This is what I want to share with my sisters here. Don't overtake responsibility. If I can explain that I work with many lovely women, I will find that they have such a tough time with a sense of deserving. They will take responsibility for things. That's not theirs. It's not theirs. Discern what's mine. What do I put right here? It doesn't mean you have to play the blame game. It doesn't mean you have to assign it to anybody else. You can go, "that ain't mine", and let it go. Because otherwise you're pushing your energy down. You're trying to keep the good away from you, right?

Kimberly: I love that. That's really taking your power, sitting in your power. The discernment with what's really my responsibility, what do I own up to. There's a big difference.

Samantha: Women at the core, we're such nurturers, we've got our ancestral patterns, we tend to, oh; I made him mad, or I shouldn't have done that. I should've known, but it was like, okay, it's a lesson, it's learned, you got feedback. Don't do it again.

Kimberly: So good. When you're able to do that and even with beliefs, it's the same thing. Those beliefs aren't always yours.

Samantha: Most times, if you haven't done the work, you haven't done work. Almost none of them are yours.

Kimberly: That's such a profound thing to realize too, is because when you recognize it's not your belief, you can literally shift out of it. Tt's simple at the very forefront of it when you recognize what it is. It's difficult to do, but it's doable. That's important to understand. You're talking about it in relationship to being responsible for what you're responsible for.

Samantha: I think like, you're saying it is the concept's really easy, like running a marathon, concept's easy, lace up your shoes and go! I can't run a marathon. I can barely make it six blocks. I'm not a runner. Give yourself some grace. Notice this, then go ahead practice your new belief. That's the thing, it is replacing the old belief. I used to believe that, now I.... Now I... and you keep practicing the new belief, it becomes you. I got out of a coaching session with an extraordinary human. She said, how do you know that? I go, well, first, I'm 54. I've had a ton of practice. Second, I'm old. I don't care if I fail because I know that it's feedback. It's telling you, Oh, not this way. That decision you made. Maybe not the best one. Time to make another decision.

Kimberly: Taking out the fear. It's just feedback.

Samantha: They're just telling you not this way. They're not telling you. No, they're saying not this way.

Kimberly: That's good.

Samantha: Well, think about it this way. I think about it this way. Cause I'm kind of weird, but like I to think about scientists, you know what I mean? When they're trying to find something, the feedback is, oh, that didn't work. That blew up, or that bubbled over or that, you know what I mean? Take out that it didn't work that way. Take it out. It's feedback. It's like, we're super happy to get that information rather than to keep mixing the same crap together that keeps blowing up in your face.

Kimberly: It's testing. If you look at it, it's testing. That gives you a different feel to it. It's not failing its feedback, testing, or practicing right.

Samantha: I'm taking testing from you now, Kimberly.

Kimberly: Yeah. I love it. That's good. When you were a child, you were dealing with and watching all of this stuff. What was your mechanism? What would you say that really kept you moving forward?

Samantha: Hmm, that's a brilliant question. When you said, when I was a child, I go to elementary school age; I wanted to fit in. I wanted to be cared for; I wanted to be looked after; you know what I mean? Those things, none of those things happened. I think I would be super nice, Funny.

These are all the things that I would try to do to, plus I was really tall and awkward. I'm six foot two now. Like I said, I wasn't looked after; I showed up at school, clearly uncared for. We lived in a really pleasant neighborhood. I felt I was definitely not the kid that fit in. I was going to school in the Kmart stretch pants. My hair wasn't combed. hat type of thing. I think there might be something, the genes. My dad was tough in a good way, Coal miner, cop, good Hardy stock, as you'd call it. I also had a lot of. I will not be like her and by the way, I don't hate my mom. I don't hate my mom. I know what people think I must hate her. I don't hate her at all, but I had to put her where she belongs in my life.

I think it was a lot of I'm going to do my best to be loved and cared for. I can do this, I can do this, I can do this. There's something about that survivor mentality and there's the gift in that, as you are becoming an adult, survivor is so victim feeling and not a lot comes out of that victim energy. That thriving is where you use the gift. When I wrote the book, the writing coach, the Co-authors, the people that helped me. I dropped out of school like twice, never finished high school, or college or anything. If you follow me on Instagram or anything, you see I typo to death, anyway; I don't care. They said, tell your story. I'm like I don't want to tell my story. I want to help people. They said they need to relate to you.

Of my actual story, this is a five out of what 10 of what it would be if I told the entire story, the proper story. But you change that, surviving energy to the thriving energy. If I circle back to my mom, I'm super grateful. She really did model "what not to do" and our family dynamics. Brady bunch to me was what families supposed to look like, I guess. I hear people tell me nobody modeled for me. TV did, for me. I loved happy days. I loved all that. So sure, you had models, not in your home.

You listen to spirit, to intuition. I'll it will tell you the difference between right and wrong.

Kimberly: Yeah. Commonsense.

Samantha: Right. Well, pay attention to what your gut is telling you is the right thing? Cause that's the right thing.

Kimberly: Exactly. I'm interested, you said only telling part of your story. What parts aren't you sharing?

Samantha: Oh, the molestation, the beatings. I was getting stoned in sixth grade, taking my lunch money from my mom's purse, saving it for keggers after school. You know what I mean? In seventh grade, stuff like that. Thank goodness my kids know this. If they read this, it's okay. My kids know this, but my kids are nothing like that. It's funny. They're amazing. Breaking that cycle was pretty cool, too.

Kimberly: What did you do to break that cycle?

Samantha: I put my energy in what I would love to have in my life and be. I don't want to say deny the facts. I don't want to deny the facts. I don't energize them. I encourage people. I'm not asking you to deny your facts. I'm not asking people to deny stuff, abuse or anything. Your own shame. I'm not asking you to do that. I'm asking you not to give energy to them. If they're not serving you and others, us being stuck in our life, stuck in our issues, stuck in our old story is robbing people, because all of us have a unique gift. Every single one of us, when we play small, we're robbing people of that gift.

Kimberly: Oh, I love it. Absolutely. Thank you. What would you tell your younger self? If you could go back.

Samantha: Take a lot of pictures when your body looked that good. It's true. It's like, oh man, let me see. What would I tell her? I think I would tell my younger self it's Okay. It all worked out. Your life is going to be much more than you could ever imagine. Start dreaming of it now. Don't wait. Because I always knew I was destined for greatness, but I didn't think I deserved it. I muted myself a lot; I sabotaged myself a lot. Lessons learned. I think that a lot of women, if they get honest with themselves, will see where they sabotage themselves too. I can't because ... I would, but... Probably every single woman has done that in her life, decades of it. It's a pattern that we need to shift out of.

Kimberly: Absolutely.

Samantha: I would too. I used the excuse or whatever, remember we started out our conversation today with the universe has perfect hearing. I don't want to do that. I don't want to go there. I don't want to do that.... Oh, my God. My car won't start. Coincidence? Nope! Manifested. Be really careful with your thoughts if it is serving me and others? What am I energizing? Is this in service of me and others? Of course, boundaries are great. I would love to, but I can't be okay. I would love to, but I'm not going to, because I don't want to. That's a suitable answer, by the way. It's a good enough answer. If you are a people pleaser, write that down, ladies. I'd love to. But I'm not lying. I'd love to hang out and chat or go for martinis or whatever it is. You know what I mean? I'd love to, but I don't want to. It could be, I don't want to, because I'm having a date night, or I want to sleep, or I have to work. Also, because I said so is enough. Now I don't do that with my children. By the way, I'm not talking about cleaning the kitchen. Well, you can't go with your friends. Why? Because I said so, I'm not talking about that. Talking about your own personal boundary, right? Oh yeah. You know what? I will not do that.

I think that that›s an important thing for women too, because we are nurturers, we are givers; we are all those things, nurture you first. Otherwise, you›re depleted, be kind, that›s totally okay. I will not be there but thank you for the invitation. There›s a joke around me. I live in what used to be a kind of small town, now it›s big. But the joke would kind of be, you can invite Sam. She›s probably not going to show because..., I have become very protective of my energy, who I was around, things like that. There are people that fill me up and there›s people that deplete me, or situations, vice versa. I said, oh yeah, I›ll heartbroken if you don›t invite me, but you know, I›m probably not going to go.

Kimberly: I love that because that's an empowered space. You are holding tight around your boundaries. Your boundaries, your time, your energy. You're recognizing what fills you up and what depletes you. That's coming from such a powerful space you can say, no, it's okay. You can say no, because you want to say no, I want to take a nap or whatever it is. It's okay. I love that.

Samantha: If your friends, cause some of us have friends, some of them are new and they match our energy. Other ones, we kind of been bringing along for the years, it's really simple. Come on. No, don't be that. Don't do that to me. No, respect my boundaries. I'm going to do me, you do you. This takes practice, by the way; this is easy for me now. But I did an interview with some gentlemen a couple months ago over in Washington, DC. I talked about the same concept. They were like, you mean, you can say no. Men have the same problem, by the way. And I go, yeah. If they want a reason, he goes, he's thinking about his sister-in-law, she will pester him if he said no. Just say, my reason is, I don't want to. I say that a lot, nobody hates me. Well, if they do, they're not my people. That's cool. They would be energy sucks then if they don't get me.

Kimberly: This is good because it's so powerful. I love having these conversations because when you recognize that, you can be in that, that changes your life, you're not constantly running that rat race, or that hamster wheel, you can say no, and be like, oh, I'm going to go take a guilt-free nap. Or I just don't want to.

Samantha: I don't want this. This is what I teach people that are yes people, they take on way more than they can really handle, which by the way is bad because it depletes them as much as it might fill them up, because they're people pleasers, they're needed, and they're valued, they're wanted, they're also getting taken advantage of, and it depletes their giving, they can't do it all. Now they're falling short. Stop doing that if that's you.

Kimberly: I talk about that all the time.

Samantha: To put a bow on this so people don't feel offended, here's another thing for our businesspeople. Say, I'd love to let me check my calendar and I'll get back to you, get back to them and say, no, I'd love to, but I can't.

Kimberly: It gives you that pause, that moment.

Samantha: That Moment is for the super people pleasers, you know who you are. Start living by your calendar. Start falling in love with your calendar. Then you really can put a note down and say, Nope, can't.

Kimberly: I love it. That's coming from such an empowered space. I always tell people no is a complete sentence, NO period, or NO exclamation mark. No. It's a complete sentence. You don't need to continue that.

Samantha: I have never heard that. Yeah. That's so good. You know, I used to tell my kids when they would keep going at me, keep going at me. I'd say, asked and answered. Yeah, we're done.

Kimberly: It is. But that goes right in line with what you're talking about. Because when I'm talking about those, yes women, who are always saying, yes, yes, yes, yes, yes. Learn to say no. Your yes becomes more powerful when you really truly know you know.

Samantha: Well, I feel so smart right now.

Kimberly: You are, you're brilliant. So good. Any last tips you would like to say to anyone who's listening, that has gone through their journey, they're coming through the other side.

Samantha: You're not through the other side yet, probably. Take your foot off the brake, keep going. Do the work, do the work, we don't know what we don't know. That's it! Do the work. I was in a retreat this weekend. I heard something really valuable. I don't know if this is everyone here or what, but if you subscribe to 50,000 newsletters and really don't read any of them, it's kind of enjoy going to Costco, when we could get a sample of this and a sample of that. Commit to the transformation. If you commit to the transformation, it's like, I did a $19, almost free thing and I didn't really engage in it.

I'm not saying you have to spend a bunch of money, but basically you got a bag of potato chips. If you find you keep dabbling in snacks, you need to put forth the energy and invest in the meal. That's where transformation takes place. It's not. I get 60 emails delivered to my inbox every morning that I scan. I'm going to come back to that word that we had a few minutes ago, discern. This isn't magic. It is magical, but you need to decide what you would love in your life. Put on the blinders, no distractions. If you are clear in your decision, you don't see all this stuff on the sides. You are focused - on going forward.

Kimberly: I love it, be all in, lean in. Thank you for your brilliance and for being here with me.

Samantha: Thank you for having me. I appreciate it.

CHAPTER 17

It's Never Too Late

Dr. Shelia Craig Whiteman

Dr. Shelia Craig Whiteman DPT, CLT, is a Doctor of Physical Therapy who specializes in working with clients with pelvic health issues. Dr. Whiteman has treated hundreds of women for pelvic floor disorders and presently works with clients to reduce and eliminate urinary incontinence. Dr. Whiteman is the two-time best-selling author of" To Pee or Not to Pee?" The Guide for Reducing and Eliminating Urinary Incontinence and "Stop Worrying about Bladder Leaks. Her online program, Stop Your Bladder Leak, educates women of all ages with strategies to reduce and eliminate urinary incontinence.

Dr. Whiteman, she also is a certified lymphedema therapist and a certified life coach, and a health and wellness coach. Dr. Whiteman is the host of a television show on KP Media, Living Well with Dr. Shelia, with topics to help the public live their best life.

Join me every Thursday at 12 pm EST on KP Media TV for Living Well with Dr. Shelia

www.thepelviccoach.com

IG- thepelviccoach_drshelia

FB-drsheliahealthwellness

Email: thepelvicdpt@gmail.com

**She got her Doctorate in her late forties,
a beautiful reminder, it's never too late. ~KA**

Kimberly: I am with Dr. Shelia Craig Whiteman. I am excited you're here today, you're a Doctor of Physical Therapy. Did I get that right?

Shelia: You did. You got that correct. I have a doctorate in physical therapy.

Kimberly: Talk about that first. And thank you so much for being here today.

Shelia: Thank you for having me. I actually do a lot of things. In the physical therapy realm, I am a pelvic floor physical therapist. I work primarily with women who have issues that have to deal with their pelvic floor, mainly incontinence, pain with sexual activity, constipation, or abdominal issues, really anything that had to do with that area.

Over the past two years, I started writing books. They're self-help books, they are really for the public to understand a little more about what's going on with their bodies. I found that was an enormous problem when I was in the clinic. Many of my clients were not aware of what the pelvic floor is or what it does. Many of my clients needed a resource to learn information about the pelvic region. Once I noticed this void, I wrote books geared towards the average person, so the information was easier to understand. It is important for women at any age to know their bodies. I also wanted women to ask informed questions to make it easier to make informed decisions about their health when visiting the doctor or health professional. I wrote two books, they're both on bladder leaks. Bladder leaks are quite common; they also can be easy to treat successfully. Reducing bladder leakage is one of the more successful diagnosis to fix. After years of treating hundreds of patients in outpatient clinics, I transitioned to doing the same work but as a health coach. One of the coaching programs I have is a program online to reduce and eliminate your bladder leaks. I also own a home care agency which hires certified nursing assistants to go into the homes, to care for seniors who want to remain at home.

Kimberly: Many hats, before we dive into the conversation. I want to go back. I know one of your books is called "To Pee or Not to Pee?" Is that correct?

Shelia: That is correct. Everybody loves the title of that book, and nobody ever forgets it. Once people hear it one time, I think it sticks in your mind. The full title of the book is "To Pee or Not to Pee," "The Guide for Reducing and Eliminating Urinary Incontinence." My second book is "Stop Your Bladder Leak. The Guide to Overcoming Urinary Incontinence."

Both of the books address the same topic, but provide different information, so you can have all you need in these two books about helping your bladder leak.

Kimberly: That is incredible. I want to touch on something that you already said. The conversation of talking, having conversations about those things we're not even told. We don't know what questions to ask because we're not informed of how our body works. Especially as women, there're many things going on.

Shelia: I have seen this most times. Women don't talk even among themselves about the challenges that happen as our hormones change during our lifetimes. Pre menopause and Menopause will happen to all of us if we are lucky to live long enough. Pre menopause begins in your forties, so changes start happening earlier than most of us expect. Many women notice mental and physical changes and because we are not educated about the symptom, you are thinking normal symptoms are abnormal. You're not really feeling well; unexplained symptoms are happening to your body. I think it's important that women realize that a lot of these things will happen. They happen. It doesn't mean that the symptoms are something you have to live with. If you're not comfortable with any of them, there are interventions you can do to help you feel better. Interestingly, during perimenopause and menopause many women also have increased emotions, positive or negative. If this, is you, no you are not unstable. But that's what a lot of women think. Thoughts of "What is going on with my body?" "Am I going crazy?" "I can't think" or "I can't enjoy sex because it hurts? Waning hormones can cause many issues that are common but because we don't talk about it, so we don't know. There's no reason for us to suffer in silence, especially these days when there's so much information out there and there are many resources to help.

Kimberly: I love it. I'm going to have on my show, a conversation all around that.

Shelia: I will be happy to have that conversation because I tell you, I talk about it a lot. I do public speaking, talks to women's groups, and senior talks, those are mostly only on incontinence. But when I go out and speak to women's groups, I do because menopause and the symptoms associated with menopause can devastate to some and it may be a matter of a few life adjustments to make all the difference in improving their quality of life.

Kimberly: What would you say is your biggest obstacle that you've gone through, overcome? And I'm curious to find out if that led you to go into what you do now?

Shelia: My biggest obstacle actually has been, I would say is time, and it has been juggling what was my primary responsibility and what I wanted to do personally in life. There was a time when there was no me, I was someone's mom primarily, or someone's wife. Now my kids are grown, I am no longer 20 or 30. I am really now coming to age to do what I want to do. I feel like I have a lot of catching up to do for where I want to be. Fortunately, though, I can enjoy the journey. I am moving forward in life with no regrets.

My children and my family are a blessing, but I think, for me finding that balance or even support, would have been great in the early years. I think that is probably why I try to support younger women work towards their goals. The women I mentor can always come and ask me any question or for advice. I actually didn't have that type of support. I think that was an enormous obstacle for me. Hopefully, that answered your question, but support and time really slowed me down. I got my doctorate in my forties, not my twenties or early thirties. I got it in my late forties because it's something that I wanted to do. Something that I knew I had to accomplish. But again, time, other commitments that many women have, depending on what your life is, sometimes change your timeline. We all have other commitments. And it depends on what your support is, values, et cetera are to, whether you can make what happens in a timely manner. As long as you are able, time can still be your friend.

Kimberly: I like you said that, because a lot of us lose our identity as we become moms and wives. And that's not talking about a lot either. Suddenly, we're mommies and that is life consuming. And then we need to fit in the husband here and there, and that's life consuming. To navigating that, and trying to not break free from it necessarily, but find that balance of, who am I, what do I want to do? Especially as the kids get older and now, you're an empty nester, there' are a lot of women that have no identity. They don't know what they like, don't know what they want to do. They don't know who they are, don't know themselves at all. Assumed that their identity was mom or attached to something else.

Shelia: The interesting thing is that their identity was mom and was wife, and actually this was reality for many of us with families. As women we have to, I don't want to say fight because fight has a negative connotation, but you have to actually fight to have your own interests and to have your own life. It it's easy to get caught up in the day-to-day duties of making sure your family is well cared for. We have been expected to take on the family as our responsibility. I always say to my children; I need to raise you to be productive adults. Now it's up to you, no matter what, to be a productive adult and be happy. When this happens, I have accomplished what I have to do, but when your children are younger and still in school, you don't really have an identity. Your name is mom.

Kimberly: Do you think, there anything in your childhood or growing up that got you to when you started having children, or did that time thing, that identity thing that we're talking about, was there anything in your childhood that caused you to feel that way even more so going into becoming a mom and a wife, or was it something that you had a great childhood and then suddenly, now you are just a mom and just wife, and it's about trying to figure out how to get all that balance in.

Shelia: I grew up in Buffalo, New York and I guess we would have been poor, but we didn't know it. We had what we needed, and it was enough. There were not a lot of opportunities growing up there, so I moved away after college. When I had children. I wanted them to have more than what I had I think that is what you find with many people who grew up in a certain generation.

This is especially true in minority populations. History definitely repeats itself. I grew up during a lot of racial unrest and tension and I can still remember it to an extent, riots, mistreatment of black people, etc. I think my childhood made me more protective of my children. It also made me want to give them opportunities that I didn't have.

Growing up poor, there were a lot of opportunities that I didn't even know existed because of lack of exposure. I wanted to make sure that they had the opportunities that I didn't have. That's part of the reason raising my children and maintaining a stable family took a lot of effort for me at least. My community growing up was remarkably close, and we didn't really venture outside of our side of the city a lot. That was fine because we were all happy, because we didn't know what we were missing.

Kimberly: I noticed in a lot of conversations that I have, that is part of the conversation, wherever you grew up, you don't know any different. This is how it is. And, when you grow up and you see outside of your four walls and you're like, Oh, it's bigger. There are more things out there. And I think parents always want better for their kids. I know that in my life, and I've seen it as well, knowing a lot of your clients are women. Would you say that is a conversation that comes up often with balance and even their physical health, do you see this correlation and stress?

Shelia: Yes, definitely. The conversation comes up a lot. The conversation comes up a lot with stress, not taking the time to take care of oneself. Especially with the type of clients and patients that I see; and it's not that they're neglecting their health or anything like that; but we all have to set priorities. Sometimes the priorities are work, family, health challenges etc. and this does not leave enough time for self-care. Even for me, day-to-day activities that are more urgent or that I feel are more important to take a back seat to self-care or relaxing things I could do instead, and stress is important to reduce. When I was in the clinic doing physical therapy and now doing health coaching, I have learned over the years that even health problems cannot be looked at as an isolated problem, it's a matter of looking at everything that's going on mentally and physically and even sometimes spiritually to help you recover or feel your best. Everything in your life is really interrelated, depending on how deep you want to get into it. Your life story says where you are today, how you accept and deal with life, and the difficulties everyone is bound to experience in life. If we look at one's backstory it many times explains about who they are now, and what they have been through, and how they navigated though life. Yes, stress management is a really important aspect of living your best life. Putting yourself on the back burner, I think is the biggest thing that I see women do regularly, because of the way many of us have been brought up. We are the nurturers and protectors first. Taking care of ourselves is second.

Another point has to do with our internal thoughts. We believe we are important enough to really work on whatever the issues and stressors in life are and then to put all your effort into working to reduce or eliminate the problem or concern. Unfortunately, women especially will wait until the stress is too difficult and affects some aspect of their lives before, we act. I am guilty of this as well. Sometimes in my life my thoughts where "I'm going to do the bare minimum so that I can keep functioning and, hopefully, that'll work out" It's only until my stress level gets really, really, concerning then it's a big priority. Why did it have to get that far for me and many of my clients to act?

Kimberly: I think you touched on something really important to not feeling worthy, that you are the priority. I always go back to the airplane, put your mask on first.

Shelia: Right. It's put your mask on first, take care of yourself first, even when we have families. This generation is not any different from the past ones that even for me, they would say you have to take care of yourself in order to take care of your family. I know we have all heard that now, but do we pay those words any attention? No, because we didn't have time or believe that self-care should be our top priority. Take care of yourself in order to take care of anybody. And number one, if you don't take care of yourself, you can't adequately take care of anybody. That's the part that I think we should change the expression to. If you can't take care of yourself, you can't take care of anybody else. Look at it like that.

Kimberly: Yeah, absolutely. And then, going back to the time, it keeps coming up, even in our conversation, it's all about the time, you've got to take the time. It's okay. You are worth it. You need it. It's a priority.

Shelia: Agreed. I thought when you first asked me about my biggest obstacle, I thought oh boy, I can pick many things, but if I boiled it down to its simplest form, that really has been my obstacle. It actually has, finding the time when I was younger to follow my purpose. I feel now I am playing catch up.

Kimberly: I feel like we all deal with that constantly in our life too. It's always about time. There's never enough of it, that entire perspective of it, change the perspective. There's always enough time, but we don't think about it like that. If you started too, that would even help ease some of that stress.

Shelia: I think you are right and that is actually what I have done. My stress level has decreased tremendously because I put that time for me in my schedule along with all my other to do's. And if I don't accomplish everything it's fine, I realize there is only a finite amount of work and output I should do on any day. Especially if you're a business owner or entrepreneur you will always, always, wear many hats and you always are going to have a million things to do. You can accomplish 10 things in a day. Then 10 more are back there waiting to be done unless you have a staff and even then, you are still ultimately responsible, everything is on you. I think to switch that attitude from, "I have to get everything done in order to be successful" to "I can get as much as I can get done, be happy, be at peace and I still will be successful" can help. By doing that little switch and changing your mindset, it helped me because many nights I would go to bed and my mind would still race with thoughts from the day. I would wake up in the middle of the night thinking I really should have called someone, but I forgot and didn't I didn't call them. Or I did I write that down? I need to contact Mr. Jones. Did I make up that flyer? You know, seriously, every thought from that day would come flooding through my brain instead of sleep. I had to consciously remind myself. No, the flyer will be there. The piece of paper I had will still be there, the phone call will be there in the morning. It will all still be there the next day. It'll be there the next week. Your business is going to move in the direction that it should when it should.

Kimberly: Absolutely. I think every woman can identify with going to bed and waking up because there's much on our minds. We need to put it to rest. Even if you're not an entrepreneur and trying to run multiple businesses, sleep with worry, with doubt, with these things, got to let it go.

Shelia: That is true. It's easier said than done because even when I started my career, I worked for someone else for a time and I thought, I don't have to worry as much about anything since I am not the boss. My mind still would not turn off at night. I think that as a woman turning your mind off at night is one of the hardest things. For most of my life I think this has been my challenge number two, because turning this voice off, and turning off the mind, is extremely, extremely difficult. I know very few women who can turn off their thoughts at bedtime and stay asleep. My mom has always done it and I envy her.

Kimberly: Yeah. I think men, men are like that.

Shelia: They sure are. I mean, that's one thing that I really wish I could do.

We even absorb some of their worry. I always think to myself, how come they're not worried about that?

Kimberly: True. how have you helped yourself in being able to go to sleep? Because many women deal with that. I know how I teach it, but I'm curious how you share with your clients. What has helped you?

Shelia: There are a couple of things I have found effective to help me wind down for bed. I now have a hard stop for work and also for electronic use. Not working until I go to bed but shutting down at least 2 hours before. I don't take my phones or my computer into my bedroom. I don't. and then the other thing is that I try to either journal or if I really have a lot on my mind, I write it down. I'll write it down before I go to bed, because that really helps me, too kind of take it and move my thoughts to the side and know I won't forget, and they will be there in the morning. I can look it up and look at it with fresh eyes. It is still a work in progress. My next focus will add in a relaxing bath to really wind down the day.

I also have a morning routine or ritual to help start the day off in a stress-free manor. I'll wake up and lay in the bed, pray, and then I'll stay in the bed for a bit in silence and kind of let my mind go, let it go and just flow. Afterwards I get up and do 10 minutes of yoga and then I get ready for the day. That has worked a lot to reduce my stress and calm me down, especially from the stress of having the home care business, as you can imagine which can be a stressor especially working with the senior population. Home care is a 24/7 business.

When I have clients who we have sent staff in to care for overnight, I bring my phone up, but it's on do not disturb except if my office manager calls, because they'll call her first, and then that phone call will go through. I try to stick to rituals, because when I do that, I sleep better.

Kimberly: I love it. I think that helps many people. If you can go back and tell your younger self one thing, what would it be?

Shelia: I would tell my younger self to pursue my purpose and dreams, pursue my dreams while I'm young. Not to get caught up in the day-to-day life treadmill. Always do something that will energize the soul. I would say that because a lot of the opportunities that I had, I let them go because I put family first, but I have to say though, like I said, it's not a regret, but I think I could have taken advantage of some opportunities that came my way. I think I could have put more effort into managing, doing that, plus even chipping away at some things I wanted to do, instead of saying, I'll leave them until later, because sometimes you don't know if later is going to come, fortunately later came for me and I am pursuing my dreams, I can't say I have regrets. I believe everything happens in its time and thankfully I can serve my purpose now.

Kimberly: Yes!

Shelia: Yeah. I've got a good life, though. It's been good. It's been great. If I would tell my younger self to laugh more, I would. We should all find more humor in life. Everything is not serious. I think I would do that and to slow down. I was one to always be on the go, even when I was younger, I used to teach at gyms. I taught exercise classes seven days a week, had my kids; went to work at a physical therapy clinic 3 days per week, 10-hour days to get my time in. I ask myself now.... Why did I do that? I look back and it was a lot. Everything in moderation.

Kimberly: Yes, But I think you're such an inspiration. You got your doctorate in your late forties, and it's never too late. And I want people to understand that too, with wisdom you can recognize and go, you know, I could have been more open to opportunity, but we don't know that back then. We know that now, you're such an inspiration though. You got your doctorate in your late forties. That's an amazing feat.

Shelia: Yes. That was tough, 40 something the mind is not as quick as in your younger days. It took a little longer to master learning all of that new material.

Kimberly: Isn't that the truth. I walk into the kitchen. I'm like, why am I in here?

Shelia: I can't tell you how many times I do the same thing. Then I will actually turn back around. I said, I'm going to go back in and retrace my steps. And then I'll remember what I was going into the kitchen for by the time I get halfway back, which I do. I honestly don't remember things like names until maybe 10 minutes after I am with the person. But truth be told, I never really remembered names even when I was younger. Maybe that wasn't a good example. No, but I remember your face. If I have met you at least once I remember your face, but your name? Never have remembered. You can remind me of that. I don't have any problem asking you what your name is.

Kimberly: It has been awesome getting to know you and chatting with you. Thank you for sharing your story and your wisdom. I look forward to hearing more.

Shelia: Thank you for having me. This has been a pleasure. I enjoyed our talk as well. It's a lot of fun. Thank you.

CHAPTER 18

Mindset over Matter

Tamara Golden

Tamara Golden is the owner and founder of Journeywork Retreats, a retreat strategy, and planning company that partners with heart-centered entrepreneurs to create unique and unforgettable retreat experiences across the US and overseas. Tamara combines 20+ years in coaching, travel, and event planning and her passion for personal transformation in working with entrepreneurs to fully harness the power of the retreat experience to grow themselves, their clients, and their business.

info@journeyworkretreats.com

(888) 960-9969

Reflecting back, she saw how
brave she was. ~KA

Kimberly: I am so excited to talk with Tamara Golden today. She is the founder and owner of journeywork retreats. Who doesn't love retreats? I'm happy you're here.

Tamara: I'm thrilled to be here. Thank you, Kimberly. I'm so excited about this.

Kimberly: Talk about your company, I think everybody should go to a retreat or should do retreats if you're a business owner. Take it from there.

Tamara: Absolutely. Well, wellness travel has been on the uptick for an awfully long time now, going into the pandemic. It certainly was hot, hot, hot, hot, coming out, it's going to be even hotter. I got early on that I was really here to do in-person retreats. That is my jam and my juju. We actually partner with heart-centered entrepreneurs, conscious companies to help them strategize, plan these amazing, unforgettable, transformational retreats. We do it across the U.S. and worldwide.

Kimberly: I love that. Yes.

Tamara: We work with everybody along the entire spectrum. We've got done-with-you course and some done-for-you kits, we've got everything up to the done-for-you, full-service packages. We really do the complete kit and caboodle when it comes to retreat planning.

Kimberly: That's awesome. I don't think people realize how involved planning a retreat really is.

Tamara: Yeah. There' are a lot of moving parts, there are several things that people have trepidation around for planning a retreat. Certainly, one of them is all the logistics. We've talked about it, you I together that, there are two brands of people. There are people who love that and love the planning piece. Then there are people who don't want to touch that with a 10-foot pole. Some people when they're further on in their companies probably shouldn't be handling all the logistics because that's not their zone of genius, right? Their zone of genius is whatever healing work or growth work, or development work or strategy work they're doing with their clients and really outsourcing the planning to someone else who's an expert or a pro in that area is the way to go. We have everything from the do-it-yourselves and helping them out, supporting them, to the done-for-you service.

Kimberly: I love it. I think it's absolutely awesome. I can't wait to get to the next retreat, right? Including my own. One thing that we talk about is really overcoming limiting beliefs or traumas or obstacles that you've had in your life. What would you say is one of the biggest ones that you've gone through?

Tamara: I gave some thought to this because this was one question you gave me ahead of time. There's only two folks. She only gave me two questions. This is all going to be off the cuff, but this was one of them. I gave some thought to this because I actually have led a pretty blessed life. I haven't had some of the trauma, some of the heartache or other experiences that I know other people who you've interviewed may have had. My biggest struggles have been the internal ones. The mindset struggles. I came from parents of divorce and there was all of that. I've had some trials and tribulations along the way, but I would say the big juicy one, the big, hairy demon, has been the internal mindset.

One for me, if I had to summarize it, would be my journey to acceptance. Acceptance, I use that purposely because, to me, it's an umbrella term. There was a long road (I'm still on that road) to accepting myself fully, embracing my gifts, my powers, and my full goddess potential. But it's also an acceptance of others. Acceptance of kind of how the world is an acceptance of divine timing and divine purpose. There's a lot when I use that word acceptance, it's a big term, but it's an ongoing journey for me, but it's that mindset piece of acceptance. I think probably the biggest one I'll start with is the acceptance of myself because I struggled with low self-esteem for a lot of years.

Coming out of that, my parents divorcing, separating and divorcing when I was seven led to a lot of anger, which led to a lot of internalized anger, which led to promiscuity, which led to low self-esteem. I'm sure a lot of us can relate to those kinds of downward spirals. Climbing up out of that, through years of therapy and years of my spiritual development, spiritual transformation work and personal development work. It's still a journey that I'm on. I think as all of us, if you're alive, on this side of the dirt, as they say, you're still on that journey. But that was for me the big one is, I'd say, starting with self-acceptance. From there accepting others, accepting the world, accepting divine timing, kind of in that order.

Kimberly: So powerful because the mindset sets you free or cripples you. It's one of those things I think I've even said, change your mindset, change your life. It's simple sounding, but it's absolutely probably one of the most difficult things to do. I think self-acceptance is an enormous piece of that because that kind of, like you said, it's an umbrella term, it encompasses that self-confidence, am I worthy? Am I enough? It encompasses all of those things. I love you used that word.

Tamara: Yes. I don't think that I really fully embraced the importance of mindset, as a business owner, the effect that it has on the success of your business until 2020. I got stark, face to face with the realization that the mindset piece was largely what was probably holding me back. It's, again, like the layers of the onion, right? We peel one back and we come to another; peel one back; we come to another. It's part of our growth journey. That's why my company is called Journeywork Retreats, by the way. The symbol of my company, my logo, is a labyrinth, because it's all about the work that we do along this life's journey.

Kimberly: I love that. That gave me chills. That's so good because when you really step into it, really embrace that, even if you embrace the idea that you can start changing your mindset and your beliefs around everything, that is one step closer to freeing yourself from all this holding you back, even though it might be difficult. Like you said and pointed out, it's a journey. We are constantly moving through it, now, we process it faster, we can go, "Oh, I'm having that moment" Let me go take a breather and say okay, now I got this. I'm going to go in this direction. It completely changes the way you're able to face life, really. Obstacles that come into your life.

Tamara: I have my secret sauce for mindset work, but I'm going to wait and tackle that when you ask me the other question that you sent me in advance.

Kimberly: She's keeping us on the hook for a moment. That's awesome. You said your parents divorced when you were about seven.

Tamara: Yeah. My parents separated when I was seven.

Kimberly: How do you think that affected you growing into your teenage years?

Tamara: Oh, God. Okay. I mentioned my parents separated when I was seven, my mother was the one who left the house. I actually stayed with my father, which was an anomaly back in those days. But my father had the stable income. My father kept the house, it was near my school, near all my friends. They really made the joint decision that this was in my best interest. I was a daddy's little girl at that point. At seven years old, I was an only child. I was attached to him at that stage in my life as well. I think I internalized a lot of pain from that.

At seven you don't really know how to process, "Okay, mommy and daddy, you will not be living together anymore". Your entire world blows apart. It doesn't sound traumatic again, compared to what some other people have experienced, but that was certainly traumatic at that point for me in my stage of growth. It became a lot of internalized anger. My father was emotionally distant. Here I was, living with him. I was a latchkey child. I would come home from school. There would be no one in the house. Initially they had some sitters, I think until maybe my middle school years and then I was alone. All of that internalized anger. I think not getting the love that I was seeking from my father, I went out and sought it from other sources; that led into that whole promiscuity thing.

That led to a downward spiral of low self-esteem because we all know that going looking for love, in the guise of sex with teenage boys, is not a really smart idea. When you look back, you know, hindsight being 2020, you're like, "Hmmmm..." Once you get into that cycle of low self-esteem, it's such a downward spiral. It's such a downward spiral because it leads to other actions that lead to more shame, guilt, anger. Then you go out, you do more. Then you get more shame, guilt, anger. I had a very rocky relationship with my mother throughout my adolescent years. We didn't become close until I was in my forties. Then we became close, toward probably the last 15 years of her life, which I was very thankful for.

I had a lot of anger toward my mother and didn't know where to put that. I had anger toward my mother, couldn't voice it against my father, my father was emotionally distant. It was kind of this whole scenario, which ended up with me acting out, and my acting out was the promiscuity. I was a straight-A student, on the track team, a cheerleader. From the outside... I mean, I got into an amazing college, my first college of choice, early admission. From the outside. I was the poster child for success. Inside, I was dealing with a lot of low self-esteem and did probably all the way through... I think I didn't really get a check on that until well into my twenties or early thirties.

Kimberly: I was going to ask you that because you're right. Once you go down rabbit hole of lack of self-confidence and so forth, it does snowball. It gets bigger and bigger, then you try to self-correct or course-correct, but it's the wrong direction. Then it gets worse. It's kind of like an addiction, you're trying to find all these other outside sources, it's not working. You said you were into your twenties when you started recognizing it. What was it for you that you recognized? What was the issue that was going on?

Tamara: When I was slated to be married to somebody who was verbally and sexually abusive; I ended up calling off the wedding. I called off the wedding only because I became attracted to another man. That was like a shear. "Oh, apparently this will not work!". But I was in that 'You've made your bed; you're going to sleep in it' going forward with this wedding. Calling that wedding off is probably one of the bravest things I've ever done. I don't think I saw it as bravery because there was this other impetus of this man that I was attracted to. That kind of was a catalyst for me to do that. But I was like, okay, yeah, I think I'm going to go get some therapy! I mean, just coming to that realization.

When I was young, one of my redeeming... I love the goddess piece of that, because I have two goddess entities in me, Athena, and Aphrodite, those are my two principal goddesses or ldess personalities... I grew up dancing. Dancing for me when as young. Was this escape? It was such an escape for me. It s the connection. It was the community. It was a place where I ild feel proud of my body, really get my emotions out through icing. It was ballet, and that was hugely important for me. en the therapy that I did in my twenties, that's where I kind of lly unraveled the emotional pieces and what really was going there.

nberly: Yeah. Wow. One, I love ballet. I was in it as a kid, but it release. It's a fantastic way, in all shapes and forms of dance. nderful way to build self-confidence. It makes you feel sexy)ugh, it's just you moving and I love it. Dance is amazing. en you said you started unraveling all the other stuff, I find it lly interesting because as a child, like you said, at seven, you n't know what was going on. You had all this anger for mom l probably for dad too because you couldn't talk to him. There s that lack, but having all of that, not knowing how to deal h that as a child really affects us later in life. It is really kind of ky because you recognized it at 20 and didn't take it deeper or ther down the road.

nara: Yeah. I was 25 I realized I had been reenacting these bad)ices with the men that I was choosing to partner with. And I'm art. I wanted to be in a healthy relationship. I saw my parents. e first marriage was not good, but my father's second marriage s great. I had one negative role model and one positive role del, at least directly in my family. I knew good relationships re an option, yet that was not what I gravitated toward. I'm ?, okay, well, I've got to figure out what's going on, see if I can a little deeper.

Yeah, when I came off of that, breaking up the marriage... I this one month prior to the wedding, everything was paid for, rything was done, and he was Italian, all his family had tickets :chased to come from Italy... it was a BFD I called this off. I actually eventually paid him back the money that we lost, that he lost personally. I think I did right by him in the circumstances, and I tried to do it with integrity, but, when I called that off, I'm like, I need to take a moment, hit the pause button.

Kimberly: That's huge, so many times, even a boyfriend, girlfriend relationship, we guilt ourselves into staying in it. You were absolutely brave in being able to call that off, especially being deep into that moment, a month away with everything paid for. That's huge... That's huge. Bravo to you. That's a lot. I had a similar situation, I couldn't, I felt guilty because of the people that were in my house, its life-changing, kudos to you for being able to recognize that in you.

Tamara: Yeah. The hardest call I had to make was to my grandmother. It terrified me because my grandmother was old school and prim and proper. I really wanted her acceptance... that was huge for me... that was the scariest call I made. Interestingly, she was probably one of the most supportive; she was amazingly supportive. My family and my friends. Their response was phenomenal.

Kimberly: That's awesome. That's such an amazing thing to do. I know it's heartbreaking on some sides of it for the marriage not going through, but that literally changed the course of your life. Everybody has that option. You can choose not to marry that person. Even up to that last moment. We've seen the stories of the girl running out in her white flowy wedding dress in the movies, and she's running either to chase a guy or to go sit on a fountain somewhere. It's okay to do that because it's an enormous commitment in your life. Even if it's the last moment, not to say that you need to break off your marriage if it's not going to be what you're wanting, but really take a moment, make that decision because it's definitely life changing.

Tamara: Like I said, it was not physically abusive, but it was a sexually abusive and a verbally abusive relationship. I knew the longer I was with him; I would have these battles going on internally. Those of us who have been in these positions will understand. My insides would scream at me, "You cannot go forward with this!" I would squish it back down and I would soldier forward, soldier through. But I knew in my heart of hearts that I was about to make a huge, disastrous decision to move forward with him. When I broke it off it, like I said, it's one of the best decisions I've ever made.

Kimberly: Yeah. Such an important thing you said too, listen to your body, your body was screaming at you not to go through with it. Huge! My body was screaming at me. I ignored it completely; it changed the course of my life. You're saying that you listened to it. So, so important.

Tamara: Intuition is always correct.

Kimberly: It is; I've tested mine many times.

Tamara: I think we all have, we all stayed in relationships, marriages, contractual relationships, business relationships, far too long because we give them the benefit of the doubt. Or we talk ourselves out of what we know our intuition is saying. Intuition is always right, let's face it. You can't sidestep that one. You just can't.

Kimberly: No, not at all. How do you think what you've gone through has helped you in your business, because you chose the path of retreats, healing retreats no less? What is it for you that really took you down that path?

Tamara: I've never attached my childhood experience to what I do today. It's more the journey of where spirit and source have brought me throughout my days all the experiences that it has given me and the skills that I've been allowed to develop. This comes together for me in the work that I do around creating retreats, helping people strategize how to embed them into their business. But I will say this. To me the mission behind my doing the retreats is really to help raise the energetic vibration of the planet, because I believe retreats are this powerful, magical platform that my Light workers {as I call my coaches and healers and transformation leaders} can really leverage in achieving speeding up outcomes for their clients, doing this deep dive work, also grow their business, all three together.

To me, it's usually the connection and community piece of what happens on a retreat that is one of the most important elements. I think that comes from having been an only child, a latchkey child, as a latchkey child at the end, feeling alone. Connection and community are huge to me, they're absolutely huge. I think being with people on a retreat, not only receiving the healing, growth, inspiration, and transformation from the facilitator, but feeling yourself as part of a community of people who are on a similar journey as yourself, feeling that comradery, being held in that space of people who understand what you're going through, at whatever level you're going through it. Whatever you're there to learn, grow, take away is an important part of the retreat experience.

Kimberly: Absolutely. It allows for transformation, it's the sacred space that was created for that time for you to step into, be open to it as well.

Tamara: Yeah. Who's along for the journey with you is just as important.

Kimberly: Absolutely. I love all that you said about it. So amazing. If you could go back, tell your little self-one thing, what would it be?

Tamara: Well, I love this question. It actually ties in directly with the mindset work that I do. I'm glad that you're asking me this, because this is something I really want everyone to hear and take in. What I would go back and tell my younger self is to develop and practice a direct, open channel of communication with Source. If I had done that much earlier on, learned how to do that, it had been role modeled, it would have saved me a lot of pain and struggle in my life. Because that's the only thing when I talk about mindset that gets me through. Mindset is tricky.

Affirmations are great, but you can't stand there in the mirror going, "I'm happy today." Life is good. And "I'm prosperous." when you have like $2 in your bank account. To me, what really gets me past... because ego is still at play there... the only thing that gets me past my mindset struggles, the only thing is to meditate, go inward, upward and connect with Source, understand why I'm here. What I'm here to do. Ask for a next step, ask for some reassurance, ask a question that may weigh on my heart and get an answer. Because that's literally the only thing that will get me past all the ego trickeries that come into play. When we talk about mindset, I go up to the Source. If I had started a practice like that when I was seven, eight, nine, ten, I don't even know where I would be now, but I'd probably be a hell of a lot further ahead.

Kimberly: Right? Isn't that interesting? Kids, especially in America, I would say they're not taught that, they don't know. I recently have seen where schools are starting instead of a timeout, they have them go meditate, it's changing, shifting how these kids even behave, consume their work, get better grades. I think it's something that should absolutely be discussed, but I love that's what you would go back and tell her, because that's such an important thing for little kids. Even they have stress, they have anxiety; they don't know what the heck to do with it. Like you said, at seven years old, you had all this anger building up. You didn't know what to do with it because we don't know how to process that or let it go. If you go inside and meditate, it's life changing.

Tamara: Yeah. I don't care if you call it prayer, meditation, whatever your religious leanings are, but to find a connection with something that is bigger than you, that you understand that you're not alone in this universe, you're not alone in this world, but there's someone, some entity that you can ask the answers from and receive, receive wisdom, receive guidance. I think I don't want to offend, but you probably don't have any atheists in your audience, but I think that we've got to go outside of ourselves to look for the answers, it will not be in your friends and your family. It's not going to certainly be in the modern-day media. The only place to really go for those unbiased answers, the ones that truly will be in your best interest and your highest good, is to go directly to Source.

Kimberly: Absolutely. Let me ask you this then. How do you do it? Do you go sit in a special space? Do you journal? There are many ways to sit in that, but I'm curious about you. How do you do that?

Tamara: Yeah. I love to journal. I love to journal; I love to write, but's a lot of ego's mind. It's like that allows me to process, get my analytical stuff going. To really get a blank slate, I meditate. It's getting quiet. Usually, I do it sitting down; I get to a comfortable place that's quiet. I allow my mind to go empty. I do some things with my body that kind of get me in that space. Sometimes I have some words of affirmation that I sort of breath in and exhale and breathe in, exhale. I say these phrases that kind of quiet my mind; they get me into that centered space. Then once I'm in that centered space, I relax. Sometimes I'll either stay sitting or I'll recline back and be opened to receive.

Kimberly: I love that. I was going to ask you how you quiet your mind because that's the joke that there's so much chatterbox going on in there.

Tamara: That's where the affirmations, the breathing come in. For me, that's what was important for me as a dancer is to get from that...my mind will go a mile a minute, trust me...into my body. Some people do it by getting out in nature, like walking or sitting outdoors. But if I can get into my body, I'm swaying and I'm saying these words, it will allow me to stop that chatter and quiet that. That's part of what that rhythm, that routine allows for me. To stop, to turn this off, and get to my third eye, my heart space and opens up the whole Chakra line and allows myself to be open.

Kimberly: I love it. Really there's no wrong way to do it. I want people to know that there's no wrong way to do it. However, it works for you. Going out in nature, sitting under a tree, could walk along the beach. It doesn't matter. Hiking a mountain, if that's what feels good to you. Again, journaling, many people can journal, get those answers. One thing that I do is I, sit in gratitude to quiet my chatter down. I start being grateful for everything. Even the tiniest of things, like the breeze on my face or the birds chirping outside. Anything to bring me to that space of being in full peace, which allows me to be open. It definitely is a life changer, it helps with that mindset too, for sure.

Tamara: Really, it's a game changer, it doesn't have to be like an hour. It could be, if all you have is 10 minutes, take your 10 minutes. There are, sometimes I do 10 or 15 minutes to calm myself. If you have a busy day, try to do it in the mornings, because sometimes your day can get away from you. I try to meditate and exercise wherever possible in the morning because once your day gets underway, different things might come at you and you may not find the time. Even taking 10 or 15 minutes, quieting your mind. I love to do it when I first wake up. Like sometimes I'll do it even laying down in bed. You asked me where, because I do it two places, when I'm still in that theta space from coming awake, I'm lying-in bed cuddling my puppy dogs. I kind of have a talk with Spirit then, or if I'm doing a kind of more formal meditation, I'll go sit down and do it later in the day. Have those two times when I do it, or two ways of doing it.

Kimberly: That's exactly me. I did that this morning, laying there in bed. I think that's such a great time because you're already laying down. You're already there. You're already kind of still peaceful. As you're waking up, you can kind of shift your attention to being in that deep peace, seeking those answers. I love that. Even if you have a cheat sheet on the side of your bed and go, okay, what do I need to say? By all means, go right ahead, do that.

Tamara: My boyfriend does. He's big into guided meditations. Not my thing, but there you go. We both have had these significant benefits from our meditation practices, but they look very different. Again, do you, do what works for you. The thing is, just do it.

Kimberly: Yeah, absolutely. I love it, Tamara, thank you so much for being on here with me and sharing your story, so important. The mindset is such an important topic.

Tamara: Yeah. If you don't handle the mind, the external, literally everything.... I have this right here on the side of my desk. I'll share it with you guys. It says: 'When we create harmony in our minds and hearts, we will find it in our lives. The inner creates the outer. Always.'

Kimberly: So good. Thank you. Thank you so much.

Tamara: You're very welcome.

CHAPTER 19

I Grew Past Her

Toni Moore

Toni Moore Esquire is an attorney, business coach, writer, and women's empowerment speaker who truly believes that a business is a vessel/asset women can use to up level their money game, power, and success. Over 15 years after Toni lost a sister and almost died herself, she became committed to becoming the businesswoman of her dreams. Whether helping women create a business, protect a brand, or develop a sophisticated legacy protection plan, Toni shares from her soul to help others make their dreams possible.

Contact info:

@tonimooreesq

tonimooreesq.com

mstonimoore.com

She grew past her, freeing her soul wounds from childhood. She is creating her own fairytale. ~KA

Kimberly: I am here with Tony Moore. She is an attorney and a business coach. I am looking forward to this conversation, Tony. Thank you so much for being with me today.

Toni: Thank you for having me.

Kimberly: So, Talk about your business.

Toni: I'm a business attorney and intellectual property strategist who helps clients go from lawless to flawless by covering their assets, fixing up where needed. I also serve as a business coach to help business owners—especially start-up owners—appreciate rules, regulatory and strategies as they grow their business. What I've found during over 20 years of legal practice is that is one thing to be a corporate attorney working with managers, partners, and everyone else who knows what needs to be done. Quite another to help dreamers become CEOs. There's usually like five or six steps to get from plans to profits and often startups don't know it. I became a business coach, as well. I had gone through a lot of stuff on my own, going up the corporate ladder, then starting a few businesses from scratch to success. I know where most need to go to manifest more cash flow. That's how I jumped into the foray of business coaching; it feels good to help others do good.

Kimberly: It makes sense too. I can imagine when people are finally getting to you, especially, I love what you said, the dreamers, I'm pretty sure I fall in that category. We're constantly doing stuff, especially as a solo entrepreneur and we're backtracking when we finally discover you.

Toni: Yes; there're three types of dreamers. Dreamers who are chasing fairy tales who haven't gotten schooled by flaw. Then there are those who have been there, done that, learned a few lessons they can never forget. Now when they're going to deep dive into another venture, they're like, look, I've already gone through business divorce, gone through bankruptcy and through tons of mishaps in business. Now I'm going to do it right. Then there are the creatives. I'm a creative, and I attract creatives. This third type of dreamers are people who are writing books, creating music, writing plays and don't fully appreciate the business games. I've been in the legal field since 1993 and can spot where a person is in their business as far as startup to succession plan framework. Most people don't because they are in the framework and can only appreciate their own experiences. Most don't assess or evaluate why rules are in place, how their failure to adhere aka lawlessness can keep them from becoming successful in their enterprise. Legal is almost treated as a distance cousin.

Kimberly: I don't think we realize sometimes, especially as entrepreneurs, how important that step is. It's like you said, we think of it as a distant cousin. We don't want to talk about what might happen to us. Or think that is won't, maybe sometimes is the attitude, it's surely needed. I'm really excited about you being here and your message. Thank you, let's dive into it. What would you say is one of the biggest obstacles that you've had to go through or experiences that you've had to overcome?

Toni: I mean, there's many of them. But for me, for this session I realized that my thoughts of my training as a lawyer. In law school, we get indoctrinated by the billable hours, everything is billable hours. If a person calls it billable hours, research, development, negotiations; it's all billable hours. The fee from each transaction was billable hours, but business is about transformation and results. Well, at least in the author, speaker and coach sector its more about transformation vs transaction. To hear people say that they charge thousands of dollars per hour, my logical brain was like, how do you charge thousands of dollars an hour? What are you offering people that doesn't violate the Federal Trade Commission's rules?

Then one day I met a business coach. I actually saw what she did. I see how her billable hours could have been calculated so that she could technically make $15,000 per hour. Now, of course, my logical brain would probably go a little further and be like, well technically how many hours or whatever. But even with the hours, even if she offered 10 hours, it was a group coaching program. That was a big logical leap that my logical brain had to overcome—charging for the result versus the billable hour transaction. Because I could not get past X hours multiplied by Y rate, I sabotaged my cash flow potential because I kept charging for the transaction while delivering transformative results.

Kimberly: Interesting. It's even goes to that am I worthy and then, I am enough when you're building up.

Toni: Yes, yes, absolutely. Because even within law firms there are still certain pedigrees that you're always comparing. I don't mind the competition, but sometimes with enough Ness, like, wait a minute, I'm supposed to charge someone like $10,000 for something equivalent to 4 hours of work. In my legal brain, its $300 billable hourly rate multiplied by x hours to get to $10,000. But in my business brain, I'm reminded that people pay for what you know, how you can help them achieve results they want to have or avoid. To go from lawless to flawless, there is usually always a problem with money or that results in a monetary response. Well, as an energy person I don't want to say always going to be a hiccup—because we see what we say.

But at least for me, I've had to overcome a lot of money mistakes, and mind blocks to overcome one milestone after another. Thankfully, I'm no longer the poor girl who is afraid of losing money because I've made money. I've lost money hoping to achieve success. I spent more than $175,000 in my quest for success if you include law school, classes, training and business coaching. In losing, using, earning and investing money, it's not that it's more okay, now that I'm no longer the fostered kid. However, money is a resource that requires each of us to respect the risk of loss at various levels. Once you master your level, you can increase and up level at each new level. Even if you're not ready, Universe/Spirit will guide you by opening doors as if to say it's time to make more money. I've been granting myself permission to increase that, I'm now at the Oh my God, Toni, who do you think you are level.

Now I'm getting to where I'm like, I'm enough. I'm not the foster kid. I grew past her. I'm not the person who is vying to be a partner. I grew past her. I'm no longer trying to go up the corporate ladder. I grew past her. Now I'm thinking Toni, it's not a glass ceiling. It's a diamond ceiling that I need to conquer, shatter and overcome with souvenirs to show from my encounter. Each time you shine, you have time to rise to the next level. That's until the day I die, it's always going to be a constant battle of old me versus new me to get to what's meant for me.

Kimberly: That gave me chills. That was good. I love what you're saying about how you grew past her. I grew past her. I grew past her. That's really powerful. That's really powerful. I love these stories, these conversations, is it's not that we're holding on to, what happened to us, or our story. It's we've learned from it. We know a new level; it gives us that experience, that know how, that's part of what makes us unique and brilliant in our own way, how we can help, share with others. I love you, said that, so powerful. Do you find that you, because you keep saying you grew past her, do you find there're moments where you're like, oh, she shows up again, maybe the lack from poverty, or the lack from the foster care, or, that constant comparison because of that, attorney world which is super competitive?

Toni: She comes sometimes to serve as a gatekeeper when I'm going to a place that leads to another milestone. I appreciate old me will always be there to protect me. But mostly, I let old traumatized me grow up. Now I've merged them, old me and new to me, that I could evolve and grow into a more powerful version of myself. In fact, I recently shared with a group that hurt is part of my story, but it's not my hook. I realized if hurt was a hook, then it was just going to always keep hooking me with hurt people and roping me into their stories. I literally had to go into the belly of my soul and go back to my ten-year-old self to heal her spiritually, so my soul could grow past the hurt and the abandonment, the abuse, the rejection. I literally had to mollify myself and work out my healing.

I guess I did not know that my soul was stuck in hurt loop much like Groundhog Day where I could get to a certain point, but then I got relegated back to the hurt and the harm, the abuse of being a fostered kid who did not wanting to get beat, rejected, or mistreated. I did what I needed to do to avoid getting kicked out of someone's basement or someone's house or someone's loving circle. I also tried to people please with pricing. Or showing up in business as not to offend to ensure I wasn't rejected. Even when people were distressful or manipulative, I tried to please and appease. Once I realized that a lot of who I was showing up as in business had a lot to do with my trauma as a child, I took the time to work on myself. I wanted to be the woman of my dreams in business. In order to get there, I had to go to the root to assess what was holding me from becoming the fullness of who I am.

Kimberly: let me ask you this, how old were you or at what point did that realize, that's what you needed to do. Go back to that 10-year-old girl. Cause that's really hard for many people. I would love for you to share a little more about that.

Toni: It was a couple of years ago, two things happened. A few years ago, Darren P Henson actually helped us walk through our wounded souls. Some people call it healing your inner child. I never heard of either. However, Henson helped us heal our traumatized selves. I now call it walking through the wounds. You go to the first time you ever recalled being harmed. When I first walked through my wounds, I immediately went to the first time I was molested at five. But that wasn't. My traumatized self was stuck at the violation I experienced at ten-years-old because I had run away. After I had gotten beaten for something I didn't do, I ran away to have a good life with my god-mom. Much like the fairy tales, I thought she would make all the hurt and pain go far, far away. But it never happened.

My ten-year-old self later watched the movie, Annie, which depicted life got better when Annie had a rich daddy who cared. After seeing Annie, I was looking for a rich Daddy Warbucks who cared about me. I had a lot going on throughout my childhood. But I lost my father figure through divorce and my mom's drama. I thought my life would be better if I had a Daddy Warbucks in my life, such as a drug dealer, lover, or a partner; someone outside of me. That was the first thing I had to heal. Then a few years ago, I got kicked out of one of my foster families, it really hurt me so much. During this time, I attended a business meeting—hurt and all—one of my clients had introduced me to one of his potential clients. I thought it was because it was a business lawyer, and she may have wanted brand protection because he was doing brand makeovers. I wasn't sure. We had a totally random conversation about how she overcame her family drama that kept her stuck in a traumatized state as it related to her soul care.

The client woman shared how she happened upon a personal development training. The course facilitator had introduced everyone to their present self, their old self, and their future self. Somehow, client woman was used as a case study. While she and facilitator walked through her childhood trauma, she realized her younger traumatized self-had taken over her present decision making. If she allowed it to go unchecked, it would continually sabotage her future growth and potential. For client woman, she realized her soul was stuck at a place where her biological father told her family member that he could not care less if she got adopted upon the death of her mother.

After hearing her story, I burst out crying because I realized I was tiptoeing on eggshells in my marriage, my business, my surroundings—including with some friends. I had learned in or about 21 years old the pain of losing a family circle when I shared my true feeling. I didn't want to get kicked out of a family that wasn't even mine. It took me a little while longer to identify that my traumatized self-had taken over my present situation to ease being left alone to fend for myself. To ensure you're not in a state of Arrested Development, you must always assess and acknowledge yourself.

If you go to a certain part and you're like, okay, this is what I need to fix, then fix it. If you're experiencing hiccups about your self-worth, net worth and wholeness about who you can be, then there's a still a snag that has been impacted by hurts hook somewhere in your soul. What I know for sure, we have the power to heal ourselves. But we must walk into our wound. We must walk into the darkness to Embrace, Enlighten and Embolden ourselves. Even though I was successful at a level, I kept getting pushed back into the wounded person who was tipping toe and wanted to be a people pleaser. Once I realized that my blessings in business and in home are not contingent upon anyone allowing me to do what I wanted to do.

Kimberly: So impactful it's interesting as we walk along our journeys, those little, tiny things that happen, that was a significant moment in your life. And that was two, three years ago. Like it just happened. Even for you to recognize it's that little girl that you needed to heal, I love you said you didn't know what age she was, but you recognize it was something from your past you needed to walk into and reach in and grab her and pull her out of it. I love you were opened to finding her and not knowing how old she was. I think that's really a significant thing you said. You mentioned there were certain things that happened younger and even older, but it was that one, you had grown past the other ones. But here she was, that she needed help. So important to recognize that. You're right. We go through so many things. It's a lifelong journey. I really liked that you pointed that out about the little girl. Now that you've had that time to heal her, do you feel like this whole new world has opened up this entire new level of you, and has broken free.

Toni: In my talks with my fellow boss ladies, I remind them that as receivers we don't have to accept everything. If we're going to take on the pain, we need to remove it. I've realized that for me, because even my mindset has changed, my business has changed significantly. I feel like I'm a kind of like the unleashed version of myself now. I no longer let that wound became a tomb of my possibilities. Now that I know I'm worthy of healing myself, I now fully appreciate that I'm worthy of living dreams. If I'm worthy of living dreams, I'm worthy of wealth too! Now I've walked myself out of the womb, I am no longer stuck.

Much like me, most people have suffered trauma as a child. In fact, the CDC says that 60% of adults suffer some level of child trauma, not everybody appreciates it because they're like, oh, that's the way it is. Or that was life. But once I realize I don't have to please everybody, it's okay if someone shuts the door on me. I'm okay with being rejected now. The universe is like, okay, now you're ready. Because at the next level, you're going to get the door slammed on your face. In listening to women, who were looking for VCs, venture capitalists or angel investors, they get the door slammed on their face all the time. They cannot be like the foster kid tiptoeing and saying, does this look pretty? Or will you accept this? You know what I mean? You must get to where you're okay with hearing no and being rejected.

Kimberly: That's hard. That's really hard. I can see why it makes sense for that healing. You've found where that healing needed to happen. Because even if you have a cushy life, I don't know many people that do, but even if you did, being rejected, it's horrible. We don't like to be told, no; we don't want to be rejected. You're in a business where you're going to hear that a lot. I think a lot of women, even in sales, let's say, people don't like to talk about sales because they're afraid of the rejection part of it. If you know that it's okay, it's okay. You're not for everybody. Everybody's not for you. You have your tribe, your tribe is calling to you and you'll click and connect and align perfectly and magically like you're supposed to, but to be okay with that, it's huge, I love that.

Toni: We totally have to make room for what's ours. Unfortunately, if we keep saying yes to everything, we can never be the magnet that we're supposed to be for the right thing, the right one. I don't know why it almost 50 years to figure this out. But everything happens for a reason. Chris Jenner said that she didn't even start keeping up with the Kardashians until she was 52. Seemingly, I'm right on track.

Kimberly: Right. We gain wisdom as we get older. It's part of things. It's the cycle of things, all that wisdom. We're building up going through that journey, things that we're meant to go through to have that wisdom and experience. Oh, I love it. Amazing. If you could go back and tell your younger self one thing, what would it be?

Toni: I get asked this question, it's really hard because the very thing that I would want to heal is the same thing I needed. I would tell my younger self to stop chasing fairytales. But the fairytales were the very thing that kept me when I was down. Fairytales kept me when I was crying. Fairytales nurtured my hope when I hoped that someone would kiss me and wake me up, such as or a Prince Charming. I didn't care, fat, tall, skinny, whatever, as long as they could take me far, far away. Because I still had that fairy tale dream, to speak, that' nurtured me, my trauma when I was growing up through trauma, cultivated by chaos but believing getting more from life was possible.

Even when I was eating off the grounds, but hoping my temporary circumstances would not dictate what destiny offered me. I had time to go back. I wouldn't want to mess it up. I mean, I watched too many shows where they'd go back in time and they're like, whatever you do, do not see your old self. I would be like, well, I don't want to stop believing in fairy tales. Perhaps, I might tell my younger, undergraduate self, not to kiss so many toads because no one in grad school or in college becomes a Prince. Oh. Maybe I would tell a younger attorney version of myself to not leave that job 20 years ago, making $75,000 without at least finding out about marketing.

I literally left the job thinking I would end up with clients in overflow. I didn't know. But I could always see the dream, envision where I'm supposed to be. My younger self didn't have the mechanics and the milestones for what I had to do throughout the in-between. But because I believe I was meant to live happily ever after; I made success happen. With that being said, I would continually allow my younger self to believe in fairytales. I would allow her to keep reading fiction and keep her in the land of the centaurs and keep her thinking that eventually something good was going to happen. Without the nurturing of hope to ignite my imagination, I don't know if I would still be who I am.

Kimberly: That's powerful. Because it gave you hope. Yes. At every turn, it gave you hope.

Toni: I know people laugh at it, but the fairytales fueled my hope, which ignited my faith. Hope, hope nurtured my soul. You know what I mean? I can't, I can't take that away from me.

Kimberly: I love that. I like every step of what you would tell each one. I love that we're talking about in the middle, that gap, because we forget that, especially as creatives and dreamers and I'm in that realm that I see, so big that I'm trying to get up there and I'm trying to figure out all of this behind me, in the middle of me and around me. There's so much of that, that we miss, that we forget, we don't know about. We're not prepared to take on. That's an important piece to embrace. How about this, Embrace the now?

Toni: Yes! Absolutely. Absolutely embrace the now. Now is what you have, anyway. So, you might as well live in it by embracing it.

Kimberly: That's good. I'm curious really quick. Before we wrap up, is what prompted you to step into that space of being an attorney?

Toni: When I was younger, looking for my rescuer, my mom actually saw it too. She sent me to the school called Milton Hershey school, which is in Hershey PA. I was there for three years. During a career day, I heard someone talk about lawyers. I knew nothing about lawyers. Thought I was going to be a hairdresser and hookup with a drug dealer. That's the life I knew, that's what I was going to do. But someone had done research on a lawyer and it resonated with my soul. Initially, I wanted to be a lawyer so I could help other children avoid living similar to the trauma that shaped most of my childhood experiences.

I thought I was going to help children by becoming a family court judge to serve as their advocate. At one point I was a divorce lawyer. I advocated for my client's children so they could be on solid ground. I actually tried to work in dependency for five months. That triggered my trauma. I left. Then when divorce law got too messy, I exited that situation as well. Unfortunately, your soul can be persuaded to forget because your ego is always there. But your spirit always remembers. It's always going to be looking for opportunities to give you glimpses of what could be. I was like Goldilocks, tasting and seeing, trying things out and seeking what was comfortable to me.

Eventually I settled into the estate planning side of legal, which showed me a huge dichotomy in net worth. Sadly, based on statistics, if women are going to be wealthy, we're going to inherit it or we are going to marry it. There's 20% that build it ourselves. As a creative, who is a passionate advocate, I enjoyed empowering women to boss up in business so that they can go after better pay, wealthier estates, and more profitable businesses by building wealth through entrepreneurship. I enjoy feeling extremely comfortable where I am helping my sister girls up level in business. Statistically, when women make money, we make sure our entire camp is helped. We give to our moms; we give to our sisters, we're hiring babysitters, we're teaching our kids about financial independence, we're always thinking community. Of course, in my brain, wealthier women, wealthier world. We can't get ejected from this game called business.

Kimberly: Different from rejected. Wanting to make that they're staying in the game. I love it. You are amazing. I totally loved this conversation. Thank you so much for all you and being so vulnerable and sharing. It was amazing.

Toni: Thank you for having me. This is like really great. P.S. lawyers are goddesses too.

Kimberly: I love it. Thank you so much.

CHAPTER 20

The Defining Moment

Vanessa Klinger

Vanessa is an Intuitive Life Strategist, Author, Life Coach, and TV Host of the Ride Along w/Vanessa Morning Show Fridays 8 am Est & Spiritually Speaking: Sundays 7pm Est Both streams are broadcasted live via the KPMedia TV Network. Vanessa is gifted with the ability to provide spiritual enlightenment using the scriptures and other sources to enrich, empower, and encourage her viewers and clients. Her gift allows her to help her clients address those root cause issues by helping them identify those soul deficiencies which prevent them from becoming more. Her one-to-one coaching gives her the ability to see into her client's souls by utilizing her intuitive gifts followed by providing specific strategic direction that assists her clients along their life's journey.

Contact info

www.vanessaklinger.com

She learned to love herself.
Then everything changed. ~KA

Kimberly: I am excited today to talk with Vanessa Klinger. You are a transformational life strategist. I love it.

Vanessa: Yes, intuitive life strategist, my area of focus is soul transformation, because everyone has a soul. I discovered that your soul is your essence. It's who you really are. If there are deficiencies, it can negatively impact your life's journey and all of your relationships, all of your encounters, your jobs, your money, all of it. Fortunately for me, I was introduced to this. I have to give credit to, pastor Carl Lance Lentz.

When I discovered that missing component of the soul, which is your soul, which comprises the mind, will, and emotions. When I realized I got to work! This discovery set me on course to discovering why I felt unloved and why my soul was so deficient. That's when I realized I needed to transform my soul, because somewhere in my soul, love did not live there. I realized I had to go through the transformation to understand the transformation. It really is your mind, your will, and your emotions that comprise you. I realized that if my soul was not right, then I could not be in harmony with myself and my world.

Kimberly: Right on, I love that. Let's jump into the conversation because I have a feeling it kind of has to do with what you do. What would you say is your biggest obstacle you've gone through?

Vanessa: My biggest obstacle was loving myself, it's interesting because I'm a Libra, right? We're all about love yet. I did not love myself for the greater majority of my life. I was seeking validation from others. When I realized it seems obvious now, but I didn't know it, I didn't know that I had to love myself in order to receive that love back from my world, from the actors in my play called life. I didn't make that connection, that what I felt and believed about myself mirrored through the people I interacted with. Once I took my power back by falling in love with Vanessa, that's when I saw it being emulated and mirrored by my family, my friends, all the people that I would encounter. They were mirroring everything that was going on inside of me. When I did all the inner work, I needed to fall in love with me and every little dimple, pimple, crease, and crevice on this body of mine is when I learned to appreciate and love everything about me.

Kimberly: Is there a time or an age maybe when you realized you were lacking, that you didn't love yourself? Was there this aha moment that made you realize you weren't loving yourself the way you do today?

Vanessa: I think the realization had to come when I did the work. I started meditating at an early age, but then I dropped off in my teenage years. I guess it really became a practice of mine in 2008, 09, 10. I awakened and realized, wow! It wasn't them. They're not the bad guys. I created those bad guys. You mean to tell me I'm that powerful, it's me I'm the master of my world and my soul and that I dictate how people are to treat me. I made the connection, thank goodness. Meditation and visualization, I really stopped, adopted those practices, and believe in those principles. It really set the course on me, even birthing Stay in love motivations, which was birthed in 2012.

Eight, nine and 10 were the tipping point years for me to really define who I really am appreciate and love who I really am and by doing, I could be awakened to my purpose. I think there are many people, if they would realize that once they take the time to do the self-work of whatever spirit is requiring of them to do, everyone's journey is unique. Everyone's story is different. Everyone's soul's requirements are different, but if they take that time to really focus on that, then their purpose can be, they can notice the purpose. I think it was 08, nine, 10. Yeah. That's when I realize I was the culprit in my life story, my nightmare. I was the culprit.

Kimberly: Dive deeper into that because there is this, fear almost in this resistance to owning that, to taking full responsibility of stepping into that space of, I'm creating this. Would you say that you've noticed the change in you regarding that? It's hard for anybody to accept full responsibility and go. Oh my God, I allowed that; I did that. Like you said earlier, people are mirroring what you are dealing with.

Vanessa: Yeah. I think that comes with self-awareness. I can only be self-worth, you can only arrive at self-awareness meditation, cause that's when you can really go within. My co-host on my show spiritually, Michelle Washington, she says, go within, you don't have to be without; you go within. What I learned from meditation is going within is that, now something that I do with my clients is I walk with them inside too, because I can only serve as a conduit, I don't know what someone needs until we take a deep dive into that, but spirit will make them aware of it. What happened with me was that I went in, spirit took me in there, I recognized, see every (I call them demons) you confront your demons, the scary things about yourself, the things that you didn't want to heal from and confront. I had to accept the fact that I was responsible for that because even things that happened as a child. I honestly believe that it was all karmic, and it's my story. That I agreed to it. It was a part of my soul's contract before I even got here that

I had an agreement, a conversation with spirit. We wrote in and mapped out my life from end to end. We included all these noble characters in these experiences, these plot twists, all this drama and all of this great stuff. I accepted I signed off on it, before I took on human form, that really helped me to own, be more conscious of my actions and how I treat people, everything, because I think when people finally assume responsibility and take ownership and to be who they are, then they really can control, dictate, really monitor, and stay in tune with how they behave.

The aim for any spiritual being that's here is to adopt the principles, practices of love, and to be as much as whatever that looks like to you, that's love to you, then that's your aim is to be love and to express light, to guide others who are in the dark, guide them out, you know? Once I accepted that, that's when things really got exciting.

Kimberly: I think it offers you a different perspective as well, because then it helps you be able to assume responsibility using your words, because you have this, okay. If I agreed to come into this life, deal with all this stuff, horrible trauma, all these obstacles, experiences, these characters, our story, then you can go, okay, I may not remember that, but I'm here, I'm in it. What can I do about it? It's part of your journey.

Vanessa: Yeah. You know what my approach is, I no longer react. I want to say a hundred percent of the time, but 90% of the time I'm less responsive, less reactionary. I approach it as if I'm watching a movie and if someone approaches me or I'm looking at it from that perspective, instead of being totally engaged, because then that helps you to maintain your sense of power and then you can choose how you respond or react to whatever you are viewing. It really helped because we, women, are emotional, we're emotional creatures. We can be reactionary instantly, and saps our energy. It takes away our light, our power, because if we're always reacting to everything, getting engaged in things and getting sucked into other people's drama, it's debilitating, it depletes you. It really does. When you finally sit in that position where, okay, I'm not going to, I will not react. I'm going to view it differently and not get engaged. Then when you're sitting in that space, you're in that space of power and able to go within and tap into and to know how to respond to whatever's coming at you. It takes practice. It takes years. I mean, however long it took you to get jacked up. It's going to require a sufficient amount of time for you to heal and improve and become. Give yourself some credit, but every day that you wake up and say, today I assume my power, I'm going to approach it as if I'm watching television. That was what I used to be my mantra. Because I was so reactionary, I felt depleted. Then I'm like, well, I felt it. I felt I wasn't getting anywhere. I wasn't being productive. It was because I was using all of my energy on these distractions, things to where I didn't have the energy to focus on me, what it does that I need to do. Then when I drew a line in the sand and say, you know what, no, then I had more time for myself. I found that when I am sufficient, then I can serve others better.

Kimberly: Well, I think what you said was really important, is you maintain control? If you watch things from an aim point of view, not jump right into it, take pause, see how you're going to react, because you can, one, you can only control so much. One thing that you can control is your reactions, right? Your thoughts, emotions, actions, reactions. I think that's a really powerful point that you were saying is holding back and watching. I love it like a TV show, because you're able to really absorb everything that's going on. Then, taking that step of how am I going to react? How am I, what am I going to say? What am I going to do? You're coming from a place of love and power for yourself. That is so powerful. I love that.

Vanessa: It really works. It really helps me because we've been conditioned to react, instead of really going within saying Spirit, what is that coming at me? From that approach, really what is it, instead of just, okay, all right. It gives you that power and then you're able to; I call it; you're shielding yourself from the energy that's coming at you. If you engage immediately, you're making yourself available to absorb and consume that energy. You don't know what kind of energy that is.

Kimberly: I think too, by realizing that you're in that moment of pause in deciding how you're going to react, sometimes you don't even react. You let it go. You're maintaining that power within you, talk about a complete perception change, shift in your life because when you choose not to react, or you choose the right way in that moment for you to act, you've got more joy, you've got more happiness, you're loving yourself. When you say you realized that what you were lacking is love for yourself, how that's changed your perspective in everything you do. Do you see it trickling into everything?

Vanessa: Absolutely, my entire world changed the characters in my play called life. Some of them are no longer here, but the main characters, my family, my loved ones all changed, I changed. It took several years for me to really come to that realization for me to realize that, hey, who changed in this scenario here? Did they change? It was me; I loved myself. I saw them through my eyes of love. It was as if someone took off these blinders and I could finally see their love, before I couldn't see it because I was wearing these glasses of low self-esteem, low self-worth. That is what I was seeing, even though they were expressing love to me. I couldn't see it. I couldn't see it, but when I fell in love with me, I was like, My God, they love me the whole time, the entire time. But because of, I'm getting misty, because I did not love myself. I could see all of this wonderful love that God has promised us because we accepted the mission of being human. It's everywhere. It's everywhere. We have to dust off our eyeballs, learn to love and value ourselves. When we do that, then our entire world can change.

Kimberly: I have chills up and down my body. Absolutely, that was so good. I like how you talked about, when you realized you started loving yourself, you discovered that the people that were already telling you; they loved you. It's like you could break open and receive it on a completely different level.

Vanessa: It's because, you know, this came to me. I'm not a genius, but this came to me, their love language. I could interpret it after I fell in love with myself. Self-love is the key to interpreting other's love language. Why? Because love is a universal language. It is an energy. When you allow that energy to possess you, then you can interpret all different love languages. The reason you can't see and recognize genuine love from what kind of love that is because you haven't allowed love to you. You haven't become love.

Kimberly: That's good. Do you find when you're even talking with your clients and for yourself, when you're sharing about how to love yourself, how would you say to love yourself? Because for many people it's such an outside thing.

Vanessa: Well, I mean, honestly, I've spent most my life alone. I've had the privilege of being able to sit with Vanessa. I allow spirit to come in any time and knock on my door and say, hey, what are you thinking about? I have conversations. I would have to say the first thing is to really get still, really sit, really go inside yourself and ask the right questions. If you ask the right questions, you'll get an answer. The reason you're not getting answers is that you're not posing your questions correctly. You ask the right questions. Not why did they do what they did to me, but why did I have to have that experience? See, that even feels different. What's the lesson inside of it. What was I supposed to learn? The change of your question, why don't I love myself, not why don't they love me? What don't I love myself & the scary one, what's right with me, not what's wrong. What's right with me. Then you'll start, your spirit will bring to your recollection everything. That's right with you. You have a great sense of humor; love children; are genuinely kind, all these great attributes instead of wrong. You're able to focus on that. Then you fall in love with all of those qualities of you. I fell in love with the fact that I love people. I genuinely care for people. When did that happen? Is that yesterday?

I really love people. I appreciate, really grateful for who I am, how I am. I think that we have to silence the noise of what we've heard or what we've been conditioned. That requires work because you clear that all out so that you can replace that with the truth. You have what you choose to affirm yourself. You're saying that how can they, how can they find this love? But then you got replace it with and override it with everything that you have taken on and conditioned and heard for the first seven years of your life that's modeled and defined you. The reason you're in that situation where you're feeling unloved during that situation, where you're around people that aren't good for you, is because of what you have believed, been conditioned. What sculpted out you the first few years of your life, which dictated your life up till now. Are you willing to put in the work by really looking at it and say, you know what, I'll close with this. I really asked spirit; I said, look, I don't have the strength to, okay. I'll share, I was on drugs for several years. I remember when I really wanted to quit. I don't want to do cocaine anymore. I remember I said, okay, okay, God, please, God; I don't know how to say no. Please keep them away from me until I'm able to say no. 30 days went by; I got a call. Hey girl, you want to go to a party.

I'm like, this is in the eighties. You want to go party? I'm like, no, I don't party anymore. When I hung up, I was proud of myself. Then I thanked spirit because he answered my prayer. If you feel that as if you need a little support, ask the spirit to keep everything away while you build up your spiritual strength so that you can stay in and confront it. Because the only thing that you're confronting is you, they're playing apart. Remember? You created these characters to appease to whatever you're sending out. I was sending out; I wanted to party and have a good time. I attracted those types of actors when I wanted to change, flip the script on my life, by me, by operating and being a sober person, someone who did not do cocaine anymore, then I had to take that time rewrite that script so that when I received the phone call, I'd have that line already ready, did that makes any sense.

Kimberly: It's perfect. It's perfect. It's powerful, and that makes sense. Again, we're always looking outside of ourselves to feel better, to feel loved, to feel anything. When you go within, there's the power that power lies within you and love is at the cornerstone, to love yourself. We talk about it all the time and lots of different scenarios in front of women. I love you shared that. Thank you for that. What would you tell your younger self? If you could go back.

Vanessa: You know, that's something that, have a part of the program that I take my clients through is I have them go back to a time when they were a little child. A scenario that I have is, I took myself all the way back to when I was five or six. I got sexually abused by my uncle. I'm sitting there on the bed, I sit right next to me, say you know what? I know you don't understand what happened, but it's all a part of your story, it's not good what happened. What I want you to remember this one thing that you loved more than you can ever really imagine that all of this is going to work out for your good, where you're going to be a wonderful person. And with this experience, you're going to use it to help others. I love you. I give myself a kiss and I come on and back out to my present moment.

Kimberly: Woo. I have chills everywhere.

Vanessa: Well good.

Kimberly: You know; it's about healing that little girl inside. We go through things we don't understand. It can totally change the course of our life because we don't know how to process it.

Vanessa: Yes. I really believe that. I really believe that if you can go back and heal that part, that little moment, it recreates your future.

Kimberly: We could go on. We could have started there and come this way. You're amazing. I love your story. Thank you for being powerful, strong, and sharing it. Thank you for being a part of this.

Vanessa: Absolutely. Pleasure.

CHAPTER 21

Following Your True-Life Path

Virginia Earl

Virginia Earl is the founder of Seven Mystic Rings in Murrieta, California, where she lives with her daughter and their dog Chaos. Clients who seek her spiritual gifts have high profiles, a broad spectrum of beliefs and come to her from all walks of life. Her spiritual path took her as far as Asia and Central America, where she immersed herself in the teachings of the Akashic Records guided by her spiritual teacher and received her certifications. She combines her spiritual gifts with an ancient technique called The Akashic Records to identify the "why" behind her clients' roadblocks and to get them unblocked so they can live a life of purpose and clarity.

She is featured in The Hollywood Digest and is a recipient of She Inspires Me Awards, London; Women Appreciating Women Hall of Fame Award, London; and is listed in the highly coveted and well-respected publications "Who's Who Among Hispanic Americans" and "Who's Who of American Women." In 2001, Yogi Bhajan blessed Virginia to live with the spiritual name of Guru Soorya Kaur, which means "Princess of the sun who brings one from darkness to light" — a fitting name honoring the spiritual services she offers her clients by bringing that which hides in the subconscious mind to light — from past lives into the present.

www.sevenmysticrings.com
https://www.facebook.com/spiritualhealervirginiaearl
https://www.facebook.com/virginiaearlspiritualhealer/
https://www.instagram.com/sevenmysticrings/
https://twitter.com/7mysticrings

"She felt a deeper calling. As she helped heal others, it healed her too." ~KA

Kimberly: I am here with Virginia Earl, the founder of Seven Mystic Rings. Thank you Virginia for being here.

Virginia: Sure. Thank you for having me.

Kimberly: Let's talk about Seven Mystic Rings. What is that?

Virginia: Seven Mystic Rings is a spiritual business. I'm a spiritual healer. I combine my spiritual gifts with an ancient technique called The Akashic Records to help my clients identify the "why" behind their roadblocks so that they can live a life of clarity and purpose. The Akashic Records energy has been around for thousands of years, all the way to the pharaohs in Egypt, to the beginning of Creation. That's the energy that I tap into, the energy of Akasha to help my clients through any obstacles that they might experience in this lifetime, whether it's with their relationships, their business, their career, their health, any trauma, or chronic blockages that they might have come through into this lifetime from a past life — if you believe in past lives. I tap into the energy of their past lives to see what obstacles they might experience in this lifetime, how those obstacles are affecting them in any area in their lives.

Kimberly: I love it. It's such a profound insight.

Virginia: Thank you. I also offer meditations. My favorite one is the journey meditation. We go through a series of landscapes. I don't want to reveal the rest.

Kimberly: They can get ahold of you for that. I'm curious then. First, how long have you been doing this and what was your calling to step into that?

Virginia: Ever since I was about this size on my mom's lap, a few days old, I remember I had a [spiritual] experience. When I share this with people who are still alive to this day and who were in that room, they cannot believe that I still remember what happened that day. But anyhow, it's been a lifelong journey. I think my catalyst point was when my husband passed away in 2015. Well, but even while he was still alive, I was being directed by spirit to the spirit world. It was amazing the way it happened. To someone else it might sound a little strange [but not to me] because there were a series of things that happened throughout my life. Then one day I was in Temecula driving North on Winchester Road, coming home from an advertising agency. I was working out at the time in Huntington Beach. I turned on the radio and they were talking about The Akashic Records. I couldn't even pronounce the word. It sounded something like Akash ... something. I was driving. I couldn't take notes, and so I listened to their entire show. I thought, oh, that's interesting. Then the next thing I did was I talked to a friend who was into ghosts. I told him about it. He's like, no, no, no, don't get involved with that. I'm like, well, why not? You use your mirror to talk to people from other realms. Why shouldn't I do this? When you tell me not to do something, I'm going to do the opposite. So I did.

The next thing I knew, I woke up one morning, and I googled the Akashic Records. I listened to this entire video about someone who is now my spiritual teacher. I told my husband, "I'm going to Guatemala [to learn about The Akashic Records]." I went, and then from there, the following year, I went to Asia and spent a month there. I went to a retreat, and I learned about The Akashic Records, my spiritual gifts and what they were. The first trip to Guatemala was very revealing, but the second trip to Asia, to Bali, was even more so because a lot of messages came through [for me]. It was an amazing experience for me. I got certified [to read The Akashic Records]; I started doing this for myself. Then, after I came back from my trip, my husband progressively got sick, that's when I really delved into the healing energy of The Akashic Records.

I didn't want to talk to anybody or see anybody [after my husband passed away], except for the people who were coming in and out of the house to talk to me about his stuff and his business. I went through a lot of difficulties; it was as if someone put their finger on the remote control and there goes Virginia non-stop. And, as if someone put the finger on the remote controller [and never took it off]. I was like the Eveready [Energizer] Bunny. I kept going, going, going ... I never... stopped, I didn't really mourn him. I came back from that trip. I delved into the healing energy of The Akashic Records. That really helped me. It was kind of an addiction and still is ... to get out of this room and go all the way up there to be spiritually connected ... Because it's a unique energy altogether; I love it. I realized how it was helping me. Then I thought, well, I talked to some friends, who said you should do this for a living. I did. I was hesitant because I have a background in journalism. I'm a writer, editor and I also translate copy, anything under the sun, from English to Spanish. That's my other second business. I'm kind of like sidetracking right now. We also translate [documents and digital copy] from English to European, Asian, Middle Eastern and South American languages. We're certified by the State [of California] and the Federal Government to submit bids. But anyhow, so I had this... Where was I?

Kimberly: You were talking about how you kept going and you tapped into it.

Virginia: Yeah, the Eveready Bunny. I realized how it [the healing energy of The Akashic Records] was helping me. I thought, OK, fine. I'll start with Seven Mystic Rings. I talked to some friends, and that's how we came up with the name... I wanted seven in there because of the biblical connection. It's a very spiritual number. Once I started, I was kind of like in the middle. OK, should I do this? Should I not do this? Self-sabotaging myself.

I live in, as you know, in Murrieta, in Southern California, it's sort of like a Bible Belt area. I have a Catholic background. I was going to a Christian Church, I thought, well, what are people going to think? What about this? What about that? That's where I was at the beginning. Now it's like, I really [see things differently]. I believe in God [always have and always will]. My soul is an incredibly old soul. Now I don't care what people think. You cannot live your life wondering what people are going to think of you. What people are going to say about you because then you're not living your life. You're not living your true self. That's where I am. I get people all the time asking me, "What do I do? I feel like I'm moving more towards the spiritual world." Follow your path because if you're not following your path, you're not being true to yourself, you're not helping yourself and you're not helping others. If God gave you the gifts that you have, use them to help others. The more I started offering my sessions, the more I saw I was helping other people. It made me want to continue doing it. I will not stop doing it. I know that I've done this in a previous life. I've been told by many people. I see how it helps other people. Everybody's gone through trauma. Everybody's had something going on, either in this lifetime or a past lifetime. We don't want to dwell on what happened six months ago. We don't want to dwell on what happened in another life, either. When I go into their past lives, I see images.

I get the messages. I share them with them. Sometimes there are things that come through that have nothing to do with a session [meaning specifics about past lives may or may not be relevant]. But the messages overall are perfectly aligned with what's going on with them in their life right now. They need to know these messages so that they can figure out how to move forward in this lifetime. I provide them with clarity and guidance for that. But it's not good a thing to be living [dwelling spiritually and emotionally] in the past, whether you're in this lifetime or in a past lifetime, because those things pull us backwards. They don't help us move forward. They create blockages. Not only they create blockages, but they also slow down whatever needs to happen for you in this life, whatever God wants to happen in your lifetime, whatever life God wants you to live in this lifetime. It's going to push everything back. It's going to delay things. That's what I'm trying to say.

Kimberly: It's Perfect. One thing that I ask in this conversation is, what is one of your biggest obstacles or hurdles that you've gone through? I didn't know your husband passed. Is that one of them?

Virginia: Yeah, there is another story behind all that. My body's getting cold as I'm talking to you about it and it's OK. I can talk about it now. A few years ago, I probably couldn't because it took me until last year [for me to fully mourn his death]. He passed away ... think about this ... He passed away in 2015. Last year, it took me this long to finally let go. I drove by his office. His office was over in Temecula, on Winchester Road. He had an insurance brokerage business, and it came to me. I drove to his business. I sat in the car, and... whoosh, I let it all out. It took me that long [to mourn him]. In December of last year, I also did a ceremony for him. We did a memorial, of all places, all the way out in Calipatria, where he used to go hunting. Yes, my husband was a hunter.

For those of you who are not into hunting, I'm sorry. I wasn't crazy about him shooting the little cute duckies up in the sky. Anyhow, He had a duck club, a hunting duck club, Cazador Duck Club, that was in Calipatria. It's still there till this day. He used to go hunting there with his father, with his brother, during hunting season, October through January. I would go with them whenever they had room because they had little cottages and they would rent them out to the hunters. I was invited when there was room for me to go. We had a lot of great memories. My daughter, when she was incredibly young, she could go there as well to experience it. I did a release. I released some of his ashes. Before I did that, I was tossing back and forth with the idea. Should I release all of them or some? Spirit told me no, just release some. He even guided me to release some and why. We released some. I got some white doves, I also got some butterflies. When I talked to your book designer yesterday, she said she's going to have some butterflies [on the front cover of the book].

Did I answer your question?

Kimberly: Yes, if that's what you wanted to share about it. Absolutely.

Virginia: We released butterflies. It was beautiful and at the end of the ceremony, someone who was very close to my husband, and one of his best friends, said to me, "Well, consider [he owns a networking business] doing these kinds of ceremonies. I have someone I can connect you with who runs a funeral home. Or whatever. I don't know that I'm really going to do that. I took a lot of my stuff from the house. It was a beautiful ceremony, but it took me that long to do that. Towards the end, my brother-in-law said, "I don't think I would have been able to do it right away after he passed away." I'm glad that I waited as long as I waited. Do you want me to tell you about the butterfly story?

Kimberly: Sure.

Virginia: I shared this with Genevieve yesterday. You will enjoy this. I have a habit of putting stuff on the steps in my house. Whenever I go upstairs, I pick up whatever's on the first or second step; I take it upstairs. For like two days, I went up and down the stairs. I saw this thing that was kind of triangular. I kept looking at it and I'm like, OK. I was too lazy to bend down and pick it up. By the second day I touched it, it flew away. I thought it was a moth. My daughter was upstairs, she said...

"No, mommy! No, it's not a moth! It's a butterfly!"

I'm like, what? A butterfly! Are you kidding me? In the house? How the hell did the butterfly fly into the house? Normally when I'm outside, I'm sure you probably have noticed the same thing, we normally see the little white butterflies, or the Monarch butterflies, every once in a while. But no, this one was different. I went upstairs; I tilted the light fixture and I'm like, OK, she's in there. How the hell am I going to get her out of there? I went downstairs, and I got the pasta strainer.

Kimberly: That works.

Virginia: My daughter tilted the light fixture. I picked her up gently and her wings were open. I actually took a picture of her. She was kind of dark brown and had a yellow trim around her. I picked her up, put her inside the strainer. Then we covered the strainer. I went outside. I thought for a moment. OK, what do I do with her now? Where do I release her? I released her. I have a plant that has like these little, I don't even know what the name of the plant is, white flowers; I stood in front of it,

I let her fly. She parked herself on the little white flower. As I stood there, all these red orbs surrounded me. Then I knew it was a sign of something, that it was my husband sending me a message. I looked at her. I stood there in awe. I couldn't believe it. (Actually, in February of last year, I was also going up the stairs. I think I might have a portal on the stairs, I guess, because all these red orbs [surrounded me on Valentine's Day].) I was standing there in front of the plant, looking at the little butterfly perched on the white flower. I gave her a little lift; she flew in the center of our street. Right after, I saw these two royal blue hearts, right in front of me, like floating, obviously up in the air. Then she flew away.

Kimberly: Incredible. I think the butterfly you're talking about it, isn't that a mourning cloak?

Virginia: That's why I sent Genevieve a picture. That's exactly what she told me it was. Yeah. When she told me, she was going to have butterflies in there; I was like, oh. Interesting.

Kimberly: I love that story. I love how you recognize, especially in what you do, you recognize signs all around you. I love sharing that with women to pay attention to signs, they'll help you grieve. They help you move in the direction that you want to, or they're little signs, like happy hellos. I love that you brought that up. I found it interesting going back really quick, when you were deciding whether to do this business full-time or not, a lot of women have that same conversation. What helped you in those moments to really go, nope, I'm doing this? No longer allowing yourself to waiver because we do that all the time. Women are changing careers. They're not sure what they want to do. What was it for you that really helped you anchor in that this is what you're doing?

Virginia: Because I saw how I was helping them. I release and let go of what was blocking them. Because they share with me some of their most intimate secrets. Some stories are amazing. Some stories are not so amazing. They're horrifying. I am flattered that they come to me trusting me, that they're making me a part of their journey, a part of their change in their lives. When they tell me, "Virginia, you've changed my life, you've made a difference in my life." That's huge! That's confirmation that what I'm doing is helping them, that it's working. And so no, I will always continue doing what I'm doing. Like I said, I've done it before. Sometimes what happens is really cute. It's kind of funny. The session's over. I had one [client], I will not say who, of course, but the session was over. She sat there looked at me, with this huge grin on her face and wouldn't want to leave, and that happens often. They don't want to leave, and that's OK. If it's too extended, then I need to make a move to stand up. Then they ask me, can I give you a hug? Of course, I say, yes. I haven't denied anybody a hug, even during the pandemic. I'm very careful who comes to see me because it's in my house.

Kimberly: It feels like to me you're a part of their healing journey, but it also has helped you on yours.

Virginia: Yes. Because you know what? It has helped me understand that I'm not the only one who has been through all these traumas. I've been through many, but because I've been there, I understand what they're going through; I understand the pain. It's an amazing thing to see that their lives change. After they see me, ... I keep in touch with them. I'll send them a text. How are you doing? What's going on? Then there are times like the other day I was at a [virtual] conference. You know how they put you in these rooms and things. There's a woman who was in distress because of something personal that had happened. I was able to let her know that I was holding the space for her. After a couple of days, she sent me a message. Can we talk? I said, sure, of course. I didn't charge her for that because you can't charge for everything. I love what I do. If I can help someone, I will, of course.

Kimberly: What would you tell your younger self if you could go back?

Virginia: Uh, so many things, so many things. Yeah.

I went through my memes. I'm going to read something to you that I wrote, "There is a quiet little voice that doesn't use words. It's called intuition. Use it. Pay attention to it because it's there for a reason. That's like your inner guide. When something doesn't sound or feel right from the very beginning, it's for a reason. Follow that intuition, always. It's coming from your higher self. If you don't like something, simply remove the power — your attention. Stay true to yourself, to your purpose. Remember, nobody will ever give you an award for living someone else's life, but they might admire you, respect you, remember you for having the courage to follow your purpose, to help others along the way, to speak your truth and make a difference in this world. Your courage and determination alone will be an inspiration to others."

Sometimes we give attention to the wrong things, they keep coming back and back and back because we're allowing it. We need to build, have limits, barriers of what we allow into our energy field, into our space. So it doesn't bring us down into a deep dark hole. Here's another one. And this one's a really tricky one, "When the tide peaks, remain calm. Listen to the silence within. The answers are there. And so it's written." So that's where The Akashic Records comes in. The Akashic records are about your past lives, present and future. It's about your soul's journey. What happened to you since the inception of your soul, how that is affecting you today? We're all connected. We're all really connected through energy. If you can imagine this massive energy floating all around us, that energy picks up your emotions, anything that's good or bad, your emotions, what you're feeling, what you're seeing, what you're saying, what you're doing. It sort of records it into that energy field. It's sort of like a massive floating recorder. That's the energy that I tap into. It's the energy of Akasha, the energy of The Akashic Records. It's one of the highest realms you can access, through the secret prayer of The Akashic Records.

I use it [The Akashic Records] for myself all the time. It's better than going to see a therapist. They work amazingly well too, but sometimes there's more stuff that is deeply rooted in there. The only way you can really look at it is by sometimes going into your past lives. I've had sessions where people, my clients, whatever I'm seeing they're seeing at the same time. They're seeing the same things I'm seeing; those are really magical sessions because they're really spiritual people. Those are my favorite.

Kimberly: Well, I appreciate you being on here, sharing your story and sharing your wisdom. Thank you so much.

Virginia: You're welcome. Thank you for having me. It's been a great day. Did I answer all your questions and some?

Kimberly: Yes you did.

Kimberly: Thank you.

Virginia: You're welcome.

Who is behind Fizzy Beard?

Originally from Valais in Switzerland, where the mountains and vineyards are sources of inspiration, Olivier Fardel scratched his first guitar at the age of 13 years. Self-taught, he set himself the challenge of learning the entire repertoire of Steve Vai and Jimi Hendrix. An impossible challenge that allowed him to progress technically and to train his own style. This experience made him understand that he did not want to play the music of others, but to create his own.

Oriented exclusively to Rock and Metal, he worked at Citydisc, a rich place of musical discoveries where he had the chance to meet incredible and passionate people.

This experience gave him the opportunity to expand his musical universe and realized that he could find quality in every style of music.

He fell in love with electro music and started producing music with synth and machines.

He released his first album "Therapy" in 2017, followed by the second one "23" five months later.

The young multi-instrumentalist composer dedicated his last album "Goddess among us" to seven talented and inspiring singers, allowing them to share a musical and spiritual message.

Having chosen the same title as Kimberly, this happy "coincidence" is the reason you're reading this book right now. It was a privilege and an honor to work with these beautiful souls and make this project alive.

This book is dedicated to my mother, a true Goddess since I was born and long before.

Fizzy

Goddesses Among us
2 Soundtrack

1. *Less than endo* – **Liz Hanks**
2. *See Youth* – **Vita and the woolf**
3. *Alone is my home* – **Meira Loom**
4. *Aqua* – **Jessanna Nemitz**
5. *Cassure* – **Imen Gardouh**
6. *Fairy soul* – **Clara Schild**
7. *Everything's ok* – **Vita and the woolf**
8. *Find the peace* – **Mia Oud**
9. *13* – **Vita and the woolf**
10. *L'alchimie* – **Joelle Mellioret / Jessanna Nemitz**
11. *Never doubt you* – **Vita and the woolf**
12. *Je suis colère* – **Charlène**
13. *I'm free, am I ?* – **Vita and the woolf**
14. *Keyboardless* – **Mia Oud**
15. *My mind is screaming* – **Lisa Labour**
16. *Remember this night* – **Enlia**
17. *Riviera's path* – **Liz Hanks**
18. *Rodeo* – **Victoire Oberkampf**
19. *Under heat* – **Enlia**
20. *Wrong choice* – **Vita and the woolf**
21. *Gratitude* – **Fizzy Beard**

Afterword

Book 2 of this series, Goddess Among Us, is truly a blessing to myself and everyone it touches.

Allow the words in these conversations to resonate with you, allow yourself to be open to the wisdom and let it guide you into stepping into your power. Don't wait to make a change in your life, the choice is yours.

If these Goddesses could go back, this is what they would say; "stay open because you will be completely different. Stay open to surprising yourself." "You are amazing, powerful, and beautiful. You got this! Trust it, trust you!", "How proud I am of my younger self for listening to that inner guidance, to still my mind, and to find that way." "Don't be afraid to be you. Own you, every ounce of you." "Be more confident." "Do not let my past determine my future." "Everything that you want, it's already done, you are smart. You do not know how creative you are."

They would also say, "Believe in yourself and do what you're meant to do, stepping to it. Don't be afraid and it's okay." "You are special, God loves you. And you are strong. You have a purpose!" "Do not let fear stop you." "Stop trying to save everyone. Save yourself first." "Be patient, slow down, life isn't going anywhere."

"You are worthy of every beautiful thing that the Lord has placed on this earth, don't stop believing." "Love you more, love you more than enough because God does." "You're enough always and forever." "Trust yourself. You're on the right path of success and all that you are dreaming of and more." "Your life is going to be so much more than you could ever imagine. Start dreaming of it now. Don›t wait." "Always do something that will energize the soul." "Develop and practice a direct, open channel of communication with Source. It would have saved me a lot of pain and struggle in my life. ""Believe in fairytales." "You loved more than you can ever really imagine, that all of this is going to work out for your good, I love you." "When something doesn't sound or feel right from the very beginning, it's for a reason. Follow that intuition always, Stay true to yourself, to your purpose."

"Change your mindset, change your life, believe in yourself and speak your truth. You are a Goddess!"

Many Blessings

Kimberly Anderson